Jon Goulding is an Assistant Head teacher in a primary school whose only other published work is a book of practice test papers for 10 year olds.

He is a self-confessed football addict and sees the somewhat insane nature of football support as a perfect escape from the somewhat insane world in which we live.

He lives in Cheshire with his wife and young son.

Further information at

www.jongoulding.com

and

www.1fcnuk.com

FOR BETTER OR FOR WURST

Jon Goulding

FOR BETTER OR FOR WURST

Vanguard Press

VANGUARD PAPERBACK

© Copyright 2009
Jon Goulding

The right of Jon Goulding to be identified as author of
this work has been asserted by him in accordance with the
Copyright, Designs and Patents Act 1988.

All Rights Reserved

No reproduction, copy or transmission of this publication
may be made without written permission.
No paragraph of this publication may be reproduced,
copied or transmitted save with the written permission of the publisher,
or in accordance with the provisions
of the Copyright Act 1956 (as amended).

Any person who commits any unauthorised act in relation to
this publication may be liable to criminal
prosecution and civil claims for damages.

A CIP catalogue record for this title is
available from the British Library.

ISBN 978 1 84386 551 3

*Vanguard Press is an imprint of
Pegasus Elliot MacKenzie Publishers Ltd.*
www.pegasuspublishers.com

First Published in 2009

**Vanguard Press
Sheraton House Castle Park
Cambridge England**

Printed & Bound in Great Britain

For Herbert who brought it with him, Angela who showed it to me, and Tommy that you may one day understand.

Acknowledgements

Had John Logie Baird foreseen the almost global obsession with the television nearly 100 years after he had invented it, he may have been somewhat surprised. James Watt would have been no doubt rather gob-smacked by the way our world has been shaped by and since the Industrial Revolution which was powered by his steam engine. And maybe Alexander Fleming would give himself a pat on the back for the amount of lives saved by Penicillin.

It seems that we have so much for which to thank the Scots and it is a lesser known, though no less great, compatriot of the iconic trio who is responsible for many of the adventures in this book. The crazy idea of creating an official fan club of a German football team came from the brain of my good friend Iain Finlayson. Through his comradeship, eagerness to mislead and be misled, and passion for beer and football, the initial momentum became something much, much more. I know he allows himself a smile when he sees what his idea has become and I thank Iain for friendship, support and for spending a night in hospital to add to the story.

To the original revellers on that first group trip to *Frankenstadion* and the city of Nuremburg – Ange, Iain, Jason, Haydn, Gail, Steve, Jon W, Phil – it was that wonderful weekend which lay the foundations for many more nights of partying and the moments of footballing frustration in Nuremburg and beyond. And along with Iain, Jason has been a prolific supporter of the cause, great friend and fine travelling companion throughout (despite his ability to poach goals that clearly belong to someone else – not that I'm bitter or anything).

My thanks go also to Trevor for his blind faith in jumping on the bandwagon without first seeing the team play and then pushing us along and overseeing the growing membership. And to Darren (a non-believer) for his excellent work in producing a website when nobody else knew what they were doing.

To the members of 1FCNUK. Without you not much would have happened at all. Those airport departure lounges, drunken nights and hungover mornings would have not been the same without so many of you sharing the same emotions and nausea. You are a truly special group of people, even though so many of you seem far more interested in the beer and Wurst than in football. Thanks to each and every one of you.

To all of the acquaintances made in Germany. Your hospitality, support, good humour and friendship have been, and continue to be, memorable. I would especially like to thank Armin Peipp for his dedication to our cause and for being an excellent host in Franconia, Liam Foster for keeping our hopes for 1.FCN in check with his realism, wit and friendship. Joe Terrell for filling our forum with so many comments about the team we follow, and Heino Hassler for supplying so much information. I would also like to thank Julius Neumann for giving his time to explain and share his experiences as a supporter of 1.FCN and President of UN94. Also Moritz and Magic for their willingness to share tales over a few drinks during their stays in England, and Audiollama for so much information and vast translations of the history of 1.FCN. Most of all I thank Jürgen Bergmann. Without Jürgen our trips to the football would surely not have run quite so smoothly. He has done everything he can to help make us welcome at 1.FCN matches and has also provided so much time and information for this book. A true football fan and fine ambassador for *Der Club,* Germany and Franconia.

Thanks also to Liam Foster and Armin Peipp for permission to use their photographs in the book, and to Mark Bender for permission to reproduce lyrics to Die Legende Lebt.

Finally I must thank that family. My father Bryan for his support, and excellent proof-reading of manuscripts. My wife Angela for everything (but at the tip of the iceberg are love, support, allowing me to go to matches, allowing me to spend far too much time away from home 'researching' German football and for making me get this book written). And I should not forget to mention the fact that if it was not for Angela I would never have seen 1.FCN play and would probably still maintain an element of stereotypical cynicism towards all things German. Last of all my thanks must go to my father-in-law, Herbert (and mother-in-law Elaine for allowing him to spend too much time away from home too). His love of his country, his city and his football team allied with his downright miserable attitude when Nuremburg lost, quickly struck a chord with me as a fellow football supporter. His delight and encouragement for the formation of 1FCNUK and the perpetuation of our support has spurred many of us on. I hope this book does his country, city and football team the justice they all deserve. Thank you Herbert for all of your encouragement and friendship over the last 10 years.

And to anyone missed in the above. Even if I've temporarily forgotten who you are and what you've done at least you know how you've helped. May your anonymity be your alibi.

Introduction

Berlin. 26th May, 2007

An empty stadium silently echoes with the events and legends of the past. Whether major or minor, global or local in scale, the ghosts of 'those days' creep into the imagination of the observer. The performances and performers, the spectators and the magnitude of each occasion crackle through the static of the years as one desperately tries to imagine a long gone scene. Conversely, a full stadium fuses the past with the electricity, anticipation and excitement of the present.

To be standing in Berlin's *Olympiastadion* would have been, as sports fans and tourists, a moment to reflect on the grand history of the place. Reflection on the famous 'Nazi' Olympics of 1936 and the four gold medal haul of Jesse Owens. And how about, albeit less significantly (unless you are French, or Italian for that matter), Zinedine Zidane's World Cup Final head-butt on Marco Materazzi? Moments and people now etched into the stadium's memories for eternity.

That the time for such reflection on the past was only fleeting was due to the importance of the present. Not on a global scale, maybe not even on a national scale and certainly without much interest beyond the borders of Germany. But in the Franconian and Schwaben areas of southern Germany, for the thousands of fans on the fan mile stretching westwards from Berlin's Brandenburg Gate, and for the 74,400 fans in the old stadium itself, for that afternoon the significance and spectacle were difficult to surpass.

Three decades of living away from his native Germany and four decades in the footballing wilderness for his hometown team had somewhat hardened Herbert Schauer to the emotions of football. However, to be standing (for despite the provision of seats, that was how it was to be for most of the game) with fellow Franconians in this temple of sport was something of a spiritual experience. To be sharing this with his daughter and British supporters of 'his' team was a personal high after all those years of support in exile and support in isolation. Thirty years of lone moments of despair only punctuated by the occasional, and all too often cruel, false dawn of impending success.

The emotions for his friends and family alongside him in the stadium were also strong – in some ways similar but in other ways poles apart. From an English perspective, the German national anthem in a football stadium has often intensified the fear of defeat. In the past it has sometimes only been heard on television courtesy of sound technicians who managed to mask out the whistling from the opposition 'fans', at best little more than a boost to the opposition, at worst a narrow-minded display of xenophobia and nationalism. To hear the anthem sung with so much passion and pride by a whole crowd in Berlin caused a spine-tingling sensation of awe and wonder.

The anthems had been preceded by the arrival of the teams to the field of play. For Herbert this was the point where all of those emotions of the past thirty-nine trophy-less years were to flow down his cheeks as tears of pride. For those travelling with him from Britain, their support had only been but a fraction of that of Herbert, but even through that short period the support had become a passion and devotion which now caused the eyes to fill and the throat to tighten. What for Herbert had been a lifelong faith had for the rest of us started as a little eccentric fun, but now we had been sucked under, and had been barely able to catch our breath for the previous two seasons. Now, as the kick-off to the 2007 German FA Cup Final approached we held our breath with the fellow hordes of supporters. That we managed to breathe at all during the ensuing 120 minutes of football is a miracle that only truly devoted fans who have nervously watched a major game can ever understand.

Olympiastadion, May 2007

Chapter 1

Sowing the seeds

My first time. October 2002. Standing on the *Nordkurve* terrace, a real treat and a nostalgic feeling for the *Englander*. Yes, I remember terraces. Standing shoulder to shoulder, packed in tightly, generating atmosphere as well as vital heat on a cold day. Then the playing of *Three Lions* before the game. Nostalgia turned into a sense of the surreal. Here I stood in a German football stadium with those around me singing what had become a very English football anthem. Maybe the popularity of the song in Germany was exactly because this English football anthem highlighted England's lack of footballing success. Were they laughing at me? I started to feel uneasy. A guy in front of me struck up conversation. I was lost and a little scared. How would a German be accepted on a British terrace (had they still existed)? My German speaking partner came to the rescue and explained that I was English to which the Aryan's response was to hold his finger to his lips as a warning not to publicise the fact too loudly.

I stayed obediently quiet for as long as any football fan can but then, armed with the courage of a few beers (sold by a vendor who casually walked around the terrace), and the increasing incompetence of the officials, I joined in with the tirade of abuse, albeit in a different language. *Abseits* (offside) was the only word I knew and still use more than any other to this day, ironic for someone who advocates the beautiful game and the elegance of fast attacking football.

The stadium was only half full, or in the context of the performance and the fact that 1.FC Nürnberg would be relegated come the end of the season, it is safe to say that it was half-empty. What was I doing? I was actually shouting in support of a team other than my beloved Port Vale. In fact, not only was I shouting for another team, it was a German team; a German team who were getting outplayed by their German opponents VfB Stuttgart. And I was actually enjoying myself.

My fiancée had not visited her hometown of Nuremberg for some eighteen months, and despite a dwindling family there she was missing the place. We booked a flight and were soon in a beautiful city, surrounded by the toned down, European version of hustle and bustle. A brilliant blue autumn sky looked painted in the year's final warm rays from the sun, their fading heat only betrayed by the shaded areas which still held on to the previous night's frost.

So schön ist Nürnberg (So beautiful is Nuremberg) proclaims the title of one of the many guide books available about the city. Indeed, as this guide book and many others point out, its central European location has always been key in providing the city with a healthy economy and culture. An important trading centre throughout the middle ages saw it become a focus for intellectual and cultural forces in the fifteenth and sixteenth centuries. The paintings and graphic works of Nuremberg's famous son, Albrecht Dürer are evident in tourist shops and on postcards. Even the other souvenirs on sale are rather more tasteful and better presented than one would necessarily expect from a city in which the tourist industry thrives. There seems to be no evidence of supposedly humorous T-shirts ('My friend went to Nuremberg and all I got was this bloody T-shirt'). Gifts are more classy with a prevalence of wooden Christmas decorations (even in the height of summer). Having been into Christmas shops and having stood outside them on many more occasions, it is easy to make the judgment that such establishments survive mainly on the trade from American tourists and my wife, although Nuremberg is particularly famous for its toys and Christmas market.

Despite becoming a provincial Bavarian town with no say in government from 1806, enterprise still came to the fore, none more so than through the development of the first German railway in 1835. As the industrial revolution swept across Europe, Nuremberg was to become an important city once again. The role of the city in Germany's history was recognised in 1852 when it became the location for the Germanic National Museum and the historical aspects of the city seem to be constantly celebrated in a variety of exhibitions. In fact, so rich is the history of the place that it really is shocking that, over the many subsequent visits I have made, I have not engaged with it more. If you live somewhere or visit often enough then it is easy to take much of a place for granted. Why visit an attraction today when there is always tomorrow or next time?

Walking around the cobbled streets among the timber-framed buildings of medieval Germany, it is easy to see why the city was considered to be the Holy Roman Empire's treasure chest. As the smell of the traditional *Bratwurst* floats between the shoppers and tourists, tempting them to part with their cash and succumb to the small *Nürnberger* sausages with a bread roll, one gets a sense of the 1000 year history of the city under the watchful gaze of its fourteenth Century castle perched atop the sandstone hill north of the River Pegnitz.

And then there is the approach to the *Frankenstadion*, lined with symbols of the darkest era of modern European history, the surrounding area all part of the venue for the infamous rallies of the Nazi party during the 1930s. Hitler's unfinished *Kongresshalle*, the *Zeppelintribüne* and parade ground all still stand as important reminders of a time we should never forget. But they also stand semi-derelict, like ghosts that time has failed to exorcise. Semi-derelict as if nobody is exactly sure what to do with them. Despite this, the area is instantly recognisable from the film footage and photographs of the 1930s and the Second World War. To think that this was once the city of the Nazi's rallies and that the major players of the era had all at some point been present on and around the *Zeppelintribüne* (the large stone stand and podium from which speeches were delivered to Party faithful) as the economic hardships of Germany, the cleverly spun propaganda and the fearsome rule of the National Socialists provided them with the support and power to plunge Nuremberg, Germany and the rest of Europe into a terrible war. Now this large stone edifice stands at the centre of debate, awaiting urgent repairs to the 360 feet long stepped structure which now not only serves as a reminder of the past but also as an interesting feature for the local skateboarding posse on which to practise and as a grandstand for motor-racing which takes place on the wide boulevards in the vicinity.

The stadium itself has grown from the original, octagonal S*tädtisches Stadion* (municipal stadium) completed in 1928. It originally formed part of the large recreational area south of the city and was then incorporated into the Nazi rally grounds during the 1930s. It was not until 1963 that 1.FCN moved to the stadium and since then several upgrades have enabled it to become a venue not only worthy of *Bundesliga* football but also international matches, athletics events and rock concerts. From 1991 it became known as the *Frankenstadion*, reflecting the local identity felt in Nuremberg and the surrounding region of northern Bavaria known as *Franken* (Franconia). The decision to change the name to that of sponsors Easy Credit in 2006 was not a popular one.

Seeing all of this at first hand was a result of me being made aware that 1.FC Nürnberg were playing at home on the weekend of our visit. When the question of attending the game came up I was intrigued. I'd heard enough about 1.FCN from my future father-in-law to know that they weren't exactly world-beaters – I'd seen it etched into his face as he'd found out results on his German teletext in his English home of some twenty-five years. But I'd also seen the lack of quality at Vale Park, home of the similarly uninspiring Port Vale, and the contrast with the ubiquitous television coverage of the Premier League to know that there was more to the game than the third division and whatever its current branding was selling it as.

We took a tram out of the city and then a walk alongside the peaceful boating lake of *Dutzendteich* and the impressive *Kongresshalle*; yet another reminder of the Führer's vast plans for a Germany with architecture to rival that of the ancient civilisations. As walks to football stadiums go, this one was pretty special. The golden autumn leaves on the late October Sunday afternoon, the stillness of the air as icy breath pierced the declining temperatures, the calm anticipation of those few fans heading in the same direction, towards the floodlights offering a familiar comfort as the sun started to fall. Onwards past the *Zeppelintribüne* and then the wide open spaces around the stadium, with hundreds of fans now converging, carrying their flags and adorned with badges and scarves as if characters in a carnival of red and black.

The purchase of tickets offered even greater comfort to an English fan than the familiar glow of floodlights. Only eight Euros, a fiver, to get into the wonderful modern stadium. Beer and sausages were on sale at dozens of stalls within the perimeter and the huge catering operation appeared to be well-supported by clean toilet facilities at regular intervals, as my fiancée pointed out (football stadium sanitation not being high on the agenda for a male British fan). It was not hard to see why there were so many families present in the stadium. There was banter too. To me it was all a foreign language and I had no idea of exactly what the banter was about but it was instantly recognisable as football banter. Even in this home area of the stadium there were a few opposition shirts visible as 'away' fans milled around with friends or relatives from the city of Nuremberg.

All too soon the game was over. Nuremberg had been defeated by two goals to one and had probably deserved it. The atmosphere had sold it to me though. Despite the attendance being nowhere near capacity, the fans, old and young, male and female, had shouted and sung creating an atmosphere I'd rarely, if ever, seen at Vale Park. The players trudged over to the *Nordkurve* after the whistle and applauded. Most fans applauded back. And I know that my senses were slightly tainted by alcohol but there was something about it that was nice, very nice indeed. Subconsciously I obviously wanted to experience all of this again.

Following that first game in Nuremberg I started to look out for their results and felt a disappointment when they were relegated at the end of the season. But this relegation proved to be something of a catalyst. The next season my now father-in-law, Herbert, would be able to view some free-to-air German second division games through his antiquated satellite system and I became increasingly interested. 1.FCN started to put together a good promotion campaign and I jubilantly celebrated their promotion via poorly translated internet reports and live coverage of games.

'I'm going to the game in Dortmund,' Herbert, informed me. He was visiting Dortmund with my mother-in-law, Elaine and staying with a friend who was a Borussia Dortmund fan. 'Why don't you come?' he asked.

Difficult. The wife's (his daughter's lest he forget) birthday.

And then a moment of genius. Pure genius. A eureka moment.

By now recently married and running out of what Angela, the wife, would see as legitimate excuses to get away for the weekend such as stag parties (the last one I'd been on I'd neglected to tell her of the absence of a stag until it was too late) it was time to introduce to my wife a new approach. Dortmund would be a trial run. A sort of easing into the whole new philosophy. I booked the flights and explained that we were going away for the weekend for her birthday with her parents and I suppose I could accompany her father to the game in the incredibly imposing *Westfalenstadion*. And what a great atmosphere (75,000 attendance) and decent 2-2 draw (first half goals from Marek Mintal and Robert Vittek, equalised before half time with two from the impressive and eventual Nuremberg player Jan Koller) it would be. And of course I'd like to go to other games, after all they were her father's team, the team her grandfather had supported and the team from her hometown. Why would I not want to immerse myself in that sort of family history and culture?

The traffic on the motorway from Cologne where we had arrived late the previous night had made me dubious that we would actually get to Dortmund at all and reminded me of many away journeys all over England, battling with traffic to go and watch 90 minutes of football. As it was we arrived at Uli's house with time to spare and were soon joined by another fan, like Uli, a business associate of Herbert's, and his young son. On the journey to the stadium, I could sense in the car the batting forwards and backwards of football banter but again had no understanding of what was actually said. I comforted myself with the thought that it was likely to be the same sort of football banter heard in England, and then comforted myself further with the fact that whatever these Dortmund fans were saying, today we would win.

We. *We*? I'd assumed that Herbert and I were been given a bit of friendly stick for coming to follow 1.FCN in Dortmund and I'd suddenly adopted the role of a true fan. It was now us and them. We were Nuremberg fans. They were Dortmund fans. This wasn't about violence or aggression. It was purely about pride and witnessing Nuremberg win to provide us with the right to give them some stick after the game in return. With hindsight and my embarrassing lack of German (which was even more embarrassingly lacking then) it's a good job that a neutral draw ensued as I'd given no thought to how I would return the banter in the event of a win other than by childish hand gestures.

Besides, it was good to be able to sit with these new friends in the stadium. We all had tickets in the stand not too far from the away supporters, the *Clubberer* of Nuremberg, but far enough away to be in a very home fan dominated area. The fact that we 'knew' a small handful of these home fans would surely be useful, even more so after Herbert and I had been unable to resist leaping to our feet as each of Nuremberg's goals hit the back of the Dortmund net.

The stadium itself gave a first glimpse of the mass support at German football. The huge home terrace of over 20,000 fans was packed a good thirty minutes before kick-off and huge banners and flags added visual effect to the sea of noise that then emanated from the vociferous crowd.

As we left the stadium and returned to the car park I almost longed to be travelling from the game with the Nuremberg supporters who now climbed onto their buses and into the back of vans, cracking open their beers at the start of a long journey home. I'd have heard tales of how, had this decision gone a certain way, or that player had not done such-and-such, 1.FCN could have defied the odds and gone on to claim victory. I then realised that I would not understand a word of it and was grateful for the short journey back to Uli's house and the excellent hospitality we would enjoy that evening.

Fortunately, the ladies had also apparently enjoyed their afternoon having had a look around the shops of Dortmund and then a trip to the theatre with Uli's wife Traudl. Maybe my wife would have preferred the *Westfalenstadion* to Starlight Express but it appeared that the experiment had worked.

Throughout the season I paid even more attention to 1.FCN score lines, line-ups and highlights. One more quick trip to Nuremberg with Angela (albeit after the season had finished) just to ensure that there was a solid 'cultural' foundation evident for my rising support for 'her' team and the seed had been well and truly sown and was now taking root.

In October 2005, following a poor start to the season, 1.FC Nürnberg seemed to be facing a seven month fight to prevent another relegation and to preserve their *Bundesliga* status (which they had regained in 2004). Having been hooked by tales of a fantastic atmosphere, reeled in with promises of the self-proclaimed most beautiful city in the world, and finally landed by the lure of fine beers and sausages, several friends decided that they, too, would like to visit Nuremberg and attend a match. They were not disappointed in what they discovered, even though Nuremberg lost the game 2-3 at the hands of Arminia Bielefeld.

Despite the defeat, for these travelling revellers there was also a desire to return. Maybe it was the readily available refreshment in the *Frankenstadion*, the cheap ticket price, the atmosphere on the *Nordkurve*, the hospitality of the Franconian people, the beauty of the city itself or the fact that 1.FCN were unlucky to lose the game. No matter, they all knew that they would one day return to lend their support to this enigmatic German football club.

On arriving back in the various corners of the British Isles, and into the workers bars and dark satanic mills (and offices and classrooms) of England's green and pleasant land, something started to stir.

Within months, that 'something' would become 1FCNUK, the United Kingdom Supporters' Club of 1.FC Nürnberg, the

English speaking embodiment of 1.FCN for fans in the UK, Germany and anywhere else we thought we could tempt them from. A simple concept to allow a group of friends and friends of friends to join together for weekends away and enable some of us to fuel our passion for football into the bargain. It all seemed so straightforward.

British fans, German terrace

Chapter 2

Finding our feet
(in our large carbon footprint)

Going to an away game normally necessitates an early start, jumping into the car, listening to various sports shows on the radio, glaring through the windows at other cars and sitting in motorway traffic in rain or shine. All to watch a game of football. Then you have to do it all in reverse, often in the dark, probably when your team has lost. A bit silly when you think about it. But to go and give your support to a team in a different country requires even greater travelling, and because of this fact, the silliness of football support becomes a somewhat more eccentric dedication.

East Midlands Airport is, like most small regional airports, nothing special. To give it its full title of Nottingham East Midlands Airport is to make you think that within a few minutes of disembarking your flight you will be in the centre of the fine English city. You won't. Not that Nottingham has anything particularly wrong with it – like most other regional cities in England, Nottingham has pockets of culture, some examples of fine architecture, a couple of floundering professional football teams and drug-related crime. Had the airport been named after the other cities it serves, Derby and Leicester, the result would have been much the same. With no rail link at the airport, the city centres are only accessible by road, and try as you might, apart from during the dead of night, there will often be a battle with traffic to reach the football or anything else you wish to see.

However, East Midlands Airport, probably as a result of the fact that it is relatively 'no frills', does have two distinct advantages. First, it is used by several so-called low-cost airlines which fly to various German destinations. Second, it is little over one hour's drive from the Staffordshire/Cheshire border (a dubious claim to fame if there ever was one, but it was here that our fan club was founded).

"Great," you may say. Low cost airlines? Aren't they renowned for treating their passengers like cattle, herding them onto the aircraft in a fifteen minute slot, causing a stampede in the process? Don't they appear on TV documentaries showing their young, cocky staff in garish uniforms doing everything they can to inconvenience the passengers and then laughing about it when they think the camera has stopped rolling? And the passengers themselves – are they not all unemployed unemployables using their benefit money to fly abroad every three months to buy 100,000 cigarettes all for 'personal consumption'? And to top it all, are these not the very same airlines that the environmental bandwagon would have us believe are almost entirely responsible for the impending destruction of our planet through global warming?

Well of course, some of the above is true and depending on your particular flight, your fellow passengers or the newspaper you read, then the degree of 'truth' is as much about perception as it is about fact.

At check in, the staff are invariably polite *despite* having to wear garish uniforms. They might laugh about the incompetence of some of their passengers once those passengers are out of earshot but what harm does that do (as long as there is no film crew who know that it will make 'great' television). When arriving at the departure gate of course there is some jockeying for position as passengers seek any advantage to enable them to gain the best of the unallocated seats. Some are skilful in their movements, changing direction and pace as they move in and around the forming queues, much the same as a racing yacht seeks to be in the premium position when the race starts. Others are downright rude and will shove and push, curse and moan in an attempt to beat the skilful and less skilful alike by expending as little energy and courtesy as possible. Finally there are those who don't care which seat they have. This group can be divided into two sub-categories. There are those who just sit down and wait, happy to let the rest of the passengers board, safe in the knowledge that they have paid for a seat on the flight and that there will, therefore, be a seat on the aircraft for them when they finally saunter down the aisle after the initial tide of passengers has subsided. Then there is the sub-category of passengers who know they have a seat, don't want to queue and would happily wait until everyone else has boarded but are incensed by the arrogance of several passengers who are elbowing and pushing. In fact so incensed are they, that they have to make a stand and join the queue close to the front just to make a point to those evil queue jumpers, thus often gaining a greater advantage than most other passengers and ending up with the extra legroom seats and the pick of any free newspapers handed out as they step onto the aircraft.

All of this, of course, takes place after the interior of the airport terminal has been circumnavigated in a matter of three minutes. 180 seconds of searching for somewhere to get a coffee, beer, bottle of water or anything resembling a snack for less than £5 before remembering that retailers will charge what they want because the next nearest shop is fifteen miles away at the motorway service station. You then realise that catering facilities in small regional airport terminals and motorway service stations are siblings in the 'overcharge the public' family and you therefore hand over your £1.50 for a packet of crisps before joining the mayhem of security checks and departure gates.

You're now probably feeling slightly aggrieved. This will be for one of a number of reasons. You may be the general manager of a small regional airport and totally disagree with the comments made above. If so, please be aware that these are the views of some people and do not necessarily reflect the views of the author who probably likes your airport very much and would like it even more if you could personally ease his passage through your terminal on his next visit. Maybe you're aggrieved because you are reading this book in an airport terminal and have been observing all of the comments made above (which are, remember, the views of some people) and you too are now beginning to share such views, particularly as your flight is now entering its third hour of delay. However, you are probably more aggrieved than anything at the fact that you purchased a book which you thought might have something to do with football but instead you are now reading an amateur sociological rant about airports and low-cost flights. What indeed has this got to do with football?

Well actually, it goes with the patch if your patch happens to be supporting a team overseas (unless you are Roman Abramovich and you decide to support and buy a trendy London team – I assume Mr Abramovich does not make much use of the Russian equivalent of Easyjet, Aeroflot Lite, or whatever it might be called). If your patch is supporting a team in the German *Bundesliga* but you live on an average income in England then regional airports and cheap flights are important tools in your footballing kit bag.

The city break was the travel success of the 1990s – a way to immerse oneself into a different culture for a couple of days before beating a retreat to the mundane nine to five job and the house in suburbia. Budget airlines and fierce competition to fill flights played a major role in tempting the middle classes to dip their toes into the life of another city, safe in the knowledge that however much they liked or disliked the place, the hotel, the food and the locals, they could soon be sitting back at their desk telling their colleagues about their latest 'adventure'.

The opening up of Eastern Europe added to the growing array of destinations on offer and this proved to be the start of another travel boom. Stag parties and hen parties decided that it was almost as cheap to fly east and consume vast quantities of cheap, tasty local beers and spirits than have a weekend in a traditional British holiday resort, previously the mainstay of the hen and stag industry.

When that group of my friends suggested that they would like to go on a city break to Nuremberg and, in doing so take in a game of football back in October 2005, it seemed like an eminently sensible suggestion. The beautiful city, cheap flights, great German brews and a game of footy would have had any stag (or hen) party getting extremely excited. Despite the fact that we had no stag or hen in our group, we were determined to make it every bit as exciting as a pre-nuptial weekend away, and by the time we arrived in Nuremberg we were determined that on this break nothing was going to stop us having fun. That we took in a game and 1.FCN lost is of little relevance now. That all of the party – male and female – enjoyed the atmosphere, enjoyed the food, enjoyed the company and enjoyed the beer, cast some sort of spell, a spell which took its real hold over the next couple of months when some of us hastily put together our UK based fan club of 1.FC Nürnberg.

Officially launched on 1st January 2006 with just seven members, it was expected that no more than twenty or so friends and relatives would be coerced into joining to give those of us with a growing obsession for the *Bundesliga* team at least a tiny bit of credibility. And so they were coerced into joining and it took little persuasion to get them on a plane as we decided that it was time to go to another game.

On a wet Friday in early March 2006, nineteen members of 1FCNUK gathered at East Midlands Airport (at last the link is made). Our pre-booked, low-cost, large carbon footprint of a flight would take us to Cologne for the following day's match between FC Cologne and 1.FCN. The airport and flight experience was as good and as bad as all of the aspects of the regional airport/low-cost airline combination promises and the 11p.m. arrival in the centre of Cologne (via a cheap and efficient train service from the airport) set us up for a good couple of nights in Germany's third largest city.

The excitement of a match day is always special. Waking up, finding the scarf, pulling on the shirt, meeting friends, maybe a beer or two before the game. That Saturday morning in Cologne saw the excitement slightly dampened by the sub-zero temperatures and further tempered by the trepidation of what was to be something of a journey into the unknown. And most of us had a hangover.

Nineteen of us that day pulled on our newly commissioned 1FCNUK polo shirts plus several other layers of clothing. Our first Scottish member, chairman and co-founder Iain, donned his kilt. Meeting in a city centre bar, who knows what the locals thought? Seventeen-and-a-half Brits and one-and-a-half Germans (the father-in-law had of course got involved from the outset, the wife was thus far going along with the whole thing) supporting the visiting team, taking photographs of each other with a Union Jack with that team's badge sitting proudly in the centre. The thought crossed our minds that had we been German supporters of an English team carrying a German flag on a visit to another English stadium, we would surely have been incarcerated by the local constabulary before our suicide mission had any chance to bear fruit. We took a couple more photographs and put the flag away. Even then, there was the nagging question of how fellow Nuremberg supporters, the travelling hardcore of the club, would take to these Brits standing with them shouting on their team.

Before leaving the UK there had been email contact with a representative of 1.FCN who would meet us at the stadium. This would surely work absolutely fine with German efficiency bound to bring our man to us in the correct place at the correct time. We arrived early and then realised we had a problem. We had no idea what *he* looked like and for that matter *we* would be just more faces in the growing crowds outside the stadium. There was only one thing for it – the flag had to be unfurled to act as a beacon and ensure that we actually got hold of our tickets. (Looking back now, it could all have gone horribly wrong. Had we not managed to locate our tickets, our fledgling supporters club may have simply faded into oblivion even more quickly than it had been formed.)

As the flag came out, so the crowds closed in. Several of them reached into their pockets surely to pull out knives or knuckledusters. Our flag would probably be slashed and burned and who knows what our fate would be apart from making the headlines as supposed hooligans causing a riot.

Then the first hand withdrew from its pocket, and the next, and the next. The would-be assailants stopped and gestured to us all to stand closer to our flag. Then the 'weapons' were pointed in our direction and mobile phone cameras took photographs from all angles. Hands were shaken, friendships were forging (or at least as much as friendships can be forged with a travelling football fan who has just stepped off a coach after a five hour journey throughout which he has consumed a crate of beer). Our initial fears about our reception seemed to have been ill-founded and the goodwill continued throughout the match, at least from fellow Nuremberg supporters.

Suddenly there appeared a moustached man, clearly bearing the stresses of organising 2,500 travelling fans.

"Welcome to fucking Cologne," he called, his 'good' English failing to belie the fact that he was somewhat hassled. It was to our relief that Jürgen Bergmann, who has ever since done everything he can to assist our regular pilgrimages to Germany, handed us the match tickets.

Jürgen is the 1.FC Nürnberg *Fanbeauftragte*. His role is everything concerning the fans of *Der Club*. He is the fan's representative both home and away, doing everything he can to ensure the fans are treated well and that they behave themselves. By liaising with the clubs, fan groups and police he is not only proactive in his role but also reactive to a whole host of issues during and after the matches. All clubs have to have a fan representative working in the same capacity as Jürgen. In the *Bundesliga* and at some second tier clubs the role is now generally full-time although when we first met him, Jürgen was essentially doing the role as a volunteer in his spare time and working full time in the club shop and ticket office during the day. At least he got to see the games for free though and as a fan of 1.FCN it was surely a dream role, although that day his face hid it well if that was the case.

Of course, we had requested standing tickets because we'd been denied standing in the UK for so long, but sometimes it is not hard to see the advantages of having a seat at a football match. When you enter a standing area and try to squeeze between the already packed-in bodies to find a few square centimetres of concreted prime real estate on which to stand, the only thing that gives you the will to continue is the excitement of the impending match. And this small piece of real estate – 30cm by 30cm of concrete, let's say at £10 for ninety minutes of football plus the halftime break and the waiting around before and after the game. If you think about it in rental terms, that's approximately £120 per day, £3600 per month for somewhere to stand! Let's face it, even the most prestigious office or living accommodation in the world compares favourably to football terrace prices. Imagine if you wanted a very modest living space on the terrace – a three by three metre bed-sit for example – £360,000 per month rental or £4.3 million per year. But, there is no luxury in the space you rent for a couple of hours, the space you have to defend vigorously throughout that time as every small ripple of action on the pitch is magnified into a fully blown tsunami of bodies on the terrace. Wherever you rent your space you seem to have a decent enough view of the pitch, over the rooftops as it were of your neighbours. And best of all, there appears to be no space for any further construction work in your neighbourhood so at least your view will remain unimpeded for the duration of the game. But then, as the pre-match anticipation turns into either excitement or foreboding some time during those thirty seconds either side of kick-off, a huge tower block is plonked straight in front of you. And the huge tower block has had a few too many in the pub (hence his late arrival). Furthermore, he seems to think that he needs even greater height advantage by intermittently standing on your toes or leaning on the shoulders of the person in front of him. He requires an oil change for his hair and then opens his mouth and starts uttering the most unbelievable gibberish about the game which he obviously sees completely differently than those around him (or at least those who can see *around* him).

At half-time one has to make a crucial decision. Do you risk surrendering your prime spot and joining the ridiculous queue for the toilets or do you convince yourself that you can wait until full-time (knowing subconsciously that you will last until the seventy-eighth minute and then have to push your way through the terrace again, finally reaching the toilets in the eighty-fifth minute as a goal is scored, forgetting all rules of hygiene as you run from the toilet still fastening your zip, trying in a forlorn attempt to glean information about the goal which you then realise will be the same information you could have got another thirty seconds later without having peed down your jeans and on your shoes)?

And then there are the problems associated with eating and drinking on the terrace. You buy a pie (or *Bratwurst* in Germany) and a plastic glass full of coke (or beer in Germany) and you somehow manage to find your standing place without spilling anything. Then it's time to eat. Now you still have your wallet in one hand, as well as the change from your purchases in the other, and your pie (or similar) and your drink. And it's the drink that is the real problem here. You clearly can't put it down as so much as a pass from your midfielder that even nearly goes to one of his team-mates will cause the forest of feet and legs to bounce and swing and destroy anything in their path. So you have to keep hold of the drink and try to manipulate all of the other items with a dexterity only ever attempted by a football fan. Your loose change falls to the floor and roles away between the undergrowth of boots, trainers and shoes on display. The ketchup or mustard on your food drips onto your hand, sleeve and trouser leg. A large piece of pie crust or sausage falls to the floor and is quickly squashed by a heel. Your wallet falls to the floor and all you can do is firmly place your foot upon it until such time that you have a hand free enough (and clean enough) to pick it up. Finally, the plastic vessel in which your drink is held provides a cruel twist in the saga of the football terrace epicure. While you get mildly annoyed about dropping the change (let's say £1.20), don't notice the spillage of sauce until later when you have inadvertently wiped it on another item of clothing, which in turn you don't notice until even later (usually when it is pointed out by an attractive member of the opposite sex), you are actually quite pleased with the trapping of your wallet beneath your left foot. Unfortunately, throughout all of this, you have been squeezing the drink and now realise that your cuff is saturated and half of the liquid is now on the floor and your footwear, a fact that really gets you incredibly irritated. A total of £5 for half a pie or sausage bun and half a glass of barely drinkable cola flavoured drink.

But for many, to stand up at a football match is the way in which the game was meant to be viewed and all of its discomforts and inconveniences are outweighed by the banter and atmosphere.

In Cologne, the relief of having the tickets in our hands was now as much about getting into the stadium to find relief in the form of the toilets and relief from the cold in the form of the packed terrace.

Compared to our previous experience in Nuremberg where we were yet to see a full house, the excellent away support for *Der Club* resulted in a heaving standing area similar to that described above. The main exceptions to this were the price and the fact that rather than squeezing through to find space for oneself, we moved onto the terrace trying to find space for nineteen which incredibly we managed to do (and in doing so spoil the view for many behind us). But we were there and despite the crush there was still a beer seller, pushing through the crowd with a barrel on his back and a tap in his hand. Our newly coerced members, while being somewhat puzzled by the attention and discomforted by the cold, were starting to warm to (or be warmed by) the crowd and the pre-match atmosphere.

As the teams took to the pitch the bemused look on the faces of those of us to whom a bit of frost was a signal to wrap up and make yourself look like the Michelin man was not shared by the fellow *Clubberer*. Perched on top of the fence at the front of the terrace was a young man with a loud hailer. It would be his job to whip up the support from the travelling Franconians, leading the songs to support the team on their travels. This seemed somewhat odd for two reasons. Surely anybody sitting on top of a fence (when they existed) at an English football ground would have been swiftly removed by the truncheons of heavy-handed policing tactics, but that was not the case here as the stewards and police simply looked on. However, what was even more striking was that this guy had removed his shirt to clearly show the sacrifice he was prepared to make for his team (although he may have done it to allow the perishing cold to distract his mind from what must have been the huge discomfort of straddling the fence). Throughout the match he yelled and gestured with his back to the pitch inevitably missing the majority of the game. He'd obviously set his video for the highlights programme later.

The highlights would be worth watching. If the cold, the crush, the eccentricities and surrealism of the day to this point had bemused many of our members then the game itself was surely sufficient to turn even the biggest sceptic into a fan. It went pretty much like this as Nuremberg sealed a 4-3 victory (having taken a 3-0 lead): a hat trick from Robert Vittek, two penalties, moaning players (Streller and Podolski of Cologne), an excellent goal from Ivan Saenko, strong defending from Mario Cantaluppi, moaning players (Streller and Podolski of Cologne), poor decisions by the referee (for both teams), seven yellow cards, one red card, moaning players (Streller and Podolski of Cologne), diving (from Streller), moaning players (Streller and Podolski of Cologne), missed easy chances by Stefan Kiessling, and to put the icing on the cake – an orange ball when it snowed!

The main Nuremberg characters on show were Slovakian striker Robert Vittek (he of the hat-trick), speedy but temperamental Russian forward Ivan Saenko, defensive midfielder and club captain Mario Cantaluppi and promising young German forward Stefan Kiessling (he of the missed chances). As you will gather from the match 'facts', it was popular opinion among the travelling support that Cologne's Swiss forward Marco Streller dived and moaned and was joined in the moaning by (at that time) the great German hope and soon to be Bayern Munich player Lukas Podolski. Were they really as bad as I make out above? Probably not but during that game some of us were getting into the whole thing so much that amidst all of the shouting, barracking and singing we maybe lost some objectivity. We were bothered about the result and some bias was coming into our judgment because all of a sudden the games of 1.FC Nürnberg were starting to matter.

Later, following banter and singing over a meal in a Cologne restaurant, we inadvertently found a bar in which we met Cologne fans unhappy with the outcome of the game. Most German football teams have their club 'hymn' which is blasted out at home games before kick-off with much flag-waving and scarves held proudly aloft, creating scenes akin to those on the Kop at Liverpool as the fans belt out 'You'll Never Walk Alone'. These hymns are usually pretty rousing stuff and ignite the atmosphere, whether they are about hatred for the opposition or the long suffering of your own team. Some are shockingly bad others are just bad. The 1.FCN hymn, *Die Legende Lebt* (The Legend Lives) is tolerable and when a full stadium is singing it with scarves held high it's pretty powerful stuff – but then again, remember I'm a Port Vale fan not accustomed to much in the way of rousing anthems.

Ein Fels in wilder Brandung (a rock in wild fiery surf) it begins,

Der alles überstand (surviving everything)
Er hielt in vielen Jahren (holding on for many years)
So manchen Stürmen stand (surviving everything)

Another verse of similar sentiments follows before the crescendo of the chorus:

Die Legende lebt (the legend lives)
Wenn auch die Zeit vergeht (although the time passes)

Unser Club der bleibt besteh'n (our club remains standing)
Die Legende lebt (the legend lives)
Wenn auch der Wind sich dreht (even if the wind turns)
Unser Club wird niemals untergeh'n (our club will never fall)

Had someone simply changed the word 'club' to 'love' and encouraged a male/female duo to sing it in traditional dress to a backdrop showing images of snow-capped mountains and alpine meadows, then surely this would have been an ideal Eurovision entry guaranteed to finish somewhere between tenth and fifteenth place. As it is though, in its raw state in the stadium it sounds quite reasonable. Unfortunately it all becomes a little more dubious when performed on electric guitar pre-match or when it becomes the subject of a radio competition in Nuremberg for different artists to perform their own version. Both have happened and believe me they do not make for easy listening. In fact the Eurovision idea sounds quite appealing in comparison.

We'd heard the Cologne anthem in the stadium before the game and thought little of it. Now, at 10p.m. escorted into a packed nightspot and through the crowds to the bar by an old friend and resident in the area (who incidentally has no interest or understanding whatsoever about football or its rivalries) we heard a vaguely familiar tune begin to play. The hordes then started to sing and we realised that we were standing among several hundred home fans singing with passion but still hurting from what they saw as a harsh defeat (evidently agreeing with the moaning of Streller and Podolski towards the officials). At this stage we could have simply pleaded Englishness and would have been welcome to drink, sing and sulk with the locals but unfortunately, beneath our heavy winter jackets we had our Nuremberg shirts and were now rapidly tucking away our red and black scarves.

Other than a handful of fans shouting down and spitting at our terrace after the final whistle and a few others banging on the side of a tram carrying Nuremberg supporters back to the city centre, we'd not witnessed any hostility or trouble. But now, whipped up by their anthem, the fans were not happy to realise that we were clearly hiding something beneath our outer clothing as we sweated and tried to drink our beer as quickly as possible. When a straggler from our group entered the bar a few minutes later wearing her Nuremberg hat, it was time to make a sharp exit to a tirade of verbal abuse.

This was a situation that has been generally isolated. Of course, there are idiots attached to German football but, given the fact that we have now visited matches in various cities across Germany as away fans and then spent plenty of time in and around the cities after the game (as opposed to travelling back to Nuremberg with the majority of the away following), it is maybe surprising that we have not met more aggression or abuse. Certainly it is not the same if you do a similar thing in the UK, although this probably says more about the differences between British and German drinking culture than it does about the so-called 'hooligan' elements attaching themselves to various football clubs. Rarely have we witnessed or heard of any city centre brawling in Germany, although then again, rarely do we see alcopops being consumed in the fashion seen in many British town centres. It remains the case that we have been welcomed almost everywhere and that the only time we have felt uneasy is because, as could also be the case at home, we've made the wrong decision (usually inadvertently) about the bar in which to drink.

Incredibly, despite the cold and the clear fact that some of those coerced into the trip to Cologne had little or no interest in football, they all seemed to have enjoyed themselves. For those of us who seemed to eat, drink and sleep football, the game had been something of a spectacle if only because of the wide variety of incidents and talking points it contained. Furthermore, it was now absolutely apparent that, despite our love for our 'own' teams back in the UK, there was no way of going back on our support for 1.FCN. They were now also *our* team and we wanted to see them again as soon as possible.

Herbert Schauer with the 1FCNUK flag

Chapter 3

Welcome to the family

For many of my formative years I'd had a tabloid tainted relationship with Germany. I was intelligent enough to know that Germans were not bad people and I knew that the war was long since over. I was even pretty sure that Germany itself was a nice enough country, although I'd never been there. In fact I was known to have said, and rather daringly out loud, that the German national team were very strong and could actually be admired for their teamwork and dedication. That I survived to tell the tale was probably due to the fact that in any encounter between the English and German football teams I would join in with some of the anti-German sentiment, not because of a hatred for Germans and Germany but because it was the easy and popular thing to do. I didn't believe most of it but certainly didn't shy away from it in the heat of the moment.

And then I met my wife to be. I had no inkling about her German roots. Her lack of accent, Hispanic skin tones, dark hair and brown eyes cunningly disguising the fact. It would not have mattered of course if I had known immediately but I was still to meet her father.

The day would arrive soon enough when, following a car crash in which Angela and I were both involved (I was driving but blameless), I visited their family home. He saw my approach from his balcony raised above the roadside. I was unprepared.

As his Germanic voice boomed down questions of whether I thought I was Michael Schumacher I contemplated turning around and disappearing to seek out an English girl for myself. But horrendous media xenophobia had taught me two things: that the English do not surrender in the face of a German onslaught and that allegedly the Germans have no sense of humour. So I laughed it off and was soon to be welcomed into the family, with newspaper influenced nonsense giving way to good-natured banter over the years that would follow. It would be seven years later that all of us would be welcomed into an even larger family.

In the early years Herbert often told me stories about the football team he supported. The ups and down, financial crises, managerial changes, departures of key players and so on. It sounded very similar to Port Vale. I sympathised as he told me of the latest defeat, marvelled at the wonderful history of his team and felt genuinely sorry for him when he could clearly not get over the relegation of 1999 when on the final day of the season Nuremberg had started the day in twelfth place. They hit the post in the final moments of their game against Freiburg and lost 2-1 while Frankfurt scored three in the final nine minutes against Kaiserslautern ultimately condemning 1.FCN to sixteenth place. They were relegated not even on goal difference but by virtue of the fact that Frankfurt had scored four more goals over the season. My sympathy was there but as a Vale supporter I had plenty of football worries of my own to have time to think too much about events in Germany.

A few short weeks after we had witnessed the victory in Cologne, a resurgent 1.FCN played Kaiserslautern at home on Easter Sunday. Having climbed almost majestically away from the relegation zone which they had propped up only four months previously, *Der Club* had lost just one of the last six games and were scoring goals almost at will, mainly as a result of the blistering form of Robert Vittek. (Vittek had not found the net in the first half of the season but then went on to score sixteen *Bundesliga* goals after the winter break – a new record.)

In Nuremberg, word had by now started to get round that there was a fan club based in the UK and when we requested tickets for the game we got more than we bargained for. The confirmation of tickets came with an invitation to the *Fansprechstunde* (the fan speaking hour) at which we were to be guests of honour and officially welcomed into the 'family of fan clubs'. Such an event occurs before every home game with representatives of the club, and sometimes players as well, answering questions from a gathered audience about all matters related to the running of 1.FCN.

As fan clubs of German teams go, ours is quite distinctive, largely because we are not German (apart from a few members) and we are not based in Germany. However, we have come across the Bali fan club of FCN, unfortunately in Germany and not in their Bali fan pub from which they watch Nuremberg matches on TV. We've also met Klaus, the founder member (and only member at last count) of the Florida fan club but, in my slightly biased opinion, neither of these groups is quite as prolific as 1FCNUK. However, in comparison to many of the German based fan clubs our prolific-ness pales into insignificance. There seems to be a never-ending social calendar in which the fan clubs hold competitions and drinking sessions often having players or other club representatives attending their events. Their pride comes from supporting 1.FCN, and they do so with an amazing level of commitment, often basing their whole social life around fan club activities.

On a later visit to Germany we would be welcomed by the Grüner Baum (Green Tree – after the name of their fan club's home bar) who treated us to a night of drink and song with handshakes and friendships the inevitable outcome. Like many fan clubs, the Grüner Baum was founded by a group of

Nuremberg supporters in their local pub. All it seems to take is a willing landlord and willing fans, plus a few beers to make it a success. Some of the Grüner Baum members were quite clearly accustomed to the beer side of membership, one even complaining that an apartment opposite the bar played the music so loud that they could not drink with the bar windows open at 10a.m., although he did reassure me that it was normally more peaceful in the afternoon.

Another fan club had a football team (of sorts) who we have played for on more than one occasion. We have been taken to the Nuremberg *Volksfest* by another fan club and, following a train and car journey out of town we were guests one pleasant afternoon of the Buchschwabach fan club. While each club has its idiosyncrasies, each has at its heart a devotion to 1.FCN. Our club is no different at its very core but beyond that many of our members are less bothered about the football but more interested in the socialising at home and particularly in Germany.

In April 2006 at the pre-match *Fansprechstunde* our numbers largely consisted of the Nuremberg supporting hardcore of our membership. The forum takes place in a convenient room at the stadium, usually the Max Morlock *Stuben*, a purpose built bar in which fans can drink just inside the turnstiles. The fan clubs are represented by members of the FCN *Fanverband* and the club itself is represented usually by the Vice-President, Siggy Schneider. Open to all fans, the greatest surprise is that it is not completely packed. However, apart from those with an interest in the running of fan clubs and the specific interactions between the club and fans, most stay away.

In our excitement prior to our welcome we had flown into the city on the Friday night. This time, the only budget flight we could get involved a four hour drive to Stansted airport (don't worry, if I started on Stansted there'd be no room in the book for any more football). The wise choice was to drive or 'navigate' the long car journey, both options necessitating a separate seat in the front of the car rather than an uncomfortable crush in the back. In this respect, going to matches in Germany is like an away game in England. Unfortunately, the end of the drive sees you holed-up in an airport terminal awaiting the next leg of the journey rather than the game itself.

There are, of course advantages that outweigh the extra travelling. Our Friday arrival gave us all plenty of time the next day to investigate the city and its culture, largely that of the local bars, more vigorously. Although we had no clear idea of what our fan club was about, apart from supporting Nuremberg and getting to as many matches as logistically and financially possible, we had a nice website and wanted to use it to recommend 1.FC Nuremberg and 1FCNUK to anyone who happened to come across it while surfing the internet. It was either a cunning idea or a lame excuse when we decided that we should research the bars of Nuremberg to provide website visitors with useful information in case they visited the city. Nigel, a hardy and well-built member, who was no stranger to a beer, took it upon himself to make notes as we visited each bar. It was only later that we discovered that he had given scores for the beer, the price, the barmaids and the ambience for each establishment. Unfortunately the accuracy seemed to diminish as the day went on, largely because what was supposed to be an investigative pub crawl of a quick and small drink in many bars, turned into a long drawn-out affair as we started to become accustomed to the fact that the pub-crawl is a rather British past-time, the Germans drinking as much but preferring to stay in one place for several drinks. Our problem lay in the fact that we managed to combine the two cultures, having several drinks in each establishment before moving onto the next. Such was the commitment to our research and forging friendships with the people of Franconia.

    We'd even printed a small fanzine explaining in English and German (but mostly English) about our fan club and our adventures thus far. The fanzine was not met with disdain although the 1 Euro price put many off (only later would we discover that the full colour match programme is just 1 Euro and other fan clubs handed out their flyers for free). We managed to sell a few copies to people who approached us and were curious as we sat gently supping during the afternoon. Looking like, although certainly not acting like (despite the beer intake), typical British football yobs with our flag across the table in each bar we visited, it was clear that there was a good level of interest, bemusement and respect for the fact that we were bothering to come several hundred miles to lend our support to the local team. Outside one bar, a British ex-pat informed us that our visit had already been mentioned in the local press and showed us the small article. People came up to us in the street and some people even wanted to be photographed with us.

By early evening, tired of carrying the fanzines around and with German beer making us believe we could even sell snow to Eskimos, we embarked on a bit more hard-sell and shifted the majority of the 100 copies we'd taken with us. Our newly adopted readers were treated to a welcome page (in German), an introduction to 1FCNUK, current views on the team and puerile football-related humour (all in English). It was certainly far from ground-breaking and the reliance on our own language (the title *Der Spieler* – the player – probably lured a few Euros our way before the buyer was aware of the English content) was something of a barrier, but some customers were seen to be flicking through it and laughing occasionally. And the sales would maybe cover the cost of our web space for a couple of years.

Partying into the small hours with friends old and new is always a fun experience, particularly when there is no specific plan in place other than to go with the flow.

Unfortunately, as we awoke late on the Sunday morning to prepare ourselves (at leisure) for the 5.30p.m. kick-off that afternoon, it became apparent that one of our members had not made it back to the hotel. It would naturally be kind to not reveal his identity here, but in the true spirit of football focused banter and piss-taking, it has to be said that it was our Chairman at the time, Scotsman Iain. A little out of character but maybe he had got lucky with a local girl and had continued his evening long after the rest of us had called it a night. We tried to call him a few times but his phone was well and truly switched off. No doubt he would roll up at some point during the day with a coy smile and resolve not to discuss his dalliance, at least until he was next drunk.

Then I received a text message:

In hospital. In a bad way.

Panic set in immediately. Here was a good friend clearly in some sort of trouble.

Had offence been taken to a Brit supporting the team? Had a gang of German thugs dragged him into a back alley and inflicted damage as a warning to us all that we should never return? Had an angry and jealous boyfriend caught him as he was mid-dalliance? Or had he been injured escaping from a bedroom window? The thoughts were spinning as several of us gathered around my mobile phone. I was worried. I read the message again and a new thought struck me.

Iain always has the habit of using full words and correct punctuation in his texts whether through a crusade to uphold good English or to be pedantic, and this one was no different. However, I was now left wondering what my wife was about to verbalise. Which hospital was he in? My thumb started to work over the keys of the phone as I dialled to call him but his phone was once again switched-off.

And Angela's question about the identity of the hospital was only the start of a tirade of angry interrogation from her, most of which was rhetorical regarding how much had we bloody well had to drink and why the hell had we let someone, albeit a grown man, out of our sight.

Angela's language skills meant that when she had calmed down I needed to get her into a taxi to accompany me on a possible tour of Nuremberg's hospitals. We got lucky with our first choice. The receptionist informed us that indeed a Mr Finlayson had been admitted to the *Klinikum Nord* but could not help us any further unless we were family. I'd got the gist of what she was saying before it was translated for me and was starting to panic. Christ, how serious was it? Was he dead? Had his text been his last words? As I had understood the receptionist without translation she also seemed to understand me as I raised my voice and rather rudely asked her to tell us where the bloody hell he was and what was wrong. After further admonishment from the wife, I then watched as she explained the situation to the less than amused receptionist and was eventually given a map and directions to another building.

We wound our way through the hospital grounds looking for a building of which I can no longer remember the number that was printed on a map. No name. No title. Just a number.

We arrived at the building and approached the door. I read the sign which to my relief identified that it was not the mortuary.

Klinik für Psychiatrie und Psychotherapie read the small notice. Relief turned to bewilderment as we entered the building. As there was nobody to greet us we made our way along a corridor where we were approached by a nurse who must have quickly realised our mission and scurried off to be replaced a few seconds later by a doctor. I was under orders to keep my mouth shut as Angela explained the purpose of our visit in German.

"Ahhh, You've come about Schotty!" laughed the doctor in English.

He continued to laugh to himself for a few seconds. This was a relief to my ears. It was not the menacing laugh of a maniac which would have suggested that we were his next victims but the chuckle of someone trying to remain professional and find the correct words to describe a silly predicament.

Apparently Iain was ok and had been picked up by the police in the small hours after they witnessed him trip in the city centre. He'd broken his nose as he instinctively used it and his glasses to break his fall, not wanting to use his hands as they were carrying a kebab and a can of Coke. When the flow of blood would not stop the police took him to the hospital for treatment. However, the sight of a drunk, kilt-wearing Scot covered in his own blood had caused something of a stir and strapping him to a bed for the night was seen as a sensible option to prevent any further self-inflicted wounds.

Now in a far lighter mood myself, relieved that Iain was safe and upbeat that I had a great story for the others to hear, I informed the doctor that we'd now take Iain off the hands of the hospital and return him to the hotel where he would no doubt catch up on a couple of hours sleep and then head off to the match.

"Oh no. Not yet," I was informed. "We cannot let him go until the alcohol has gone from his blood."

I decided it was best not to protest that his blood had not been alcohol free for years and asked instead when the doctor thought that would be. "Maybe later this afternoon," was not the reply I wanted to hear, especially as we were refused access to Iain to reassure him that we were there for him and that he could meet us at the stadium if he could escape in time. We left the hospital without him and returned to our hotel.

As later that afternoon came round, fearful that jumping up and down in the stadium would not be conducive to helping him recover, the hospital authorities refused to release him until it was too late to go to the match and he was, therefore, to miss our big occasion. He didn't even eat the kebab he had saved as he fell, though he remembered last seeing it in the hands of the police officer.

And so, with one man down, to the stadium. The flag was held open as we passed by the increasingly familiar landmarks. The excitement was clearly building for our fan club and the thousands of other Nuremberg fans approaching the stadium, yet my mood was a little sombre, maybe fitting for the surroundings from an era of indisputable evil, except my mood was not even reflecting on these times. I was subdued, even a bit pissed off; this was a big day for all of us but a prominent figure was missing and I felt dreadfully sorry for him. It was a throw away comment from Iain about having a fan club that had cranked my support for 1.FCN up to the level of today's events. This was his day as much as anybody's and now he was awaiting release from hospital and unable to attend the game. The stupid bastard.

Once again, our Union flag was drawing more interest and more photographs and on arriving at the venue it was taken from us and hung with pride by our hosts. After a few minutes of standing around as people took photos or asked questions we were ushered to stand in front of the flag as a Vice-President of 1.FC Nürnberg and the President of the fan association made speeches. The gathered audience nodded approvingly in our direction every few sentences and applauded when prompted to do so. If it felt strange to be the centre of attention then it was even more strange to have no idea what was being said about us. Maybe the nods of approval were in agreement to comments by the speaker that we were completely insane and should be treated with a mix of caution and sympathy as he surely pointed out that we were all slightly unstable travelling all this way to watch a game of football. Had he made such comments he could certainly have corroborated them by adding that our chairman was indeed in a psychiatric unit as he spoke.

It was then Herbert's turn to take to the floor in his capacity as our President. The locals applauded Herbert's words and gasped as he predicted that we would one day reach a membership of 100. We just sniggered at what, at that time, seemed such a preposterous prediction. As Herbert then launched into what was quite probably his life story, the welcoming party were finding it difficult to prise the microphone from his grip but eventually, despite his pride and excitement he was persuaded to relinquish the floor to enable the officials to present us with a signed shirt and ball and the certificate confirming our new status as an official fan club of 1.FC Nürnberg. Much hand-shaking followed with officials and the gathered fans, and reporters asked questions about our support, the logistics of it all and the contrast with English football.

The press interest continued the next day. We'd seen our pictures in the local papers over breakfast and I was shocked to see that I had been completely misquoted by one reporter who somehow took my comment about the German football we had witnessed thus far as being more exciting than much of what we got in England as meaning that all German players were soft and dived around too much. As we left a café we were excitedly approached by another photographer who claimed she had been looking all over for us. She then proceeded to take photographs, adopting all manner of positions and vantage points before asking a few questions and disappearing with what appeared to be for her something of a scoop. It was all rather surreal – what had started as an excuse for a few beers and weekends away had seemingly turned us into sought after and well-respected fans of a famous German football team. On a small scale, the paparazzi were pointing their cameras at us and even the pitfall of misrepresentation in print had started to sweep us along in a whirl of minor celebrity status. Although it was all a bit difficult to comprehend, it was somewhat exciting and quite enjoyable. For now.

It was probably more than fortunate, for our popularity at least, that we had arrived on the Nuremberg fan club scene at a time that the fortunes of the team on the pitch were on the up. It was also quite clear to the fellow fans we spoke to that we were not just tourists or some sort of gimmick and we were knowledgeable about the club and players, and more importantly gave our heartfelt vocal support from the terraces. That weekend, amidst all the attention surrounding one fan club, 47,000 fans witnessed Nuremberg beat Kaiserslautern 3-2 with two more goals from Robert Vittek, his second, Nuremberg's third, the winning goal eight minutes from time after *Der Club* had been 2-1 behind. The atmosphere in the stadium was incredible and the size of the crowd was in sharp contrast to the previous game we had seen there less than six months previously. The spirits of the team and the fans were high and somehow we were made to feel that we were becoming a small part of the unfolding story. On the terrace fans shook our hands, offered us beers and cigarettes and delighted in the fact that their team was somehow attracting interest from overseas. When Thomas Paulus made it 2-2 in the sixty-second minute, crashing the ball into the net from the edge of the area, I was just taking a sip from a newly acquired, full, plastic beer glass. As the net bulged, the crowd surged and the young woman standing in front of me was saturated. She was not the only one. After Altintop had scored his, and Kaiserslautern's second just after half time, the crowd had quietened somewhat and many people were nervously sipping at a beer as there seemed to be no immediate threat to the opposition goal. But what's the problem with getting soaked with beer when your team have just got themselves back into the game and are pushing for another victory? And despite the initial look of displeasure on the girl's face, today the beer had been spilled by at least one of the

British contingent and today they were seen as something of a lucky charm for 1.FCN.

Our personal celebrations were slightly muted out of concern for our injured companion. The result itself had lifted my mood, especially as Iain had been contacted and was now back at the hotel. It was there that we found him to be bruised, shaken and somewhat disturbed by his mishap and night in hospital. We genuinely felt for him but at least he was alive and on the mend. And he'd managed to see the goals on TV. As his story unfolded, our sense of pity for our good friend became masked by the broad smiles that spread across our faces as he explained that when admitted to hospital the nurses had asked him to remove his kilt before he was put into bed, and were clearly so terrified by what they saw that they then strapped him in, either to save themselves or to prevent him wandering off in the unfamiliar surroundings. With his tale told, we left him to rest and headed off to celebrate.

Before we caught our return flight to Stansted on the Tuesday afternoon, we decided to visit the Club's impressive *Valznerweiher* training facilities. Each week the 1.FCN official website published a timetable of the training activities of the team (or at least the ones it wanted the public to know about anyway) and it just so happened that on this sunny April morning there would be a training session open to public viewing.

The *Valznerweiher* facilities are not just used by the 1.FCN football team. The several football pitches are obviously used by the whole range of reserve, youth and ladies teams as well as the first team. Furthermore, there are facilities to satisfy the needs of teams performing under the 1.FCN name in a variety of other sports. Of even greater interest to many fans is the fact the there is also a small pub on the site, extremely popular on match days and sometimes used by the club for press conferences.

Impressive though the set-up may be, in the past it has proved something of a millstone around the neck of the club. In the 1967-8 season the completion of the double over Bayern Munich with a 2-0 away victory saw *Der Club* crowned as champions for the ninth and, thus far, final time. Unfortunately things then went downhill rather quickly and without warning. The relative mediocrity (at least when compared to previous decades) of the 1950s and '60s at 1.FCN suddenly gave way to an almost coma-like sleep.

For the 1968-69 season, the state-of-the-art training ground was built. Coach Max Merkel allowed many of his championship winning side to leave to enable him to create a team to challenge for the European Cup. It all went rather horribly wrong. Success eluded Merkel's team who failed to gel as well as his previous charges. Finishing bottom and therefore becoming the first (and to date only) champions of the *Bundesliga* to be relegated the following season, on the pitch failure led to off the pitch debts as the fall in status caused financial hardship.

Recriminations still ring among the Nuremberg faithful as to what went wrong. Many fans blame Merkel and at least one player has claimed that goalkeeper Jürgen Rynio was bribed in a crucial game. Merkel himself apparently put at least some of the blame with the club itself, believing that they were only interested in making financial gain from their hitherto last championship, frightening away players as the purse strings tightened. The debts, caused partly by building new facilities, certainly did not help in the aftermath. It would be another nine years before Nuremberg regained *Bundesliga* status.

Rebuilding of the stadium in 1991 and the addition of a hotel at the training ground provided another facelift for the facilities but again financial misery followed, this time even more pronounced. During the 1995-96 season while in *2.Bundesliga* (the second division) six points were deducted following an investigation into previous financial irregularities, resulting in relegation to the *Regionalliga Süd*.

Of course, the facilities cannot be held entirely responsible for the club's problems over the last four decades, and have surely played a positive role in the sporadic successes over this period. The buildings no longer look state-of-the-art but clearly serve a purpose and despite the hotel with its large Hilton sign, this is clearly 1.FCN territory. Rarely does one visit without seeing at least some fans or players milling around and the club badge is ubiquitous here. I'm yet to stay in the hotel, but it is advertised as having rooms with views over the adjacent forest or the 1.FCN training pitches. There's no contest really is there?

The 10a.m. start of training and the fact that we'd done our fair share of imbibing over the past few days saw us, for once, forgo an opportunity to once again sample the pub, and instead we got out of our taxis and walked straight past it to the training pitches.

Several players and coaches were already out there, stretching and jogging in front of approximately 150 people who stood behind a rail alongside the touchline or waited along the path from the changing rooms for other players to make their way to the pitch. We stood around behind the goal for a few minutes and did not join in the excitement as a few kids asked for the autographs of approaching players on the fringes of the first team squad (well we did not recognise them and nobody else showed much interest so we assumed they had a relatively lowly status). However, there was more excitement when the head coach appeared. Hans Meyer had been responsible for masterminding the change in fortune since taking over as manager in the previous November and was fast becoming something of a Messiah in the city of Nuremberg. Certainly as far as Herbert was concerned, he *was* the Messiah and, despite the fact that Meyer seemed somewhat uncomfortable with the adulation he was receiving from close quarters, Herbert threw himself at the coach and in one breath apparently told him that we were the British fan club and that he would now pose for a photograph. Somewhat bemused, Hans Meyer agreed, or at least stood still for long enough for me to get a picture of Herbert and the coach and even sneak onto one myself. Although the whole incident lasted just a few seconds, Meyer looked a relieved man when he got away and could get on with what the results were showing he was clearly good at – coaching the team.

One player we wanted to see was not yet on the training pitch. The midfielder Jan Polak, with his silky skills and boyish good looks had been a key player for *Der Club* so far that season and had become a firm favourite with one of our members, LD (an abbreviation of Little Dick if you must ask – his name is Richard and he was short when the nickname was given – unless anyone knows differently I assume this is why LD has stuck for several years). LD had seen Polak's hairstyle in Cologne and decided, against his better judgment, to copy it. For anyone copying celebrity hairstyles or fashions, please heed the following warning. If it looks daft in a pop video or on stage then it will look even more daft when you're walking down the street or are at work. If a professional footballer who has to keep in peak physical condition because of the nature of his athletic job sports a hairstyle that looks somewhat silly, then you can bet that the same hairstyle will look somewhat sillier on somebody for whom exercise means walking to the pub or the take-away. However, we all told LD that his diagonal, bleached stripe of a low-rise Mohican cut in the style of that of the influential Czech international midfield player, looked cool. Well what are friends for? Initially disappointed that his hero, who had been injured during Sunday's game, had not appeared, LD's face then lit-up when Polak emerged. It was a shame that Jan Polak did not greet LD like a long lost brother, but at least he posed for a picture with him (getting players to pose for pictures doesn't require much in the way of language skills, just the ability to say their name, put one arm around their shoulder while pointing towards your mate with the camera). The photograph of the 'two Polaks' does not show much resemblance, although at least LD still goes to watch *Der Club*, whereas his one time hero moved to Anderlecht in August 2007.

Photographs taken, we then watched the training session. It was nothing too vigorous but we were pleasantly surprised by the fact that we could get this close to professional players doing their job. Can you actually watch Liverpool, Manchester United, Arsenal or even Port Vale at such close quarters when they are training? In fact, although it is good to be able to see some of what goes on, would you really want to watch many training sessions? It does allow you to appreciate better the power with which the players hit the ball but in reality, at least in these 'open' sessions, nothing much is given away.

Hans Meyer was now completely at home, working with his players and, one gathered, working the audience a little as well. Sarcastic comments and well-chosen phrases (all of which had to be translated by Herbert) caused ripples of laughter among the gathered spectators, but as already has been mentioned, it was a beautiful spring morning and *Der Club* were on the up. As the session started to wind down defensive midfielder and club captain, Mario Cantaluppi, decided to have a go in goal. As his team-mates fired in shots at him, he made a string of highly creditable saves to some applause from the small crowd. Meyer was unimpressed. Whether this was because there was a danger of 'Lupo' stealing his show was unclear, but the coach quickly suggested that his captain should perhaps take up the position more permanently after his mediocre display as an outfield player two days before. The crowd laughed, Meyer was still their hero and training was over, or at least officially.

As some of the players started to make their way to get changed and do whatever they would be doing for the rest of the day, we managed to grab a couple more players for photographs.

It was only after this that we noticed one of our group, Tim, a rather large body-builder (unimaginatively nicknamed 'Titch'), had made his way onto the pitch and was standing in between the posts as a couple of players gave him no chance with several shots that easily beat him. The rest of us wandered onto the pitch, watched and had a few shots ourselves, got some more pictures with which to adorn our website and then realised that we should leave.

The whole weekend had been a rather surreal experience. Not because we were star struck in the presence of the players or felt like we were the centre of attention for much of the time in Nuremberg. I think we were probably a bit too old for that. It was that the few days had felt almost like a wedding. Everyone laughing and joking with each other like you do with people you know you should know but don't really have any clue who they are. The fans and players of 1.FCN seemed to accept the British guests but could not quite put their finger on why we were actually there. Just like a wedding though, everyone politely shook hands, smiled for the photographs and everyone was everyone else's friend. There seemed to be a lot of love in the air.

The concept of going to watch Nuremberg play and giving them our support was in itself a beautiful, albeit slightly off-the-wall, pastime to engage in. As a purely footballing trip it was possible to do it for a reasonable price. However, we were firmly setting ourselves a standard which would not only allow us to support 1.FCN but would also work out considerably more expensive if we were to continue to spend additional nights in Germany, supping, eating and socialising, preferring the comfort of mid-range hotels rather than the more affordable hostels. We would have to try and reign ourselves in a little. But not just yet.

The official welcome

Chapter 4

Vot ist die name of das Hund?

We approached the turnstiles of the stadium looking out for Jürgen. As usual he was there in his official capacity co-ordinating the hundreds of Nuremberg supporters who had made their way by coach and car.

"I bought a book... I bought a book," then a laugh.

"I bought a book," more laughter as the mock English accent became even louder and more pronounced.

Jürgen had spotted us before we caught sight of him. He persevered a little more with his phrase, adding, to further laughter, "Sorry I forgot." He repeated it all again. As we approached he singled out Jason and changed from piss-taker to teacher – "Ich habe ein Buch gekauft, Jason, ich habe ein Buch gekauft" – then back to his piss-taking Queen's English – "Sorry I forgot."

Jason smiled. He was now accustomed to the stick he was getting as he had been on the receiving end of it for a few weeks ever since a BBC Midlands Today feature showed some members of our club, Jason included, practising their German at night school.

"Jason, can you tell me how you would say I bought a book?" asks the tutor.

"Yes, that's dead easy that is," replies Jason clearly confident that he was getting to grips with the accusative case. "That's ich habe... I forgot."

In the annals of TV history this will be a clip which will be quickly forgotten and unlikely to be unearthed ever again but in the age of the internet it had already become a popular download on our website and was attracting plenty of attention on You Tube.

Another bit of publicity for 1FCNUK and a bit of a laugh to see various members on the television news this may have been but it also highlighted issues regarding the difficulties of the language barrier when travelling to watch a foreign team.

The language required at the matches themselves was coming along quite well. It was certainly slow but some progress was being made. *Abseits* and *Tor* (offside and goal) were starting to come naturally although whereas fans the world over will shout "offside" in the hope that they might influence one of the match officials, does anyone, apart from commentators (and 1FCNUK) actually state the obvious as the ball hits the back of the net and announce a goal? Cries of "get rid of it" have now sometimes being replaced by *Aus* (out) and yes and no are easily translated to *ja* and *nein* even when shouted from the terrace. *Scheiße* will be cried by 1FCNUK when a goal is conceded and receives several nods of approval when disagreeing with a refereeing decision. Our fellow supporters are obviously appreciative of our attempt at German. Having said that, they often nod in approval when our members just can't get out the German phrase quick enough and resort to the odd "Bollocks" or "For fuck's sake", the latter receiving looks of admiration. In fact it seems that while English/American expletives are well known and understood in Germany, "For fuck's sake" is considered something of a rarity, even exquisite. A friend from Germany who took a work placement in Cheshire to gain broader work experience and the chance to further develop his already excellent English was fortunate enough to sample the delights of football at Port Vale and their Potteries neighbours Stoke City. He now claims, and I suspect only half-jokingly, that the only new English he learned came from the mouths of North Staffordshire football fans and were the phrases "Y'big gay" and "For fuck's sake" which he can pronounce perfectly in a dialect of which the people of Stoke-on-Trent would be proud.

Away from the football however, it has been more of a struggle. Having a wife, father-in-law and mother-in-law who can speak both German and English fluently should have helped me. But it hasn't. Angela is an impatient teacher and communicates the majority of the time in English because she quite rightly gets sick of me asking what the hell she means (although she has a healthy range of German expletives which funnily enough seem to get the message across to me when I'm in her bad books). So as with all of our members I've had to struggle along, picking up bits of language here and there as we have spent time surrounded by it in football stadiums and bars.

There is surely no better way to grasp vocabulary and phrases than being immersed in them and it has certainly helped as we've moved on from ordering a beer, to ordering several and even requesting *große* (large) without using a rudimentary, pointing-based sign language. *Bitte* and *Danke* (please and thank you) have become second nature now so at least we don't sound completely ignorant and 'kebab' sounds much the same in several languages. Some of us have even become confident enough to try to string a sentence or two together but this is where learning usually grinds to a halt. Not because we are unwilling to try or are afraid of making mistakes but because as soon as most people realise that we're English they usually switch to English themselves either to politely make things easier for us or to embarrass us with the fact that they have a fluent grasp of our language while we are drowning in a sea of misplaced verbs and incorrect genders. And on the rare occasion that we come across somebody who has no English at all, sign language takes over and, depending on the lack of sobriety, the conversations make surprisingly good progress in this manner.

Unfortunately then, advancing our skill in German is something of an onerous task. We have therefore been tempted by a range of other methods of language acquisition.

The first point of call for most of us, and I guess for any traveller, is to try to recall any language learning from our school days. For me personally this was of very little use. I was a poor student in all subjects as far as applying myself was concerned and school reports always started with a hint of praise along the lines of 'he is a capable boy...' quickly followed by the word 'but'. I saw no reason to push too hard in any subject, particularly those which required as much effort as languages certainly did for me. In fact it is testament to my disinterest that the only memory I have of learning French is the teacher returning a piece of work covered in corrections – on a blank Peanuts cartoon strip on which we had to write our own captions in French, I was reprimanded for referring to Charlie Brown as 'Charlie Brown', rather than 'Charlie Brun'. My quite reasonable argument that a person's name does not change because they are in a different country saw me sent from the room. The same end result came just a few moments into my first ever German lesson. When the register was taken and my name was called out I replied, "Ja Frau Gibson," and was subsequently dismissed for my alleged insolence. Little wonder then that any slight interest I may have had for language learning was all too soon pushed aside. And how I regretted it when I first started to need languages in the real world.

Next stop then is the phrase book. I am quite certain that I have failed to retain any information from a phrase book but to carry one around in a pocket is like having a concealed weapon to protect oneself from embarrassing language related situations. Or at least that is the theory. In reality the shrugging of shoulders to indicate that you have not got a clue, or that they have not got a clue, is less embarrassing than taking out the phrase book, finding the correct phrase and then pointing to it with the hope that you will understand the response given.

The content of phrase books is rather questionable too. There is normally a section on pronunciation and grammar which I assume has to be read and committed to memory before use. But if this is the case then can a couple of pages of a phrase book really sort out the myriad of grammatical issues of the German language as you casually flick through the book as your flight makes its final approach? So lacking in confidence in their products are the producers of phrase books that one of the first phrases they contain is a plea to the foreign ear:

Do you speak English? Sprechen Sie Englisch? *shpre*-khen zee *eng*-lish

Before you can even say it you need to translate the phonetical guidance and try and find out what the italicised bits mean.

One phrase book I have (I own several, often buying a new one at the airport just in case I've not packed one of my others – none of which I seem to use), takes this plea further by asking "Does anyone speak English?" and then "Do you understand me?" Another generally common phrase will appear shortly afterwards:

Ich spreche ein bisschen Deutsch. (I speak a little German.)

In fact you obviously speak no more than the four or five phrases of German already printed in the phrase book, if you could actually read them.

Many phrase books, particularly older versions, then have their very useful business section. If you ever feel you will need to ask for a fax machine, for someone's VAT registered number or for the more discerning traveller, seek out a trouser press, then you will be well-advised to brush up on the business phrases. The trouble is, most phrases in phrase books are not designed to be learned verbatim – they are generally not the phrases you will use every day and so for the amateur linguist there is little reason to learn them when turning to the correct page can give you the required phrase. You just have to hope that by the time you have found it, the person who is designed to be on the receiving end of your attempt at their language is still standing there. Most of the phrases can be arrived at with body language anyway or should even be quite obvious. The gem from the Lonely Planet German Phrase Book in the section Occupations and Studies is a delightful example. Believe it or not, the first phrase on the list of professions is *"Ich bin eine Drag Queen"*, and this amazingly translates to "I am a drag queen". The phrase book usefully tells us that drag queen is a feminine noun though surely in this case gender is all down to luck or perception!

The truly committed travelling football fan therefore needs to try a different approach to develop a worthy level of fluency. A number of 1FCNUK members have dipped their toes into the murky waters of night school learning. There are obviously great advantages in having a fluent speaker on hand to teach you, and a large group of people to try out your developing skills on and with. The pride of putting this learning into practice must be immense. *"Ich mochte ein Chef Salad,"* begins one of our female members as she appears on the same film footage as Jason, ordering food and drink in Bremen, *"und ...erm... ein Bier und ein Orangensaft bestellen."* Great. Well done. It would be easy to mock but at least it's a move away from, *"Ein große Kebab bitte."* Her simple phrase, the result of several weeks of learning, would help most of us to extend our life expectancy by politely asking for a salad rather than just agreeing to have the same as the person next to us (who has probably just ordered a burger and chips). On the other hand, in the same way in which so many modern pop musicians are plainly just not living rock and roll lives, asking for a salad quite clearly has no part in a weekend of drinking and football. But such is the cosmopolitan nature of our fan club these days that almost anything goes. Despite Jason failing to be able to remember to tell someone in German that he bought a book, another member gets quite excited during one trip as she sees a person with a dog. She is trying hard to remember the phrase she wants to say. *"Vot ist die name of das Hund,"* someone helpfully volunteers but she knows this is wrong. Then she has it. *"Wie heißt dein Hund?"* she asks before failing to be able to continue the conversation much further because the next part is in next week's class. Besides which, there is a game to get to.

Language difficulties are not just confined to the English speaking travelling fan. Players also have to come to terms with the language and with so many nationalities in the 1.FCN team there is always the potential for problems. At the club the first language of communication is naturally German, followed by English which gives most players the chance of having some of the main fifty or so words apparently required on the football pitch. I've never seen a list of what these words are but I would think that fifty is quite an excessive amount. For goodness sake – some of the English players in English football interviewed on television each week appear to have a total vocabulary of less than fifty words although from watching coverage of Premier League matches one can safely assume that in England at least the word 'fuck' is taught to all players who don't already know it as a root for a range of nouns, verbs and adjectives to direct at other players and officials. I assume in European football there is some sort of equivalent. For those players at 1.FCN who don't have the key vocabulary in one of the requisite languages then they are provided with lessons. I wonder if they teach them how to order a Chef Salad as well.

It is thought that language was a problem early in the 2007-08 season for Czech goalkeeper Jaromir Blazek who apparently had very little, if any, German or English. An own goal from Greek player Angelos Charisteas which left Blazek stranded was put down to language difficulties. The Greek had no problem having played in Germany and Holland for several seasons. Apart from trying to grab a few players for photographs by simply calling their names I've never spoken to any of the players with the exception of (now former player) Josh Kennedy, an Australian forward. When calling after him as I chased him down to give him one of our fan club magazines all he could say was, "What sort of accent do you call that?" in an Aussie twang. Git I thought. "Better than yours," I replied shoving the small booklet into his hand before walking off with a certain amount of indignation.

To be fair to our members who studied at night school, they have improved their German, although it has been commented on that there was too much focus on grammar and not enough on conversation. It seems that once you start learning about German grammar you are at the beginning of a rather long and confusing journey. If all you want is to be able to tell someone in the pub after a match that the referee was a bastard then night school classes might not be the answer to your language needs, at least in the short term.

In fact if you want to question the parentage of the referee the best bet is to ask someone how to say it because it does not really fall into the list of most required phrases of travellers. On the other hand it surely has a greater frequency than *Ich bin eine Drag Queen*. There's another problem, too. Although at least one of us has purchased a dictionary of German slang and profanity, even this does not take into account the phrases shouted by fans in local dialect. But maybe one should not put too much emphasis on the need to learn a great deal in order to be a foul-mouthed yob on the terrace. For a start there are far more women and children present at German football matches than there are in England (although some of the most foul-mouthed people I have ever come across at matches in both Germany and England have been women and children). And then one has to remember that swearing at the referee or opposition player is not a great test of semantic knowledge and understanding. Just a couple of words or hand signals usually get one by.

Before the start of many German matches the stadium announcer reads out the names of the home team. He doesn't simply read out a list in a monotone. This is often a piece of showmanship, occasionally more exciting than the football itself. "*Nummer eins*," (number one) he may call, then, managing to get his 'r' rolling almost to a buzz, he launches into the name of the Nuremberg goalkeeper Raphael Schäfer. "*Rrrrrrrrrrrrrrrrrrrrrrrrraphhhhhhhh -ae-l*," and then the briefest of pauses before everyone joins in, "*Schhhhhhhhhhhhhaaaaaaeeeeffffff-er.*" It's then optional to shout something else. If the player is in form, scoring lots of goals or gets stuck-in every game, some people will shout *Fussballgott* (football god). If your name happens to be Marek Mintal then everyone will shout it in praise of the deity-like status you have achieved at 1.FCN. Everyone, that is, apart from the away support. When away from home in Germany it seems almost customary to raise both middle fingers high in the air and when the player's surname has been read, a simple and guttural *Arschloch* (arsehole) is set forth. Most people seem to do this in good humour although there are always a few who are red faced and have veins bursting from their necks such is their apparent hatred for somebody they've probably never even heard of before.

In that respect then there is little to learn to join in with the abuse from the terrace or stand. However, if you believe that listening and having conversations are the best ways to progress your knowledge but can't be bothered to leave the house or the comfort of your car then you could always try language CDs. Some are a bit much like hard work – you have to listen to them and work through a booklet at the same time, having to rewind the track every few seconds because they speak too fast. I once purchased a CD which is a bit like a story. Three friends from somewhere in Germany fly to somewhere else in Germany for the weekend and eat, shop, drink and enjoy the nightlife. The two guys and one girl have to check in at the airport, ask for directions and bus times, purchase various drinks and so on. But then you realise that you're only listening to it to see which of the guys gets the girl and shaking your head at the one who orders a milkshake rather than a beer. After a while you just know that they're both wasting their time and you give up learning.

Other CDs slot straight into your computer and via a microphone the programs they contain can check your accent as you respond to various situations. Great if you want to speak like someone from the Prussian landed classes in the mid-nineteenth century but hopeless if you want a few quick phrases to get a bit of drink and grub.

Then there are the CDs which require no writing, no microphone; just listening and repeating, sometimes building sentences yourself as you pause them. This has been my favoured method because you can listen in the car on the way to work or anywhere else for that matter. The only trouble is, if it's supposed to be dangerous using your mobile phone when driving then it's sure as hell got to be far worst trying to concentrate on a language. I usually start the CD playing and when I reach work realise that I only listened to the first five minutes having spent the rest of the journey cursing the idiot directly in front of me whose rear bumper I am practically sitting on, or otherwise cursing the idiot directly behind me for such stupid driving as to be practically sitting on my rear bumper. Like everything else then, CDs are quite limited. You can pick up some ideas and increase your vocabulary but that Holy Grail of fluency still remains far, far away.

It does therefore leave just two options. One seems to be to commit to learning German over a long period of time in whichever way suits you, be it CDs, the internet or night school, or alternatively to just spend more and more time there picking up new pieces of language on each occasion. Of course, this latter option could also be read as not being arsed to do anything and hoping that you get to grips with the language bit-by-bit, safe in the knowledge that you never really will because you never bother with it in between trips. Immersion in the language is the only hope, and unless you are prepared to watch German TV, listen to German radio and ignore all print and every spoken word in anything but German, then without being there your chance of learning in this manner seems rather limited. Then again, the language required for the football terrace itself is rather limited in whichever tongue one chooses and as football fans we are sometimes left entirely speechless anyway.

A budding linguists toolkit

Chapter 5

Backpacking

After our first three trips of the 2005-06 season we had no plans to return to Germany until the new season started. After all, we'd already exceeded our expectations and spent rather more than we should have done to fund the fun. It is, so we are told, possible to have too much of a good thing, and we had the feeling that some people may have considered it excessive to fit in a trip between mid-April and the end of the season in early May. Besides which, the only game that we could feasibly get a flight to and not have to take time off work was the last game of the season against Bayer Leverkusen just a few miles along the Rhine from Cologne. We could hardly justify another flight to, and weekend in, Cologne just two months after our previous visit. And, of course, the next season would be along soon. With all of these subliminal messages we should have been strong and fought the need to satisfy what was fast becoming something of a Germanic travel addiction.

Hot May weather enabled us to enjoy a glass or two of the excellent *Kölsch* beer sitting in shorts and T-shirts outside bars into which we had huddled away from the freezing conditions only a few weeks previously. Having now visited Cologne on a number of occasions to watch football or to just enjoy the pleasant bars and the magnificent River Rhine flowing majestically past the city's imposing gothic cathedral it is somewhat to my shame that I (and I know that I am not alone in this) have never really done much as a tourist, other than stick my head through the cathedral door once and walk along the banks of the Rhine as an essential means of clearing my head. Sometimes, however, it has to be asked what one could possibly need other than the eating of good food and sampling excellent local drinks (preferably but not essentially in the sun) in the company of good friends. There is, in fact, nothing that could add to such an experience apart from then going to a football match.

It was to this end that our leisurely lunchtime in Cologne then saw us board a train for the short journey to Leverkusen, passing through the seemingly endless Bayer Pharmaceuticals works which line a strip of land alongside the river most of the way to the small town which has now become a suburb of its large neighbouring city. Bayer have been the major reason behind the strength of Leverkusen over recent years, with the pharmaceutical giant pumping money into the club and bringing them the success of a Champions League final, although this should not belittle the nurturing and hard work of great talents such as Michael Ballack, Bernd Schuster and Dimitar Berbatov among many others.

It's a good walk from the train station in Leverkusen to the 22,000 capacity, modern, compact *BayArena* but it was a pleasant day (and we made a mental note to take a taxi if we visited again). Outside the stadium were the usual stands grilling sausages and selling beverages and we had no fear of unfurling our flag and taking in the pre-match atmosphere.

The game itself had passed by quite innocuously until it was brought to life by a stunning goal on the stroke of half-time from Joe Mnari, Nuremberg's Tunisian midfielder, thundering the ball in from distance. The largely ineffectual Berbatov restored parity after the break and then, with the teams seemingly going through the motions as the final whistle approached, Leverkusen were awarded a final minute penalty which Berbatov slotted home. It is the mark of a quality striker that, even with a below par performance, he could still score two goals in the game, and create a fitting end to his career in Germany before a £12 million move to Tottenham. Berbatov, as with everyone else in the stadium, must have thought that his last act for Leverkusen was to secure them three points from what the Nuremberg supporters considered to be a poor decision by the match officials. *Scheiße* was all that we were able to muster as the verbal onslaught around us created a much more colourful picture, not that we understood any exact meanings. But the game was not quite over. As *Der Club* re-started from the centre circle they moved the ball forward for Stefan Kiessling to strike the equaliser with the very last touch of the game and his last kick of a ball for 1.FCN before his seven million Euros move to the host team.

The supporters of *Der Club* were happy again and the language was toned down. Hans Meyer had turned the season around and from bottom place they had reached eighth by the end of the campaign. As for 1FCNUK, we had 'pledged' our support to Nuremberg when they were a struggling team but had got carried along with the momentum that had lifted the club and its fans. The four games we had attended in our first season as a fan club had entertainingly provided twenty-one goals, great excitement and new friendships. Immediately we were eagerly awaiting the next campaign.

Optimism for everything to do with 1.FCN was high and, as the 2006 World Cup got underway in Germany, we had the added interest of games broadcast live from the *Frankenstadion*, in particular England v Trinidad and Tobago. Watching the game on TV in a packed pub, the Nuremberg link was overshadowed by the most important aspect of the day – willing England on to a positive result. The competence of the performance could be analysed later but a win would be needed to aid progression through the tournament. As a Port Vale fan, it was also an historical moment as a Vale player graced not only the World Cup but also the *Frankenstadion* turf. Chris Birchall, the first white player to represent Trinidad and Tobago (on account of his grandmother having being born there), was the first serving Vale player ever to play in the World Cup finals. (1.FCN were represented by four players in the 2006 finals, although none of them were playing for Germany.) An extremely tenuous link it may have been, but here was the briefest crossing of paths of what I considered to be the two teams in the whole universe (three if you also include the English national team) worthy of my support.

The pre-season optimism for *Der Club* also went hand-in-hand with some trepidation for 1FCNUK as we watched the World Cup. Over the previous nine months we had made several good friends and acquaintances in Nuremberg and were overwhelmed, and initially somewhat surprised, by the way in which we were received by fellow fans and the public in general. How would this be affected if hordes of English hooligans rampaged through the Nuremberg streets, throwing plastic chairs at the police and locals? Would it put an end to our flag waving and public celebrations of our support from the British Isles? None of our British based members could attend the World Cup matches, understandably having already spent various amounts of money and holidays for extended stays in Germany to watch 1.FCN play. Now we looked on, imagining that when the next season started we would maybe have to keep a relatively low profile on our visits to games and find ourselves apologising for the conduct of our nation's hooligan element.

As it happened, there was little trouble in Nuremberg, although Cologne, much more accessible from England and more suited to the lager loutish outings of those who use the football bandwagon as an excuse to have a fight, fared less well. Minor 'skirmishes', if you'll excuse the tabloid-esque phrase, certainly happened in Franconia but trouble was limited and to a scale akin to that in a small provincial English town on a Saturday night rather than the nationalistic mass-organised violence witnessed so many times before.

We followed the World Cup with the same amount of devoted interest as any football fan, changing work schedules and other engagements to enable us to see as many games as possible, spending whole evenings staring at the TV. Most of us, of course, were desperate for England to realise the potential of the 'best team since 1966' (as we were constantly told by the British media) and win the tournament. Desperate but not deluded, we knew that there was a chance but did not dare to believe that this would actually be England's finest hour. There were obviously members of 1FCNUK who would have preferred England's demise in the tournament to come sooner rather than later and eventually, with the English media bandwagon building up to its full 'we're the greatest' rhetoric, they were granted their wish as Portugal conquered the 'mother nation' of football in the quarter final penalty shoot-out.

The visits to Germany, had left many of our members unwilling or unable to participate in the normal anti-German 'humour' and sentiments that surround international football tournaments in the UK and would have liked to have seen the hosts go on to win the tournament after England were knocked out. Incredibly, this feeling was apparently mirrored by many of the English fans who had travelled to Germany and represented something of a turnaround in the way in which Germany is viewed by some, if by no means all, English people. Of course, it is doubtful whether this will end the anti-German sentiment in the British tabloid press, a sentiment which is portrayed as humour but which many of the readers take as serious propaganda as if the Second World War had never ended (and these are the very same people who would claim that the Germans are a humourless nation who take everything too seriously)! Some turnaround in general public feeling was evident however as Germany played (and lost to) Italy in the semi-final and then met the Argentines in the third-fourth place play-off, although this does raise the question about English attitudes towards Italy and Argentina! Just in case you thought that this mild warming towards Germany in football tournaments could have been something to build upon, the fact that English interest in Euro 2008 vastly decreased when England failed to qualify almost banished the opportunity to try it out. The need to create patriotism through nationalist sentiment disappears when England are not in a tournament and press hype turns its attention elsewhere. Worryingly it also provides those humorous headline writers with a chance to regurgitate their old material when the 2010 World Cup arrives, providing that England (and Germany) qualify of course. For those who were missing the tabloid fun-poking at the Germans, the BBC's Gary Lineker gave them a little hope that the old rivalry was still alive and kicking. The anchorman of the BBC coverage advised before the Germans beat Poland 2-0 that, "All games have gone to the formbook. Germany next and we're due an upset. That would be a shame."

It has been well-documented that the World Cup did much for the image of Germany. In Nuremberg, it also did much for the image of the English football fan, and when we returned to the city in August, without exception everyone we spoke to about the World Cup had praise for the camaraderie and behaviour of the English supporters. Maybe there were incidents that lived up to the stereotypical image of the England fan on tour and I'm sure not all local residents were as happy as those we spoke to, but just as the image of Germany had soared in the estimations of the average England fan, the image of the average England fan had also risen in the estimations of the people of Franconia. This was a massive boost to those of us who took delight in the fact that the fixtures threw together 1.FCN and Borussia Mönchengladbach followed by Bayern Munich and

1.FCN for the second and third games of the season, at home and away respectively.

Three of us saw this as the perfect opportunity to acquaint ourselves better with Franconia and Bavaria. The planned trip would take in Nuremberg for the home game and then various towns and cities in southern Germany and Austria over the course of the following week before winding up in Munich for the big 'derby' game in the Allianz Arena. Three thirty-somethings would be backpacking around Bavaria in recognition of the fact that we'd somehow avoided doing any such thing when we were in our late teens and early twenties. And why had we avoided it? Was it the thought of missing some of the football season? Was it a fear of the unknown? Was it the belief that one didn't need to travel very far to have a good time? Was it the fact that endless second-class train journeys and run-down hostels would break our spirit for adventure? Maybe it was a combination of all of these factors, but now we thought we were ready for it, if only for a week or so, in the name of our support for 1.FCN.

To ease us in gently we shunned budget airlines and took a direct flight to Munich with Lufthansa. This had the advantage of not only the perception of greater comfort but of also allowing us to fly on the morning of the home game from our nearest airport rather than travel for miles before we even saw a plane. It also provided us with the chance to have a pre-taste of the German rail system by taking the train from Munich to Nuremberg before our backpacking adventure started in earnest.

An initial concern we had was whether it was possible to have a scheduled lunchtime arrival in Munich and then travel north to Nuremberg in time for the Friday evening match. Do real backpackers give themselves tight schedules or are football kick-off times of no concern to them? As has become the pessimism of the British traveller, it is easy to expect delays of two to three hours (if you're lucky), at least ninety minutes wait for your luggage, a thirty minute queue for passport control, several missed and cancelled train connections, leaves on the railway tracks, the wrong kind of snow or several other reasons for not reaching the desired destination on time.

Of course, Lufthansa got us to Munich on time, there was no real queue to check our passports, our luggage was already going round the carousel after the short walk from the aircraft and the attractive girl on the *Deutsche Bahn* (the German rail network) information desk sold us our train ticket, provided us with directions to the bus link and advised us that we had time for a beer and a sausage in the bar adjacent to her kiosk. All that was missing was her making a suggestion that she should join us and, lacking any nerve or further sense of adventure than we had already let ourselves in for, we neglected to ask her. All this within a few minutes of touching down. Welcome back to Germany.

German airport efficiency has become an almost pleasurable part of our frequent trips. In contrast to many of our experiences at British airports – and apologies to the staff who *have* been pleasant and helpful in Britain – the German airport staff *are* helpful and *do* know what they are doing. Yes, 'efficiency' is a word often associated with Germany, and it's not hard to see why. Our thirty-five minute record from the plane touching down on the runway in Nuremberg to arriving in a bar six kilometres away having checked into our hotel and thrown our luggage into our room will, even by German standards, take some beating!

Munich airport does not have its own train station. You can get the *U-Bahn* (the underground metro system) into the centre of the city and go to the main station and this is what you would expect would happen in Britain. In fact this is what you would do because you would probably not trust the overpriced, unreliable bus service to a nearby village. But the bus service between Munich and Freising works beautifully. The village has a mainline railway passing through it and the considerate *Deutsche Bahn* people have some of their trains stop there to transport passengers to more northern areas of Germany. To then wax lyrical, as I could do, about the efficiencies of the German railways would probably only serve to provide a contrast with the British system. There was a time when this would have been a fair thing to do but much of the negativity surrounding British public transport is historical and in my recent experiences things are improving. But the German trains work exactly as you would expect and we were in Nuremberg with hours to spare.

Dutifully, we checked into our hotel and had a walk around the city centre, building up our strength for the backpacking exertions that would follow by eating copious amounts of the famous *Nürnberger Bratwurst*. In Germany, sausages are sold everywhere and each region is rightly proud of their local speciality. In Nuremberg, the locals take great pride in the fact that they have very small sausages, if you'll excuse the double entendre. *Nürnberger Bratwurst* are only finger-sized, in contrast to some of the meatier, thicker and longer specimens found in other parts of the country. There is a historical reason for this. Sometimes referred to as the 'keyhole' sausage, the small size dates back through the centuries to times when inns were forced to close early. Improbably (but allegedly true) anybody who wanted serving with sausage 'after hours' would have to wait until their *Nürnberger* appeared through the keyhole of the door, keyholes obviously being larger in days of old. An alternative version of this history suggests that the sausages were pushed *into* buildings through keyholes, particularly to inhabitants of cells. Now they are served in most local restaurants and every few metres at stands in the street through normal serving hatches rather than keyholes. And to avoid locals and tourists getting hungry, the small sausages are served in threes, normally in bread if brought in the street. There seems to be no better snack to break up the monotony of shopping streets and the tourist trail (no matter how wonderful the architecture and ambience may be). I'm ashamed when I think about the amount of *Nürnberger's* I've scoffed on some visits to the city, although I've reduced my intake a little now. Whether in the street, in the park, in the station or in the stadium, one cannot escape the mouth-watering aroma of the *Bratwurst*. And when tired of being on your feet why not retire to a bar (or restaurant if you're feeling particularly cultured) and eat more sausage? I'm almost convinced it's worth the flights just to sample them. Even though 1FCNUK exists primarily to support 1.FCN, there are members who claim that the sausage (and I'm sure the beer too) is their main attraction. As with every other opportunity to eat and drink on our travels, we made sure that we were partaking of this traditional fayre at regular intervals as we strolled around on this delightful August afternoon. With high hopes of seeing some marvellous football over the next ten days, we at least had the comfort of feasting on sausages if football did not bring the joy we anticipated. This relationship was for better or for *Wurst*.

And just while we are on the subject of traditional Nuremberg fayre, it is also worth mentioning the fact the city has many excellent beers. Drinking in Germany is not just a case of 'getting down' as many pints of lager as possible. Although Germany does have its massed produced beers which can be found in plenty of bars, there are literally hundreds of local brews which become extremely difficult to find as one moves from town to town. In varying shades from extremely pale to black, the range of flavours is truly astounding. While the popular city centre nightspots play it safe with middle-of-the-road draught lagers and some bottled dark beers, other establishments offer greater variety and require greater research. A few bars brew their own beers or act as specialist outlets for the myriad of small breweries in the region. This all means that the beers do not have to travel far, and whether it is an apocryphal tale or not, some believe that the lack of chemicals required for preservation over long journeys results in no hangover after imbibing too heavily. Having tested this theory on more than one occasion I can confirm that it is not true, although German beers seem more tempting to drink as hair-of-the-dog than most beers I've had at home. It also has to be said, at risk of causing some embarrassment, that 1FCNUK also occasionally partake of Martini Rosso. It was adopted as our fan club drink – well why not have alcohol for a mascot – when on an end of season trip to Gdansk our members were in part responsible for drinking a bar dry of beer. We turned to Martini, probably because someone misheard the order, and now toast each other with it every now and then. It does get some strange looks when what people assume to be lager loutish football fans sit sipping from delicate glasses. Then we get back to the beer.

Having eaten and walked away the afternoon, maybe with the odd break for liquid refreshment, we met Armin, a Nuremberg supporter who would give us a lift to the match. Leaving the city centre early made good sense, as we needed to collect our tickets, not only for that evening's game but also for the following week's match in Munich.

Even some three hours before kick-off, the area around the 1.FCN training ground and ticket office was busy with fans. Tickets in hand, we stood outside the Stuhlfauth-Stuben bar chatting (with Armin as our trusty interpreter) with other *Clubberer* on a wonderful August evening.

Having emphatically beaten Stuttgart 3-1 in their Gottlieb-Daimler stadium the previous week, with Robert Vittek having continued his scoring form from the previous season, expectations for the game against Mönchengladbach were high. The weather was hot, even at the 8.30p.m. kick-off time and *Der Club* had a new beer sponsor. The outcome of this combination of factors was, with hindsight, quite predictable. There seemed to be more beer kiosks than normal, and on entry to the stadium everyone was given a red and black flag across which was emblazoned the sponsors logo, and the beer's name was everywhere else you looked too. It would have been rude not to try some.

The stadium was almost full and the atmosphere, fuelled no doubt by the beer promotion, was electric. Flag waving and singing, the fans pushed the team (without Vittek who had been injured in a mid-week international) on to a 1-0 victory. The lacklustre performance did not concern the fans that evening because with a few favourable results the next day, Nuremberg would be going into the following week's derby game against Munich above their rivals as *Spitzenreiter* – the league leaders – of the *Bundesliga*.

Prior to the game our 'credibility' of having made the effort to travel so far to give our support was dented when we were introduced to Yohannes, a member of the newly formed Bali fan club. Through a combination of waving hands, broken German and plenty of enthusiastic nodding and shaking of heads it turned out that Yohannes and his German host Klaus would be playing for the *Rot-Schwarze Franken Oldstars* on the Sunday afternoon, a team we had also been persuaded to represent by Armin who was apparently the team's President, coach and part-time goalkeeper.

Armin had joined our club with some excitement a few months previously. His affable nature and willingness to meet us in bars and provide us with his views on the football, and his eagerness to act as something of a chauffeur were both despite and because of the fact that he doesn't really drink. That he therefore joins in with groups of people who become, at varying rates, increasingly inebriated as the day, evening or weekend passes by, is testament to his good character. The fact that he was now excited about the three 'past-their-best' Brits 'signing' for his team unfortunately places his judgment in the spotlight. Add to this the fact that the unlikely looking footballing duo of

Klaus and Yohannes were also very recent signings, then we should have seen the ominous signs of how the game would unfold two days after the glorious evening in the *Frankenstadion*. Whatever doubts we had beforehand would only be confirmed on the Sunday afternoon.

Having had all of Saturday in Nuremberg to recover from the previous evening's celebrations and then do it all again, the nausea and headaches of the Sunday morning were a harsh reminder of those Sunday League football matches we once believed we were fit enough to play each week. Now, with the August temperatures in the eighties and humidity high, the last thing we wanted to do was run around for ninety minutes. After all, when professional players have to do this sort of thing in a game in the World Cup for example, the media use a plethora of hype and computer graphics to show the physical effects and how dangerous it can be to push the human body too far in such conditions. Apparently it even causes several pounds of weight to be lost, which is probably why, subconsciously, our minds allowed us to even consider taking the *U-Bahn* several stops to a suburb from where we would be collected and taken to the game.

The thought did cross our minds that our team-mates would be so superior to us that we would only have to play a small role and avoid any real exertions. They would do all the running, they would occasionally pass the ball to us to make us feel good about ourselves and maybe they would even patronisingly let one of us take a penalty when they had created a large enough lead to comfortably win the game. Then we got to Röthenbach bus station where we would be met by Armin and Klaus in their cars. A few young men were hanging around chatting, sharing their cigarettes. They appeared to have sports bags at their feet but they did not look like footballers so we made no approach. A few minutes later, Armin arrived and introduced them as our team mates. Shock prevented us from apologising for our ignorance and I like to assume that the reason that they had not approached us was that they were not expecting us. In reality, they were probably thinking that they were about to be lumbered by another hopeless trio of ringers who would say that they could play in any position which actually meant that they could not really perform anywhere on the pitch.

Most of the team climbed into the two cars while the remaining players jumped onto a bus. As our two car cavalcade made its way to the rather upmarket suburb of Katzwang, it did not bode well when, having lost sight of the bus which clearly knew where it was going we came to a halt. After much gesturing between the drivers and telephone calls to a third party (on the bus I believe) who was able to direct us, we eventually arrived at a well-appointed sports centre. This game would surely be beyond us. There was even a track around the pitch, ample car-parking, a river running through the complex, a club house that appeared to contain changing rooms and a bar, another pitch with floodlights and advertising boards – it would be some place to play a great game of football, had we ourselves indeed been capable of playing a great game of football.

Having had our hopes of being carried through the game instantly dismissed back at the bus station, there was still hope that the opposition would be an even less convincing advert for the beautiful game than we were. It was not to be. We were taken to another pitch which could best be described as 'out of the way', a pitch where the public would not be able to see us. There was little evidence of any grass, never mind a running track. Although it was a setting suitable for our footballing expectations, I'd rarely even seen a school pitch in such bad condition. Now at least we had another excuse up our sleeve, other than being crap and unfit.

Our opposition were hanging around, no doubt wondering where the hell we had been and what our team would look like. Either their nerves were on edge or they were just fed up of waiting because when we arrived they were taking long draws on their cigarettes and hammering the ball at each other. However, they did at least look like a team, resplendent in their blue kit and most of them in clearly semi-decent physical condition despite the smoking. The *Rot-Schwarze Franken Oldstars*, on the other hand, looked more like the team of misfits and malnourished allied prisoners of war in the film *Escape to Victory*, even though some of us were clearly over-nourished. But football is football and once the challenge presents itself there is no hiding. Everyone has to stand up and be counted and show the opposition that you're ready to ruffle their feathers and teach them a footballing lesson or two. Just like those prisoners in the far-fetched David versus Goliath of a match in the light-hearted war-film, we too could defy the odds, pull-together and grab a victory in the face of adversity. Unfortunately, we did not have Pele, Osvaldo Ardiles, Bobby Moore or any of the other ex-football stars who graced the film with their exhibition of football skills if not their acting, in our ranks. But we were there, we were going to play and there's little point playing if you're not going to get stuck-in and at least make an effort to give a good account of yourself and your team.

The kit bag was slung to the floor and everyone reached in to grab a kit that would surely show our professionalism to the opposition. Unfortunately each of us pulled out a pink shirt. So badly faded was a previously red kit that we were to play looking like a rather shambolic prawn cocktail. We changed in the warmth of the afternoon by the side of the pitch. The humidity was now increasing as the sky ominously darkened beneath huge clouds. The fact that we would have been visible to each other in the dark wearing our pink shirts probably meant that we should have delayed as much as possible and waited until nightfall before kicking off. We didn't even have proper socks. They were socks without feet, a piece of elastic looping round the heel from the ankles. Things were becoming increasingly ridiculous and a ball was yet to be kicked.

The final straw was the clap of thunder just as we kicked off and the torrential, warm rain that fell throughout the game. Within moments we were soaked although the temperature never dropped. Now we not only had every other factor already mentioned going against us, but we had to contend with carrying around on our backs the increasingly heavy, wet prawn costumes.

Miraculously, we started well and not only created chances but also scored goals. So did the opposition of course. Much of it had to be put down to our lack of discipline (in a positional sense) and their lack of fear that they would be defeated (if we scored ten they must have been certain that they could score at least eleven). I personally sickened of playing in a leaky defence and started to push up the field in search of a goal of my own. Iain had just sickened and was on all fours in the far corner of the field having been substituted, while Jason was the only one making any impression by hanging around up front and scoring a hatful of goals. Our team-mates and coach were impressed with him and despite my best efforts to persuade them otherwise, they kept giving him the ball. They would not have to spend the next ten days with what we knew would become a self-proclaimed *Fussballgott*. He even managed to get on the end of a shot I'd hit against the crossbar, such is the lot of a footballer like me with more heart than skill. How I wished for the days when at least a decent level of fitness and ability to run throughout a match had made up for some of my inadequacies. At least in this game I'd got stuck in from the start and torn my leg open on the gravel surface with a fine sliding tackle after approximately ten seconds. What I thought I'd gained in footballing wisdom over the years was obviously let down by a lack of footballing common sense. During the second half, following another unsuccessful foray forward into the opposition's penalty area, Armin, through the driving rain and from his sheltered position beneath a tree, suggested that I should get back and defend more quickly. It is to my shame that, even among many non-English speakers, everyone on the pitch understood the content of what I shouted back. Iain thought it was amusing until the insulted coach suggested that Iain should now return to the pitch as my replacement. It was worth the shame of the foul-mouthed outburst as I collapsed, knackered, when I crossed the touchline.

What the final score was I cannot remember. It is irrelevant anyway. I know we were well and truly beaten. We thought there might have been at least a few drinks and banter in the clubhouse following a shower but for once it appeared that the British contingent had not (even despite Jason's goal scoring prowess) made much of an impression. There was no shower and no beer and we returned to our hotel to patch up our pride and wounds.

Clearly Klaus and Yohannes had not considered us to be too bad in footballing terms (although I'm sure they won't mind me saying that they were probably only comparing us to their own standards) and later that evening we met them for a drink.

Yohannes was in Germany for a couple of months on holiday from Bali. Klaus had met him on one of his holidays to Indonesia and had also met his own wife there. For Yohannes and his local community in Bali, supporting 1.FCN was a big thing and *Bundesliga* football is shown on TV so there is no problem keeping up-to-date with events in Nuremberg and the rest of Germany.

Klaus has followed the fortunes of Nuremberg seriously for only a few seasons although was obviously aware of his local team and even more aware of the potential for football to help his personal business interests. He was now somehow linking the support of 1.FCN from Bali with his own project to launch the promotion of Asian markets throughout Germany, using the revival of the football in the city to also capture the attention of the local Asian community. A key personality he was hoping to involve in this would be the German born (to a Vietnamese father) young centre forward Chhunly Pagenburg who he hoped would make a big impression in the team and increase interest in the Bali fan club and his projects. It all seemed rather complicated but when we were later joined by his beautiful wife we figured that he was obviously doing something right, and besides, Klaus is an extremely affable bloke with a dry and sharp sense of humour and, importantly to us, a good grasp of English.

We assumed this sense of humour was the reason he took us to an Indonesian karaoke bar. Not only did we meet his wife and friends but also a couple more members from Bali, although their links to the tropical island were not entirely clear. Maybe the same sense of humour was at play when he then proceeded to try to set Jason up with a beautiful Balinese lady who apparently lived in Germany but had beach houses in Bali and Majorca, or at least that's what Jason said after he'd spurned her advances – yes really, he actually did, obviously feeling he'd scored enough already that day.

However, despite what could have been a myriad of ulterior motives at play, our hosts for the evening also wanted to discuss football and we did so at length between a truly mixed bag of karaoke songs of which only two really stood out. For some reason a group of Philippino girls thought that The Cranberries song *Zombie* is related to sexual ecstasy as they faked orgasm at the end of each chorus – "Zombie, zombie, zombie, bie, bie, bie" being the cue for multiple screams and moans each time it came around. I am sure the lyrics are about sectarian violence in Ireland but maybe I'd missed the point somewhere as we laughed at what was probably the strangest rendition of any song. By the fourth time the girls stood up to perform it, any amusement had long since disappeared. Fortunately, this was eventually followed by the whistled opening to that very

German, very poignant song *Wind of Change* by Scorpions. For those unfamiliar with this power ballad allow me to enlighten you. The whistling leads into a song about comradeship and the ending of division, lyrics written at the time that Germany and indeed much of the rest of Europe was witnessing the breaking down of physical and nationalistic barriers. The atmospheric whistling gives way to the opening line which gives the listener no doubt that on a particular August night there is an almost tangible presence hinting at imminent and defining change. To top it all, it was being whistled and sung in perfect English by Yohannes who could only actually speak a few words of the language but was clearly an expert at covering songs. Now it might have been the beer and our physical exertions on the football pitch that afternoon, but this song seemed to represent the beauty of sitting chatting to new-found friends on a warm August night and we proclaimed our wishes that the wind of change (i.e. winning) would continue to blow kindly on 1.FCN for this season that had just begun. Thankfully, to prevent any more sentimental rubbish pouring onto the page, we then spoiled it for everyone with a rendition of *We are the Champions* ('of the *Bundesliga*' was added each time for drunken topical effect). It was definitely the beer and it was definitely time to leave Nuremberg on our circuitous backpacking adventure that would ultimately take us back to Munich for the following weekend's big match.

 Tired and barely able to walk after the previous day's kick around we hobbled to the station and boarded the train to Regensburg. Our journey began in earnest and after a little over an hour we were in our first destination. We checked into a small hotel near to the station promising to try hostels from the next day onwards. For now our aching muscles and limbs required a little more comfort. After this one night a few nights in hostels or on park benches would do no harm because we had booked into the elegant Maritim hotel in Munich for the following weekend on account of the fact that we would be meeting my wife and in-laws there.

So a somewhat painful stroll around Regensburg's old town during the afternoon ultimately led us to a beer garden where it was decided that it would be sensible to take it easy on the beers and have an early night before really getting the adventure going the next morning.

That we turned up at the Maritim hotel four days early the following afternoon was a result of the fact that we were too old for backpacking and hostels, station platforms and park benches. We could see Bavaria another time but for now it would be wise to acclimatise ourselves to Munich and take in the build up to the big game. This decision was made at approximately 5a.m. as our quiet couple of beers in Regensburg ended after several hours in a cocktail bar where they were very kindly selling their produce at half price. Once again the polite Brits were faced with a dilemma and once again we considered that it would have been rude not to partake.

We didn't look like the Maritim hotel's usual guests when we turned up but had cunningly booked our additional nights just a few moments before in a Munich internet café. Only when the receptionist realised that our booking had just arrived on her computer did the porters then decide to help us (and to think that we really did intend to carry our bags ourselves around southern Germany)!

We passed the time in Munich as would be expected with culture, food and drink, although not necessarily in that order. We also had a reconnaissance mission to the Allianz Arena and soon discovered that there was not much to do there and that it was miles out of the city. However, by stopping off on the way back, at least we found ideal places for us to take refreshment after the game on Saturday.

By Wednesday evening, newspaper stands started to bring the forthcoming game to the attention of those who did not yet know and at least for the three of us the excitement started to rise. On the Saturday morning when I met my wife, mother-in law and father-in law at Munich's main station, the place was packed with Nuremberg fans singing and creating an atmosphere which they would ultimately continue throughout the game and beyond.

After a few days of relaxing by the Maritim's pool and ostentatiously sipping Martinis in the hotel's Piano Bar, we were fully re-charged and ready for what was promising to be the chance to witness 1.FCN show how much progress they had made and that they were ready to compete once again on equal terms in the upper echelons of the *Bundesliga*.

R-S Franken Oldstars (v-necks) worse for wear post match

Chapter 6

Reaching the dizzy heights

There are four days to go and I'm alone in a hotel room. The TV is on but there's not much to watch. More re-runs of the highlights of yesterday's matches, live snooker from Malta on Eurosport or the Americo-centric CNN. Nothing at the moment to take my mind from the fear building inside. A fear that has been building for a few days now and a fear I can no longer ignore.

How can I overcome this fear in the next four days? What can one do when for years you have periodically had to back away from situations because fear has taken its grip, or else you avoided it getting a chance to? It's not always been there. I'm sure that as a young child I was alright although I know that by the age of nine or ten, I was aware that certain situations were dangerous and that death always seemed to be a distinct possibility.

How, in just four days, does one overcome a long-running fear of heights? Or to be more precise, how does one overcome a fear of falling? I like looking through the windows of an aircraft, I've been up the Eiffel Tower and the Empire State Building although admittedly I was terrified when I left the interior areas of these structures. Looking at views from high vantage points is a pleasure to behold, as long as there is a window or very secure, and preferably very high, railing to prevent anything causing me to fall to the ground below.

Mountain walking and skiing are, of course, out of the question with such a fear, even though I would dearly love to do them both. But until recently football had not been an issue. It was through a combination of carefully purchased tickets and supporting Port Vale around the low level, lower league stadiums of England, that had kept me from having the need to enter a very high stand. Following Nuremberg changed this. It was now February 2008 and in just four days I would be entering the *Estadio da Luz* of Benfica Lisbon.

For several weeks the trip to Lisbon had been playing on my mind. I wanted to go but thoughts of the stadium triggered my memory to serve me with vivid images of the local derby between 1.FCN and Bayern Munich in August 2006. The images were worrying, especially as they reignited a burning feeling of nausea each time I thought of that visit to Munich's Allianz Arena.

As one approaches the magnificent stadium, home of both Bayern and 1860 Munich, it looks like a giant inflatable UFO. Had it been unveiled in a North American desert in the 1950s, the whole of the USA would probably have come to a panicked standstill. Sitting somewhat lonely in its location in the northeast Munich suburb of Fröttmaning, in an age when architecturally anything goes and science-fiction provides us with far more imaginative shapes than saucers for extraterrestrial flying machines, the Allianz has the appearance more of fun than fear – at least from the outside.

Some would say that it is, as with many other modern football stadia, a characterless, sterile sporting arena. There is certainly sterility in the surroundings as the stadium is built some distance from anything else and is reached on foot by an esplanade 500 metres long and over 100 wide. This esplanade covers part of the car park for the arena which, with 11,000 spaces is Europe's largest. However, sterility in this sense should not be criticised. The transport links to the stadium and the general accessibility are regular features in Germany and are a far cry from the traditional British model of a stadium, packed in between rows of houses and narrow streets. Maybe if Vale Park was situated next to an 11,000 space car park then even Port Vale might get a few thousand more on their average gate, although I doubt it.

As with a number of other German stadia (and many of the new British stadia being built), the Allianz lacks the character of crumbling concrete, mismatched brickwork, rusting roof pillars and inadequate catering and sanitary facilities. It is clean, homogenous and spacious inside and out, with services on offer only to those who have a pre-purchased card. This obviously enables refreshments to be bought efficiently without the staff having to handle cash. It also gives the first insight into the fact that the Allianz Arena is not just about football *per se*. It is about the entertainment industry, providing for a much wider audience than the stereotypical football fan. It also appears to be about charging this wider audience as much as possible for the entertainment and services they receive.

Still, the ticket for the away section only cost 12 Euros and we were able to join an estimated 7,000 Nuremberg fans in the stadium for the third game of 2006-07. Of these, up to 3,000 were dotted around the stadium mixed in with the home support but the majority were positioned on the third tier in the north corner. The atmosphere was clearly going to be electric as everyone made their way up the vast stairways inside the arena to our seats in the gods. Or at least that was, everyone with the exception of me.

How something so seemingly sterile can also provide such perceived danger is a question which still puzzles me. As I was entering the seating area I looked down seeking the pitch. It was surely down there somewhere and readjusting my focus brought it into sight approximately thirty-five metres below. That in itself was not a problem. These seats would obviously provide a fantastic view of the play. However, I was more than a little put off by the gradient of the stand and could see that there was a clear danger of falling from the middle of it to the pitch. Others around me seemed completely unconcerned, oblivious to the danger as they focused on their pre-match rituals. With no chance of communicating the danger to the masses I had to look after number one and at least ensure that I did not tumble to my death. That apparently nobody has yet done so in this stadium is surely down to luck rather than any fact that would suggest that the stadium is actually safe. But now as I stared into the abyss before me I realised that no matter how long I stood coyly at the threshold to this magnificent stand, my fear of heights would not allow me to see the game from my seat. Furthermore the steward clearly had no intention of allowing me to stand clinging to the wall in what was essentially a doorway for the next couple of hours. For someone who had bravely 'backpacked' across Bavaria in the preceding week, this fear was something of an anti-climax.

My wife, seeing the fear and sensibly realising that forcing me to my seat would surely enable her to smell the fear as well, suggested that we try and find another position from which to watch the game. So the two of us, her a little fed-up to be giving up her excellent vantage point, me not convinced that there would be any chance of now watching the live action in the sell-out crowd, made our way down through the bowels of the stadium.

We had entered the stadium into a wide area in which there were refreshment kiosks at the rear of the first tier of seating. This tier was not high and had an un-daunting gradient leading down to the pitch. The seating here was for home supporters although there were several 1.FCN fans still standing around with just a few minutes remaining until kick-off. Some people milled around behind the back row of seating and from where they stood there was a good view of the pitch from directly behind the goal. We quickly made the decision to hide our Nuremberg colours, buy a drink and stand around in this position until the inevitable jobsworth of a steward moved us on, at which point Angela would have to provide some explanation of why I could not take my allocated seat, and appeal to the steward's better nature to not eject this strange Englishman from the stadium.

That day I managed to cheat my fear and it was something of a bonus that, come half-time, I had managed to watch forty-five minutes of football from my favoured behind the goal position, standing on what was a makeshift terrace with several other Bayern and Nuremberg fans who clearly knew the dangers of high seating positions, without a steward so much as even looking in my direction. Not even when Ivica Banovic headed just over Oliver Khan's crossbar in the opening minutes of the game and I threw my arms into the air foolishly thinking the ball might be heading for the net. In contrast to the way that it would be in a British stadium, the stewards and police who stood around were clearly uninterested in making or enforcing petty rules and actions to prevent other people from standing around and having a good time. In fact, for a local derby, I was surprised that there were so many fans of both teams sitting and standing together with little more than friendly banter.

The game had been preceded by a semi-haunting ritual as the Bayern Munich *Südkurve*, the south end of the stadium, unfurled a banner which slowly covered much of the stand. It was a huge Bayern Munich crest on a white background and as it rolled open from its base behind the goal a low continuous note played, adding to the atmosphere and providing an almost religious undertone to the proceedings. This ceremony lacked the carnival, spine-tingling anticipation created by the choreography of the Nuremberg Ultras before a home game but it was certainly impressive. The whole place was a cathedral of football with a congregation of 69,000 ready to worship.

The atmosphere promised to be electric but as the game got underway it was clear that the neat pre-match performance was the high point as far as the Bayern fans were concerned. Despite the stand containing the higher tiers of seating acting as a roof above our heads, the most noise we could now hear came from far above and seemed to echo around the stadium. The Nuremberg fans are extremely proud of creating an intense, ongoing noise at football matches. On this occasion, playing against the mighty Bayern with all the regional and political history between Bavaria and Franconia adding to the long-standing football rivalry, the *Clubberer* managed to sing for the entire match. From where I was standing singing would not have been advisable so I hummed the songs beneath my breath, at least happy that I'd been able to move and thus watch the game.

Eighteen months later, in that hotel room in February 2008, I started to wonder if I might be able to try a different vantage point in Lisbon. In fact, remembering my fear in Munich, I started to wonder whether it was worth going at all. After all, I didn't have to put myself through that again. So I was due to go and watch a game and the tickets were for the third tier and Row W to rub salt into my opening wounds. The solution would be simple. Either get a ticket for another part of the stadium or don't go to the game. No problem. No fear.

This would have been easier if it was not for the fact that the hotel room in which I was contemplating my choices was in Nuremberg from where I would be flying on to Portugal. Flying to a date with destiny in that huge cauldron of football with high stands from which, unlike in Munich where I'd clearly cheated death, I would, without doubt, be the first tumbling fatality.

In Munich I had known that the tickets were for Block 344 but this did not tell me the height of the stand and so I gave it little thought beforehand. Inside the stadium we had climbed stairways which were covered and curved, obviously gaining much height but with no indication of how steep the gradient was to the pitch. When I had seen the huge drop I became tense, unable to control my breathing. I stood and tried to acclimatise but it had been no use and I could not have gone any further. It defies logic which makes it even more frustrating. The instinct is to crouch down, making oneself as small as possible, lowering the centre of gravity to feel safer and less likely to topple over the rows of seating, over the edge of the stand. You simply don't get this at Vale Park.

With time ticking away some eighteen months later, I had to try to overcome this. The flights, Lisbon hotel and match tickets were all paid for. It would be crazy not to see the game. In English, maybe even German at a push, I could plead with the officials that I would be at risk of some sort of collapse if they did not re-seat me although this could naturally have the consequence that I would be simply ejected from the ground. But in Portuguese? My old phrase book, purchased for a holiday there sixteen years previously, did not contain a translation for 'Please let me sit somewhere else. I'm not going to cause any trouble but I'm shit scared up here.' And besides, I wanted to be with the Nuremberg fans.

Maybe alcohol would help: the old 'Dutch Courage'. I don't remember having had more than a pint before entering the Allianz Arena, although after a week of drinking to excess in Bavaria it would have probably taken more than a few to provide the necessary 'protection' on that occasion. But drinking could also have a negative effect. Obviously drinking so much that I feared nothing at all would be ridiculous because, even if allowed into the stadium I would probably fall from the stand, or even jump depending on whether lack of balance or belief that I could fly came to me first. So the drinking would have to be moderate at the most. But even this could be problematic. What if it worked and then started to wear off? Would I be stranded until somebody was able to sufficiently refuel me? And what if the effects were just about enough to allow me to make my way to my seat, nerves on edge, barely able to look or even move but then needing to pee after ten minutes. Alcohol alone could be a rather hit-and-miss solution.

There was only one thing for it. I had to face this fear head on. I had to be able to march up the stairs and into that stand, to my seat in Row W, praying for my safety and slaying this fear once and for all. There would be no repeat in Lisbon of that scary time in Munich. Easy. Or at least easy to think when lying on a hotel bed only eighteen inches from the floor. It would need more than just sheer, stubborn, old-fashioned bravery and religion. What was needed, and very quickly, was a modern, mental conditioning approach.

Like an athlete or successful businessman I would imagine my victory. The fear came from a feeling of being unsafe – I would imagine standing there feeling totally safe. It made me tense, barely able to breathe, panic-stricken – I would imagine feeling relaxed as I stood there immersed in the atmosphere, watching the pitch and the fans below me. The fear also made me unhappy that I could not enjoy what I wanted to – I would imagine feeling very happy, content that I could take it all in, feeling safe and relaxed, making my way up or down to my seat, standing up or sitting down as the match itself dictated I should. I would feel safe, relaxed and happy in Tier 3, Row W of the *Estadio da Luz*. It was time to begin the mental preparation.

The views of Nuremberg from the Sinwell Tower are almost breathtaking. High above the steep roofs of the re-built medieval *Altstadt* it was the first place I thought of to help with my quick-fix cerebral conditioning. Looking beyond the roofs and spires the views extend to the industrial suburbs of the south and south-west, the stadium and *Kongresshalle* to the south-east, and the airport and the *Kraftshofer* forest to the north. As I looked through the barred windows of the old watchtower I felt safe, relaxed and even happy. It was a beautiful February day. A slight drift of air from the east. A beautiful sun in a perfect blue sky.

But it wasn't only the view that was making me happy. The top of the tower is reached by an internal wooden spiral staircase, winding its way upwards, clinging to the walls with a rather nasty looking gap down the middle. However, a few minutes before, I had managed to ascend it without too much fear. Okay, I had held on with both hands and avoided looking up or down but I'd even, rather nervously I must admit, let go of one rail at a point where the old stairway became too wide to reach across. I had contemplated retreating at this point but that would have meant turning round, thus letting go with both hands, or descending backwards, neither of which were any more appealing than continuing. When I had felt the panic building I had simply stopped and taken deep breaths. Or was it panic? Maybe my heavy breathing had more to do with my level of fitness rather than my level of fear. After all, how often was I required to climb so many steps in one go.

Inside the viewing area of the tower there are a couple of benches and what even I would consider to be a totally risk free situation. The staircase however had been different. As I sat contemplating my achievement I could hear the voices of a coach load of American tourists below in the castle courtyard. I decided to stay put and contemplate for longer. No doubt if I went down feeling great about myself I'd hear one of the elderly Yanks telling a compatriot that the tower is quaint and is nearly half the size of the tower in their city which would probably be a village of 200 people.

As I sat I looked at one wooden panelled wall. Hundreds of people had obviously been so pleased with their achievement of reaching the top that they had to sign their name, and usually with that of their latest desire too. Apparently "Alexandra was here," and clearly demonstrating that she was a well-educated graffitist. Surely she meant "Woz ere"? George certainly hadn't let himself down in this manner though. Or his country. He "Woz ere from England 5-1" and must have had a right old laugh telling his friends that he had written such an amusing line. I bet he didn't tell them that he owned a glittery silver marker with which he had written it.

Somewhat to my relief, it wasn't just British graffiti. "Chrisbelle Emma Loves Pauline (Kulmbach)" incoherently but strangely provocatively claimed another silver scrawl. "Vive Paris" said somebody whose name was illegible, and "I love Annecy forever" proclaimed someone who was either extremely taken by the French Alpine town or they fancied a girl whose parents had decided she should have a rather pretentious name.

I carried on reading for a while to see if there were any references to football other than George's little Anglo-German rivalry reminder. But there weren't. A couple of endorsements of anarchy and the profound statement that "Rulez Sucks" but nothing about FCN, Greuther Fürth or Bayern Munich. When I was growing up, I'm sure you could hardly pass a wall or public toilet without reading of Leeds United or Liverpool.

Had I kept looking maybe I would have found something but now I realised I was putting off the inevitable. I had to get down from this bloody place. Down all the stairs. How many were there? Too many. I was panicking. I tried to relax. Surely down would be worse than up. I was about to visualise the whole thing – more mental preparation – but then I heard the tourists on their way up. I had to go for it.

Maybe if the chance had been there to prepare myself mentally and to prove myself at Nuremberg castle before the Munich game I would have been able to spend the game in the midst of the singing away fans, although when I was told that the whole game was spent standing, sometimes on the seats, I was quite happy to have avoided the situation.

The first half in Munich saw a highly spirited display in which both teams came close to scoring but chances were narrowly missed or saved by the almost legendary Oliver Kahn for Munich or Nuremberg's captain Raphael Schäfer who produced a series of fine saves to deny the opponents.

At half-time we decided to have a walk along the promenade on which we had stood to watch the first forty-five minutes of action. Angela told me that she thought it went all around the arena, effectively meaning that with unconcerned officials, the game could be viewed from any side or end of the pitch. I laughed this off as a ridiculous suggestion – nobody would be foolish enough to allow fans to wander around in this manner, and besides, nobody else appeared to be moving. I expected after a few yards to come across a fence or a gate and be asked for a pass to move into the next section. With hindsight it was probably a foolish thing to attempt to do. It could have gone horribly wrong had someone asked to see my ticket and helpfully escorted me back to the top of the stand.

Not long after I had sneered at my wife's ridiculous suggestion, we both stood at the opposite end of the stadium at the back of the home supporter's terrace. No gates, no questions asked. We were free to walk around the area at the rear of the lower tier of seating and terracing. Before we were moved on we called the others, sitting what appeared to be a vast distance away far above the pitch at the other end of the ground. They waved the flag in our direction although this was difficult to see from so far.

A decision was then required. Should we make our way back to the north end of the arena or stay on this terrace for as long as possible with the hardcore of Bayern Munich fans? As 1.FCN would be shooting towards us during the second half we decided to stay put. A couple of police officers stood right next to us so we figured we might be offered some safety but did vow to keep our celebrations to a minimum if the unthinkable happened and Nuremberg scored.

As it happened, neither team found the net. Dutch international Makaay went ridiculously close for Bayern, taking the ball around Schäfer before rolling it into the side netting. Schäfer continued to make excellent saves and Brazilian centre-half Glauber made a last-ditch tackle to keep *Der Club* on level terms.

In the dying minutes Nuremberg substitute Marek Mintal fired just over from the edge of the area. I held my breath, raised my arms and then somehow turned my gasp which was intended to show how unlucky it was into a mock sigh of relief as those around me thought I had been about to cheer. Fortunately I got away with it but we now edged to the very back of the terrace ready to make a quick escape as Nuremberg looked likely to score or at least hold on for a point.

Despite our position being just a few yards from the beating drums of the staunchest of Munich fans even these could not drown out the constant singing of the Nuremberg supporters. It was quite amazing that these could be heard louder than the numerically superior home support. In fact it has become something of an issue with some Bayern Munich fans who are concerned that the loudest section of their group is split between the lower tiers at each end of the stadium while the away fans are placed high up, close to the roof and clearly enjoy far better acoustics to make themselves heard.

The introduction of Marek Mintal in the seventy-eighth minute had sent the *Clubberer* into a frenzy of excitement. Here was their hero, their talisman on his way back from injury. The Slovakian international would surely be the man to cement the performances of the second half of the previous season and lift *Der Club* to greater heights in this campaign.

No stranger to success, Mintal joined 1.FCN in 2003 having being the Slovak top scorer in the previous two seasons, playing for MSK Zilnia and helping them to back-to-back championships. A loyal servant, Mintal played in the town in which he was born for seven years before signing for 1.FCN. Legend has it that the Nuremberg president, Michael Roth was purchasing a car and after the sale was complete the salesman asked him if there was anything else he could help him with. When Roth joked that he could do with an attacker and a midfielder, he thought little more of it until a few days later when he was contacted by a Slovakian who the car salesman knew. Not long after this Marek Mintal and Robert Vittek were signing contracts for *Der Club*.

The form shown for Zilnia was immediately transferred to the *2.Bundesliga* as Mintal's eighteen goals made him leading scorer and were instrumental in Nuremberg bouncing straight back into the top flight. The adoration of the fans was also sealed as the nickname 'Phantom' was bestowed upon the skinny Slovakian attacking midfielder because of his ability to arrive unnoticed and unmarked into the opponent's penalty area: a trademark skill which would lead to even more goals the following season.

Nuremberg would have been relegated again from the *Bundesliga* in 2004-05 if Mintal had not found the net on the twenty-four occasions it took him to become the league's leading scorer. Alleged interest from some of Europe's top sides came to nothing, and another season of many Mintal goals would surely follow.

Unfortunately, after just a handful of appearances Mintal broke his foot early in the 2005-06 season. He was sorely missed as the team slipped to the foot of the *Bundesliga* and Wolfgang Wolf was eventually replaced by Hans Meyer. Mintal started in the first game following the winter pause, a 2-1 victory over Hamburg. However, despite the amazing revival of *Der Club* which would follow during the second half of the season, the Slovak would play no further part, having been taken from the pitch in only the sixth minute with another break of his foot. He would not play again that season.

It was the week before the game in the Allianz Arena that Mintal made his long awaited comeback, as a substitute against Mönchengladbach. The expectant home crowd gave their returning hero a rapturous welcome. Unfortunately it would only be a few weeks into the season that another long-term injury sidelined the player.

Had he scored what would have surely been the winning goal with his eighty-eighth minute volley against Bayern Munich, Mintal would, without a shadow of doubt become the most popular man in Nuremberg, Franconia and possibly the rest of Germany for a time. That he did not find the net was of little concern to the *Clubberer* as the final seconds ticked away and the referee signalled the end of the game. I did not glance up at the section of away supporters as I was now more concerned about getting out of the way of miserable home fans who were more than a little disappointed with their start to the season. The last thing they wanted to see were the beaming smiles of two Nuremberg supporters standing on their sacred terrace. We jogged back to meet the others and listened to the chants of *Spitzenreiter, Spitzenreiter, Spitzenreiter* echoing through the stadium and down the stairways as Nuremberg fans spilled out into the open towards the vast convoy of coaches ready to head home, or the public transport back to the city centre. Today had been an almost miraculous achievement as far as these fans were concerned. Never before had I seen a goalless draw celebrated with so much passion and with so much delight. It seemed that the majority of this was a result of the great rivalry, but there was also an element of dislike for the opposition.

Throughout our few days in the city, conversation with Munich fans had been nothing more than banter but to some there was a deep hatred. In footballing terms this could be put down to local rivalry and a variety of occasions where the paths of the two clubs had crossed, none more so than the phantom goal scored by Thomas Helmer in April 1994. With *Der Club* struggling for points at the wrong end of the *Bundesliga* and Munich trying to hold off the challenge of Kaiserslautern at the top, Nuremberg visited the Olympic Stadium where both Bayern and 1860 Munich previously played. With the score at 1-1 the referee made one of the most curious decisions ever seen. As a cross came into the penalty area Nuremberg keeper Köpke was left stranded. The ball fell to Helmer at the back post but he somehow managed to mis-control it and to the relief of Nuremberg the ball trickled harmlessly wide of the target. Köpke was now in a heap in the goal having scrambled to make up ground and Helmer sportingly helped him to his feet, a nice gesture after such an embarrassing miss. However, when Helmer turned around he saw that the referee had signalled a goal. The Munich players began to celebrate as Helmer's sportsmanship was quickly replaced by a disgraceful lack of morality, when realising the points would go to his team, he raised his hands in triumph. Despite the protests of the Nuremberg players the phantom goal was allowed to stand and the hosts won 2-1. In an unprecedented move the DFB ordered the game to be replayed but the outcome was the same with Bayern taking the points, this time with a 5-0 victory. The hurt was to get much worse for the *Clubberer* a few weeks later when they missed safety by one point and Bayern won the title by the same margin.

Such an episode is often pointed to by other detractors of Bayern Munich as an example of how the big clubs hold the power and the commercialisation of football increasingly threatens the people's game and smaller clubs.

However, despite the rivalry it has to be said that this was the tamest derby game I had ever attended. I have no complaints because it is certainly far more pleasant to travel to, watch and return from a game without the threat of violence and personal injury. Even on the *U-Bahn* as we returned to the city centre fans were not kept apart and the police presence was enough for the rivalry to show itself as banter rather than anything more serious. Although the policing always appears to be relatively low key in Germany, plenty of fan groups would dispute this. Of course there are occasions when it is required that the policing is more heavy-handed but most of the time the police are able to stand around and survey the scene. This is not to say that policing of football in England is heavy handed these days. Unfortunately what seems to happen is that officials in the stadium are left to control the crowd with the police stepping in if anyone disobeys an order from a steward who thinks that his fluorescent jacket gives him the right to spoil the day for everyone.

At the end of 2007 I made the hour or so journey to Nottingham to watch Port Vale play Nottingham Forest. With the league table making the home team look like promotion probables and bottom-placed Vale like relegation certainties, it would have been too much to expect anything from the game from Vale's perspective other than a promising performance. The grey, dark day and the rain only further served to provide a grim backdrop to the poor quality of finishing in the game, which Vale ultimately lost 2-0. Although the *Bundesliga* is not as strong (on paper at least) as the English Premier League, Italy's *Serie 'A'* or *La Liga* in Spain, it provides a far higher standard than the lower reaches of English league football. And while the cup upsets, and the ups-and-downs in form of the team and individuals cause varying levels of anxiety, excitement and apathy among fans of all teams, that is probably the extent of the similarities of supporting Vale and 1.FCN.

Unlike many 'away ends' in lower league football stadia, Nottingham's City Ground provides good facilities beneath the stand. The seats themselves provide a reasonable view of the pitch and of the remainder of the stadium which itself belongs to a higher division and acknowledges the fact that Forest were once, for a while, one of the big teams in England and Europe. The vast amount of police and stewards present amongst the away following of mostly young men and youths does nothing to promote the game as family entertainment, a worrying issue if football clubs need to diversify their fan base in order to gain or develop their financial viability. The treatment of fans like animals (and Port Vale is hardly noted for anything, let alone for having a dangerous hooligan element) is of even greater concern.

Although in England the huge fences separating the fans from the pitch have long since gone, it often appears to be the case that these have now been replaced by overly arrogant officials backed by police officers. While fences were clearly an issue in situations when the stand required rapid evacuation, at other times one can observe that at least a fence does not suffer the verbal abuse of a steward or police officer from young fans who realise that handing out such puerile insults is often more entertaining than the game itself. Often this abuse is in return for the fact that the supporters are constantly being warned to sit down, facing ejection from the ground if they refuse to comply with the polite and not-so-polite requests of the officials. If one person is refusing to sit and is hampering the view of those around him then surely a polite request to sit, followed by firmer action if necessary, should be expected. But if you have a whole block of people standing to sing for their team or even simply rising to their feet to celebrate something as simple as a corner kick, then why should the stewards move in and threaten fans with expulsion? Surely this only serves to cause resentment between the two parties. This resentment is then furthered when one group of fans (often the away supporters) are constantly told to sit down while in the adjacent block or stand, the officials are seemingly ignoring the fact that elements of the home support are not only standing for much of the time but are doing so facing the away support and hurling constant abuse in their direction. One way in which to deal with this issue in England would be to tell the chief 'offenders' that whatever they do, they must not sit down quietly on the seats provided. One can imagine that relatively quickly this reverse psychology would have some of even the biggest potential hooligans sitting angelically throughout the game! But why have such ridiculous rules in the first place?

It was the Taylor Report of 1989 following the Hillsborough tragedy that rid English stadiums of terraces aimed to improve the safety of fans watching football matches. Whatever the pros and cons of terraced areas at football matches may be, it is, for whatever reason, widely regarded as being easier for a crowd who are standing to create a better atmosphere than a crowd who are sitting. This contrast can clearly be seen between the stadia of Germany and England. It is possible to witness the semi-religious atmosphere of the Allianz Arena with a standing area for home fans but apparently no concerns if, as in August 2006, the away fans simply stand and sing all match in their seated area. Similarly, the *Nordkurve* terraces and stands in Nuremberg's *Frankenstadion*, can produce a deafening atmosphere when the fans all stand en masse and get behind their team. Such scenes are repeated all over Germany, and perhaps nowhere more so than the home end in Dortmund's *Westfalenstadion* with over 20,000 packed on to the huge terrace behind the goal.

Now compare this to England where the true fans, not the so-called corporate 'prawn sandwich' brigade as Manchester United legend Roy Keane once labelled the less than vocal businessmen and women on a jolly with their colleagues, want to sing and shout for their team and create a fantastic atmosphere. In the English Premier League, the die-hard fans now have several factors against them. New stadiums have led to the dispersal of the fans from the traditionally fanatical areas of the ground as pricing and demographics of support have changed.

Even the stadiums themselves may now have reduced acoustic capabilities from the echoing tin sheds of the pre-Premier League era. And where fans do try to create the atmosphere, they often do so in fear of punishment by the authorities.

Following a 1-0 home victory over Birmingham City on New Year's Day 2007, Manchester United manager Sir Alex Ferguson described the atmosphere at Old Trafford as being like a funeral. Certainly a number of the factors mentioned above were part of the cause of Ferguson's annoyance. In response, the spokesman of the Independent Manchester United Supporter's Association Colin Hendrie, was quick to lay the blame at the door of the authorities. "You can't stand up to make a noise. If you try to stand up, you've got stewards who are ejecting you, they're taking your season ticket away from you. It's almost like a police state in a football ground now and if you do stand up, people will take your arm, put it behind the back of your neck and throw you out of the ground. Under those circumstances, what atmosphere does he want? The only atmosphere we've got is one where we're a little bit frightened of losing £1,000 for the season ticket we've paid for. A lot of people are pretty upset because it shows a lack of understanding about what it's like to be a football fan in 2008. Fergie's going back to the days ten years ago where it was absolutely fantastic, you could stand. But you can't do that now."

Yet in Germany it all seems to be so different. The huge choreographed displays of flag-waving and unfurling banners don't happen by accident. They require meticulous planning and no shortage of labour in making the flags and banners in the first place. Fan groups need to be highly motivated and organised and it is such organisation which surely causes some fear for the various footballing authorities in the UK. It is unlikely that, bearing in mind the huge business represented by Premier League football clubs, any of them have a genuine interest in providing fans with any real power. Only if it matches the business interests of the club will there be true concessions and unfortunately this is what professional football has 'evolved' into in the UK and is increasingly doing so around the world, such is the advent of global media and the realisation by the business community that big football can equal big money.

With good reason, for the protection of the public and upholding of law-and-order (as well as the reputation and dignity of football itself) there also exists a real fear of control of the stands and terraces falling into the hands of groups such as the hooligan 'firms' of the 1970s and '80s who wore violence as a badge of honour and used match days as the opportunity to engage in running battles with the police and other 'firms'. This fear could also be compounded when one considers the press coverage (and actions) of the various Ultras groups, particularly in Italy where violent clashes with rival fans and police have caused several deaths.

But are football fans like this now? As Colin Hendrie said, there is a fear of losing your season ticket. And policing is supposed to be better now, too. Not all Ultras and organised fan groups are like those in Italy. Now there seems to be a backlash against the commercialisation of football and particularly where fans are gaining control of clubs in the lower leagues there seems to be a genuine understanding of what fans want and need. These groups know that they can't turn out a team that will compete for titles and mass media attention each week but they can work towards at least providing entertainment for a couple of hours on a Saturday afternoon without the fans feeling like totally anonymous customers feeding their hard-earned money into a corporate machine. And this for the real fan is often enough. It is not an ever-increasing spiral of success that they crave each season. They know that this is unrealistic and many also realise that eventually they would have nothing left to dream about. They just want to see their club doing reasonably well but even if it goes through tough times they will still be there. The love for the club is unconditional.

As we reflected on the position of Nuremberg at the top of the *Bundesliga* that weekend in Munich our love for 1.FCN was also becoming unconditional. It was obviously easy to say in this position but we knew that we did not need them to be top of the league to want to come back for more. Then again, it was a wonderful feeling which most of 1FCNUK had never really experienced before with our teams back home.

Unfortunately it would not last long but the promise was there and the top positions were to remain tantalisingly close for the next several months. Those months would see me taking extra care with ticket purchases, making sure that I was not going to put if not my life, then at least my sanity, at risk. There would be many ups and downs to witness before I would throw caution to the wind and purchase tickets for the *Estadio da Luz*. *Der Club* were beginning to look like a team with the ability to reach the dizzy heights more consistently. Inevitably I would have to try and reach them again myself before too long.

The medieval aldstadt and the dizzy heights of the Sinwell Tower

Chapter 7

It wasn't always this nice

In our ever-increasing experience of watching football in Germany, it should be made clear, if it is not already, that we have a great time. The atmosphere is fantastic, the refreshments are delicious, the football is often exciting, the fans are wonderfully passionate in their support and everyone seems friendly and welcoming. If I were to go on about the German football experience, as I often do far too much for 'normal' people to bear for more than a few minutes, I would run out of superlatives.

Imagine walking into a football ground and savouring the smell of a variety of sausages on vast grills. Fresh *Brezel* (large salted pretzels) on sale at various outlets, beer and soft drinks (the real brands not Rollercola or some other low quality impostor) all readily available without much queuing. Imagine doing this after enjoying socialising in various bars from the city centre to the stadium with fans representing the home and away teams, the time spent watching the match an extremely pleasant interlude before returning to the city centre or another venue to continue this socialising. And imagine doing this in other cities as an away fan, wearing your club's colours, visiting the strongholds of opposition supporters and sometimes waving around a flag from a foreign country to boot. Now imagine doing this and not just managing to escape alive but actually making new friends and acquaintances on the way.

I've done some of this in England too. Believe it or not I've experienced some culinary delights. The balti pies at Walsall are excellent, even the pies at Port Vale, are rather tasty. I've enjoyed a beer pre- and post-match in various towns and cities all over the country and have worn club colours sometimes in doing so. On occasion I've even dared to unzip my jacket slightly or talk in a not so local accent. I love going to the football and have loved the opportunity to visit different parts of England over the years just to watch my team play. Win, draw or lose, there is always something to take from the experience. However, despite there being occasions of brilliance, both in terms of the performance witnessed on the pitch and in terms of the fun surrounding the whole experience, it is not really necessary to use a range of synonyms for fantastic to describe it all. It's good fun but it seems to miss something, especially these days.

Maybe the problem is the lack of novelty involved. I've been doing it for years now and it's no longer as new or as exciting as it once was. Those early days when you could jump into a car with your mates as the first, then next, then next passed their driving tests, taking it in turns to make incomprehensible journeys to distant destinations for midweek and weekend away matches. The near misses as inexperience behind the wheel and pre-match adrenalin came close to causing road traffic accidents, the endless search for the football stadium's floodlights in lieu of any proper directions or willingness to stop and ask for them. The driving the wrong way down one-way streets, through pedestrian zones, past motorway exits. Duping the driver to stop at a pub to enable his passengers to allegedly use the toilets before re-emerging with beers in hand. Those were the days. Then the novelty wore off. Maybe it was the lack of enthusiasm for cold pies and the aforementioned, flat and sickly cola drinks. Maybe it was the increasing prices. Maybe it was a combination of these and a whole raft of other factors. Somehow it just stopped being as much fun. The support was still there but the whole experience surrounding the match had become stale. It was as though we had done too much too soon; we hadn't paced ourselves and had set off going hell for leather in what is clearly a very long marathon which we had treated as a sprint. Such is the exuberance of youth. We thought we would be able to sustain it forever but hadn't taken into account work commitments, relationships, financial situations and increasing age with its increasing responsibilities. Or had we just realised how crap the football we saw was?

But then came the thirties and beyond. Horizons naturally broadened as a new, more sophisticated approach was made to regain those heady days and legitimise it with the addition of a bit of culture. And what had we learned? In some respects absolutely nothing. Why could we not just fly over to Germany, watch a couple of matches each season and be happy with that? We could even fly to different countries and watch matches in a whole range of different leagues. On the surface this idea holds great appeal; an excuse to travel, an excuse to visit stadia around the world, to see some of the greatest footballers and teams and to experience the phenomenon that is the beautiful game across a variety of cultures. It all sounds idyllic but as most football fans know, it doesn't work like that.

Watching a football match between two teams usually has the prerequisite or the outcome that you have at least a slight affinity to one team more than the other. Whether this is because a friend of a friend supports them, you feel that the referee has been slightly one-sided, one team was a slick passing side or you had a bet on the game, it is sometimes hard to be completely neutral. See your slightly favoured team for a second or third time and your affinity becomes a little deeper. You start to recognise the players and watch out for the results. When this team is not competing with your team, the club you traditionally support, and particularly if there is no chance of them ever doing so, then the easier it is to become more involved. But of course, you don't want to go headlong into a frenzied level of support that you somehow believe you can maintain forever. That mistake has been made once before.

By the spring of 2006 then, the hardcore of 1FCNUK were somewhat in the mire. We'd created this thing and, like Frankenstein's monster, we were not sure where it was going or whether we could control it. We had been taken in by 1.FC Nürnberg, both in terms of a fully-fledged support for the team and as a group of fans welcomed by this famous club. We were oblivious to the fact that we had fallen into a trap we'd unintentionally set ourselves and by the time we did realise it there was no going back. We were in deep. We'd fallen for *Der Club*. It was a rather full-on affair and we were having the time of our lives. The superlatives were flying around to describe the team, the fans, the stadium, the food, the drink, the country, the camaraderie. To put it simply (and master the understatement): watching football in Germany is nice.

However, this has not always been the case. Historically speaking, German football has had a myriad of issues with violence and racism both inside and outside of football stadiums. Much action has been taken to tackle these issues over recent years and at the most commercially viable end of the football spectrum in Germany, from personal experience, it is rare to witness anything even closely related to the hooliganism to which many writers have referred as 'the English disease'.

The niceties surrounding the whole fly-to-Germany-to-watch-Nuremberg experience are even now slightly betrayed by the fact that some of the Nuremberg fans live on (but thankfully rarely seem to live up to any more) a reputation as one of the least desirable groups of supporters in Germany. As with all football clubs it is their fans as a whole who become labelled as undesirable when the anti-social behaviour only comes from a minority. In England, Leeds fans, West Ham fans, Millwall fans and Chelsea fans, to name but a few, have for a long time held varying degrees of fear factor for fans, towns and police forces related to other teams. However, I have met fans of each of these clubs and to say that these well-behaved individuals are in the minority would be wrong. Like these English teams, Nuremberg have had groups who at times could have been termed hell-raisers and hooligans. And where such groups are present the remainder of the fans clearly get tarnished with the same brush. Take the example of the first game ever abandoned in German football (at least in the west). It was a local derby between Nuremberg and local rivals Fürth. For many this not only serves as a reminder of the historical tension between the two clubs but is also a reminder of the days of trouble and the menacing status of the *Clubberer*.

If the rivalry between Nuremberg and Bayern Munich is intense, then that between Nuremberg and Fürth is almost explosive. Whereas passions surrounding the Bavarian derby are as much about regional identity as they are about football, those that envelop the Franconian derby are historical and local rivalry based, and for many they are deep. No matter that only five miles separates the centres of the two places which in reality now almost blend into one another. Forget the fact that the first German railway linked Nuremberg and Fürth in 1835. Football it seems can override all other sentiments. In the 1920s with 1.FCN the dominant force in German football, Fürth were not far behind. Fürth player Hans Sutor was forced out of the club after he married a Nuremberg girl and when the German national team consisted of only players from Fürth and *Der Club* in 1924 the players travelled to Amsterdam in separate railway carriages. It is said that when Fürth's Karl Auer scored Germany's winner, the Nuremberg players refused to celebrate.

Over eighty years later as the players and fans of *Der Club* celebrated their 2007 Cup final victory in Nuremberg's market place the players were presented to their adoring public. Amidst thanks to the well-wishers from club officials and players, and cheers and chants from the gathered masses, defender Andreas Wolf struck a rather popular chord as he greeted the crowd with a little ditty directed at the local rivals and poking fun at their cloverleaf crest.

Alle Blumen blühen	*All flowers bloom*
Alle Blumen blühen	*All flowers bloom*
Nur das Fürther Kleeblatt nicht	*Only Fürth's clover does not*
Alles kann man rauchen	*Everything one can smoke*
Alles kann man rauchen	*Everything one can smoke*
Nur das Fürther Kleeblatt nicht	*Only Fürth's clover you can not*

Naturally it was met with rather loud applause.

The abandoned game in January 1973 seems to be written into the folklore of the club for some fans. Several people I have spoken to in Nuremberg refer to this event as a demonstration of how bad the Nuremberg fans have been in the past. The myth surrounding the abandonment of the game certainly seems to demonstrate hooligan fans in action but in reality, some fans who were actually there seem to play down the whole issue. It seems that fireworks were set off even before kick-off and at least one, but probably more, landed on the pitch during the game. Fans also spilled onto the pitch (again at least once) from the overcrowded area in which they were standing and the referee ultimately abandoned with Fürth leading 4-2. It was not even certain that the hosts would have won as reports suggest that Nuremberg were in the ascendancy having pulled two goals back in quick succession after half-time. There is a sense of some people wanting to propagate the myth to show how feared the *Clubberer* once were, whereas those who were involved would now like to distance themselves from or play down the actual events. The truth lies somewhere in between.

What is clear though is that the two most prominent 1.FCN fan clubs over the past forty years have certainly seen their share of hooligan-related troubles. The German word for waterlily is *Seerose*. Nothing violent about that you would think. Do not let anybody tell you that Germans possess no sense of humour when a group of young men out for a beer and a fight each weekend operated under the name of 'waterlily'. The *Seerose* fan club was formed in the year Nuremberg won their last German Championship in 1968. Named after a bar in which members met before and after matches, the *Seerose* fans became synonymous with 1970s aggressive fan culture, particularly in southern Germany. During the '70s Nuremberg only played in the top division for one season (1978-79) but for the majority of away games the *Clubberer* out-numbered home fans. As the second tier of German football was regional until 1981, the games played in the *Regionlliga Süd* and its successor the 2.*Bundesliga Süd* were all relatively local, easily accessible to the travelling fan and hooligan. They represented fixtures and cities with a range of history and rivalry. In some respects most games were local derbies.

In the 1980s Red Devils Nürnberg formed. Obviously not wishing to be as subtle as *Seerose* they chose a name which sounded more fearsome. Their reputation soon grew and they became one of the most feared groups in West Germany alongside the notorious fans of Schalke and Cologne.

It is interesting to meet members of these groups now. The *Seerose* members generally regard themselves as being past fighting and the Red Devils Nürnberg no longer seek trouble, although according to one member they would never run from trouble as they have their name and honour to defend. Of course most of those who were involved in hooliganism in the '70s and

'80s are now more mature and many take their own children and grandchildren to watch 1.FCN play. They became aware of the stigma attached to *Der Club* through association with their anti-social behaviour and have fallen in line with the changing face of the modern game. One member of the *Seerose* fan club, involved in violence for thirty of the last forty years told me that he eventually "recognised that the violence is pointless and then went to the other side". He now works on the Fan Project, a government backed scheme which has seen fans, clubs and the authorities work together on initiatives born out of the growing concern that the football stadiums of Germany were becoming breeding grounds for extremists including neo-nazis and racists. Some would argue that what happens at football matches is only a reflection of feelings and opinion in society as a whole but whatever the position nationally in Germany (drawing on personal experience, at least on the surface there appears to be few if any problems) Nuremberg seems generally devoid of any organised political or anti-social problems. That does not mean that issues do not occur. There will always be fans who like to fight with the fans of other clubs or even amongst themselves, particularly when fuelled with alcohol. There are also fans who are racist. However, the vast majority still shun and even activate against such behaviour. The police, too, are more organised and understand how to handle hooligan issues far better than they did in the '70s and '80s.

Now the fan-scene at all big German clubs is well-developed and vibrant. Nuremberg has over 300 official fan clubs, divided across seven 'regions'. Each region has its own leader and the 1.FCN *Fanverband* is instrumental in co-ordinating and organising fan club events and the sharing of information. Many of the fan clubs are represented in the stadium each week, their presence announced by a variety of flags and banners or on the logos on the shirts of the supporters.

Quite amazing, especially when compared to my first steps into the world of supporters' clubs.

In the late '70s while watching Port Vale I'd informed my father that I wanted to join the Port Vale Supporters' Club. After the game he took me to the hut from which the Club ran its affairs and they were only too happy to oblige, signing up another keen young fan with the hope of ensuring a lifetime of support. As far as I can remember there was no small print or disclaimers about the risk to my future happiness and sanity which would arise from my boyish enthusiasm. However, to help them be certain that they could track me down if I ever changed my mind, they obviously needed my address for their records. When I gave it to them and they realised that we had travelled all of eight miles, the exclamation was, "Bloody hell, you come all that way to watch this rubbish." It is a sentiment I have repeated in the first person on many occasions since, both when watching Vale and Nuremberg, but like a true fan (or martyr to the cause) there is a need to keep returning, hoping that next time it will be better again.

In October 2006, fifteen of us flew to Germany for Nuremberg's home game against Borussia Dortmund. Six members were making their first visit having been drawn into the idea after hearing of previous trips. As a fan club we were becoming increasingly organised. Meetings were regular and held at least bi-monthly and the membership was growing at a steady pace. Social events between trips were organised and the media in the UK and Germany were continuing to show interest (generally based on what they saw as the eccentric pastime of travelling to Germany to watch football). Members now wore our own club polo shirts or club ties, and tickets were ordered well in advance for each game we attended. On this occasion we also arrived in Germany prepared with several hundred double-sided flyers, in German, explaining a little about our club and why we supported 1.FCN.

The flyers were handed out to anyone in the city centre who wanted to know why we were following their hometown club. When we arrived at the stadium on the Saturday they were handed to anyone, irrespective of whether they were interested or not.

Prior to the game we had visited the fan bar at the 1.FCN training complex, a short walk from the stadium. The Stuhlfauth-Stuben takes its name from the legendary goalkeeper Heiner Stuhlfauth who won five championships with Nuremberg in the 1920s, playing over 600 games and representing Germany on twenty-one occasions. Statistics, eye-witness accounts and anecdotal evidence suggest that there have been few goalkeepers who could match Stuhlfauth's brilliance and certainly in his day, only Spain's controversial Ricardo Zamora could hold a light to him. Attributed to Stuhlfauth is a quote still displayed in the stadium before games and on items of clothing worn by many fans:

It is an honour to play for this city, this side and the people of Nuremberg. May all this last for ever and may the great 1. FC Nürnberg never falter.

If you want to become a footballing legend a touching sound bite is almost as important as your skill and commitment.

On this occasion I doubt any of our group gave any thought to the great Stuhlfauth. We were certainly not there in need of liquid refreshment as we suffered the now inevitable hangovers. Instead we were there at the requests of a local TV company who wanted to make a short film about us and our support. The shortness could not be short enough as the last place several of us actually needed to be that day was in another bar, but there we were and soon afterwards so were a cameraman and a reporter. Fortunately it was only a brief interview in which Herbert gave some details in German and Iain gave them something to translate from his Scottish accented English. They filmed us sitting there with our drinks (any viewers must have thought some of us were surely tired victims of a natural disaster, bedraggled and dazed following an audacious rescue) and they filmed Iain's kilt with the inevitable banter about just what he wore beneath.

It is a strange phenomenon that when a man wears a kilt he seems to be constantly asked what he has beneath. Iain had already caused a stir in Nuremberg's psychiatric ward by apparently having no undergarments, as seems to be the custom amongst kilt wearing Scots. It should be published somewhere that Scottish men do not wear anything under their kilt. And that, if it is always the case, is final. People the world over should be requested not to ask the question. Either that or each kilt wearer should be required to display a badge showing what is beneath – a simple symbol showing a pair of underpants or otherwise would suffice. I do not wish to sound like I am bothered about what Iain or any other Scot wears under his tartan – that is up to him and I certainly don't crave the attention he gets when wearing it. Obviously some pretty females approach him from time-to-time to ask or even try to take a peek which I'm sure he enjoys but there have been occasions when men have shown far too much interest in the subject which must be rather disturbing. Besides, if a man were to ask every woman wearing a skirt whether she was wearing any knickers I would think that they would be running the risk of a slap across the face and probably getting arrested too. I would incidentally not wish Iain to stop wearing his kilt. When he does so he naturally wears his sporran as well. This is in fact a very useful man bag in which the drinking 'whip' (the beer money) of a large group can be safely carried.

After Iain had been filmed walking along a makeshift catwalk between a row of tables, the stadium was beckoning. To add to the normal sightseeing, eating and drinking, on this trip it had been arranged for our flag to be paraded, with the flags of several other fan clubs as is the pre-match custom, around and onto the *Frankenstadion* pitch as the teams entered the field of play. Many German clubs have this display prior to kick-off as huge flags, several metres from corner to corner are threaded onto long, sturdy poles. With what looks like a requirement for considerable strength they are carried onto the field of play and waved to great visual effect as the teams emerge from the tunnel and the referee tosses his coin. The flags are then laid out behind the goal (where space allows) only to be waved again if the home team scores a goal.

The impending moment of pride for 1FCNUK caused a mini-crisis when our nominated flag-bearer, LD, lost his nerve and decided that performing in front of 45,000 people was all a bit too much. After an emergency meeting of senior members it was decided that Herbert should do the job as President and former Nuremberg citizen, and he was left to reflect on the various emotions he felt carrying the flag of his fan club onto the pitch in his hometown team's stadium and the irony that he was actually carrying a Union Jack with the FCN badge painted in the centre. Despite the diminutive size of our flag flying from the huge pole provided by the stadium authorities, in comparison to the huge flags of other fan clubs, it almost looked like it belonged. The welcome from fellow supporters and stadium announcements before and after the game not only instilled pride amongst the British contingent but this pride was also clearly evident in the fans we stood among.

The game itself was quite poor. We dutifully stood singing and shouting from the terrace as Herbert stood on the track behind the goal, occasionally turning to the packed *Nordkurve* and gesturing for them to sing louder if that was possible. When Joe Mnari gave *Der Club* the lead from the penalty spot in the second half Herbert celebrated with more vigorous flag waving. It was just unfortunate that as the game went into its final moments, Dortmund equalised and we were denied witnessing another victory.

Yet again however, this fan club from overseas had made its presence felt and were welcomed by all whom we met. We looked the part, sounded the part and acted the part and many people commented on the calibre and organisation of our support.

Organised, welcomed and well-thought of we may have been, but as we distributed our leaflets before the game, our fifteen strong band of members paled into insignificance compared to another fan group who were also distributing leaflets. When one of their members approached one of ours and suggested we join them for a drink at a party later that evening, our member was so taken back that he did not even think about asking where the said party was, for he had realised that he was talking to a representative of the Ultras and, as this was his first trip to a football match abroad (a Queen of the South versus Port Vale pre-season friendly in Dumfries some years earlier had clearly opened his mind to further adventures), he informed the rest of us with some panic in his voice. I guess if the only thing you know about Ultras is that they look pretty violent and dangerous in Italy, then it is reasonable to assume that an invite to a party is an invite to a good beating. However, these were the UN94 fan club (Ultras Nürnberg 94 – the 94 referring to 1994, the year of their foundation).

Wherever and whenever one watches 1.FC Nürnberg, there are always Ultras present, usually en masse. It cannot be denied that these are the supporters who create the atmosphere these days, or at least ignite the atmosphere and do their utmost to maintain it for ninety minutes. I once came across the 1.FCN women's handball team playing in the handball Champion's League as I flicked to Eurosport one day. There seemed to be a somewhat vocal crowd for a female handball game and then when the camera panned around the arena there they were, a large group of UN94 singing and shouting the team on. This, for them, was a fun experience and something of a break from the serious nature of supporting *Der Club*.

We didn't go to the Ultra's clubhouse after the Dortmund game, not because of fear – enough of us knew something of the Ultras and the people of Nuremberg to know that it would have just been a fantastic and lengthy drinking session – but we had other arrangements. I was lucky enough however to be taken there at a later date by President of the Ultras, Julius Neumann.

Of average height and slim build, Julius has no real physical presence, although I'm not certain I knew what to expect of someone who represents in the region of 3,000 or more fans. As we talked he made little eye contact and came across as almost guarded, suspicious of the motives of anybody who would want to know about the Ultras. His eyes however did appear to show signs that he'd had quite a few the night before and, as this was a Sunday and Nuremberg had played at home the previous day, it is probably safe to assume that he had and was up celebrating until the small hours. Quietly spoken it seemed that he was resting his voice after much singing at the match but his tired eyes would brighten and his voice would rise a few decibels and maybe an octave or two when he started to talk about an aspect of the Ultras that really excited him. And despite the almost withdrawn air about him, it was not hard to imagine Julius being very diplomatic and controlled.

The Ultra's home in the Gibitzenhof district of the city is in a disused factory or warehouse building. In fact it seemed at the time that several of the buildings on what appeared to be an old industrial area were empty. Railway tracks run into the area and then disappear beneath tarmac or are blocked by walls, the rolling stock having evidently not progressed into these parts for some years.

Entering through a small door which looks lost on the side of the large building and then climbing the concrete stairs one gets the feeling of entering some sort of rebel den. Reaching the floor where they have their rooms, this feeling is even more pronounced as old sofas and walls painted with symbols and slogans and covered with various posters and flags make it seem as if you could quite easily bump into Che Guevara or Leon Trotsky. I do not know in exactly what sort of places Guevara or Trotsky hung out in their time but this seemed like a good place from which to initiate a revolution if one so wished. Not that the few guys who sat around seemed particularly revolutionary. They lazed on the sofas as they watched football highlights and smoked their cigarettes. A couple sipped beer from cans while another took his fill from a jar of Nutella, the contents of which he spread thickly on his bread. For some reason Nutella does not strike me as a staple of a revolutionary diet.

In a side room there is a bar area and storage for much of the paraphernalia that the Ultras take to the games – flags and banners, megaphones, drums. A large fridge is filled with beer and snacks. A few files and boxes contain the UN94 paperwork. There are other rooms too, into which the partying can spill and there is enough floor space to make the flags and banners large enough to cover a whole section of the stand in the stadium. Originally it seemed that the club would provide somewhere for the Ultras but as time went on nothing materialised and so they moved into their current premises. As one of the first tenants in the building, Julius explained, they feel they can make as much noise as they want. They have a good relationship with the owner and although a larger premises would be ideal, any move could be a problem because of the fear of upsetting any new, already established neighbours. It is clear that Julius and the *Capos* responsible for running UN94 have a very sensible and measured approach to their operation.

I asked Julius whether the Ultras were the new force at Nuremberg and had taken the mantle of *Seerose* and the Red Devils Nürnberg. In terms of mass support he felt they had but was more careful with his answer with regards to the violence which was once the preserve of the two. Although he said that UN94 as an organisation have no violence he admitted that there are people who attach themselves to the group who like to fight. "Those who want to fight with other groups tend to do it away from the stadium and cities – it's like a boxing club," he laughed.

However, this does not mean that the Ultras don't come under attack. Returning from a cup defeat against Jena the Ultras coach was pelted with stones by a group of fans in former East Germany. (Julius is one of many people who have warned that visiting stadiums in the east is sometimes a risky experience with violence far more prevalent.) The UN94 coach stopped and the fans poured out, not to apparently fight but to frighten their attackers. It seems that it worked as the stone-throwers ran away. Listening to such a tale it is difficult to imagine but somewhere there apparently exists a position beneath the aggressive football violence and even beneath that bit of childish name-calling and chasing. It seems that for the most part, UN94 have found that happy place. However, that happy place does include at least looking rather troublesome even if officially they are not.

The Ultras were formed in 1994 but were a small group with little influence. They were not properly accepted and had little momentum. They really got going when Julius Neumann was told he could take over in 2000. Since then the Ultras have grown in size and influence. I asked him whether, like some of their counterparts in Italy and Spain, UN94 are politically motivated. Julius was quite adamant in his stance that while some people say that UN94 is anti-racist and anti-fascist, it has no official political allegiance. In fact he was at pains to add that if you are an active member of the Ultras Nürnberg you don't have time to be political, too. He also thought that it is important for individuals to make their own decisions privately although the Ultras do try to control the crowd in public in the stadium using their megaphone and microphones from the fence on which a prominent member will sit, addressing and leading the crowd. What about the racism in the penalty shoot out during a cup game against Unterhaching in the autumn of 2006 I ask? On an amateur video shot from the *Nordkurve*, racist monkey chants as Unterhaching's striker N'Diaye walked forward to take a penalty could be heard and on occasion I have heard them directed at black players from other clubs too. Julius shrugged his shoulders. "We can't control everyone," he explained with a rather sad expression. Pragmatically though, he added, "we can only ask them to stop."

The first time the Ultras mounted the fence between the terrace and the pitch and used a megaphone to whip up the atmosphere and direct the crowd it didn't go down as well as they had hoped. Beer was thrown at them because they were either blocking the view or people didn't want to be told when to sing. But the singing in the stadium then was disjointed and the Ultras wanted to change this with non-stop noise. They persevered and in 2001 Julius approached the club and asked if loudspeakers and a microphone could be set up to enable the leading of chants to be heard by more fans on the *Nordkurve* terrace. The club agreed and UN94 took advice from the Ultras Rapid of Vienna who have control of the whole curve in their stadium.

Whoever is on that fence, facing the fans rather than watching the game has to find the right song for the right moment to keep the terraces motivated and the volume high. I suggested that the person with the microphone (or megaphone at away games) can't see very much of the match, remembering the time in Cologne when the topless Ultra was straddled across the fence in freezing conditions. "No," grinned Julius, "You don't see the game that much. You have to keep looking at the replays on the screens if you can and try to read what's going on behind you so you can get the right song. We sometimes get criticised for getting it wrong. It's not easy." I'd never thought that there was that much to it but now he put it that way it was clearly more than just a case of risking injury to one's more sensitive areas. And despite the grin, the tone of voice I was hearing was telling me that this was not just a bit of a laugh but something far more serious. The Ultras had their fun, that was for certain, but for at least the hardcore the business of supporting their club was not to be taken lightly and was done with dedication and passion.

For each game it starts well in advance of match day. For the choreography before a home match there is clearly a lot of planning, hard work to make and paint the banners, and the organisation of who will do what and hold what. When these banners can cover forty or more rows of seats in one direction and a similar number of seats in each row, often many more, it is a major operation. With additional choreography in adjacent sections of the crowd then there certainly has to be a labour of love involved and an almost military-like procedure to get everything from the Ultra's rooms to the stadium and in place well before kick-off. In Berlin for the DFB *Pokal* appearance, the banner unfurled was bigger still and was mightily impressive, flanked by huge sections of the crowd waving co-ordinated flags giving the impression of solid blocks of red, white and black surrounding the main 'picture'. Not that I saw much of it at the time as we, like several thousand others were stood beneath this huge image of cartoon strip character Andy Capp.

Created in 1957 and first published in the northern edition of the Daily Mirror, Andy Capp is a working class idler. Wearing a cloth cap and with (at least in the early days) a cigarette hanging from his mouth he spends his time watching TV, drinking tea and beer, enjoying the football, having a bet and demonstrating all the traits of the stereotypical male chauvinist. The character has the rather amusing and somewhat rather unfortunate German title of Willi Wakker but the Ultras call him Jacky. A north-east England anti-hero cartoon character is surely something of a strange logo for German football Ultras to adopt. "He likes a beer, likes football and has problems with his wife," explained Julius. "Many football fans can relate to the character." Naturally. And Andy, Willi or Jacky is not the only symbol used by the Ultras. Their most popular alternative to the hard-drinking Andy Capp is a sun. Now a sun should not require much describing but just to get the exact image of what the UN94 sun has evolved into, it's best if one imagines the yellow smiley face of the acid house music scene. Add some fiery looking rays around its circumference and make the eyes appear to be almost menacingly stoned and you've got the idea. It's fun but there appears to be just an undercurrent of mischief behind those eyes, just as Andy Capp is funny but represents a cartoon strip to which many have objected over the years because of the politically incorrect sexism, drinking and smoking. I was gaining the impression that the Nuremberg Ultras had a similar mischievous undertone.

At their most visible on match day, UN94 give most other fans something to be proud of, leading what is often non-stop singing and producing the fantastic Technicolor displays which really lift the atmosphere to phenomenal levels; no mean feat in a stadium much maligned because the presence of an athletics track adds frustrating distance between the fans and the play.

But not everyone is happy. In an attempt to increase their impact the Ultras want more control of the *Nordkurve*. Their ideal is to have free-seating in at least some of the blocks of the stand to enable them to have the presence not only on the terrace but also above, taking over the seated area but undoubtedly standing throughout the game. A fine idea on the surface but objected to by many fans who have their favourite seats and want to exercise their right, via their season tickets to sit there each game without the Ultras blocking their view or taking their seats if they could. Neumann describes them as, "stubborn –

typically Franconian guys who won't change their mind." He has little sympathy with the argument that they want to watch from their regular seats without having to stand all game and endure the waving of flags all around them. It is his view that the atmosphere must come first and the wishes of the Ultras will allow this. At the last home game of the 2006-07 season the Ultras demonstrated by producing no visuals other than hanging some flags upside down in the hope that it would persuade the club to grant them their wish. It did not.

Of course, it would probably be to the financial benefit of Nuremberg, and any other club, to get rid of the terracing and install far higher priced seating, particularly during successful times when filling the stadium is a relatively simple task. From this perspective the clubs in Germany do at least show some respect for their fans by keeping terracing and providing low-cost areas of the stadium from where an earnest atmosphere can really be generated. They could marginalise these very fans for financial gain as happened in the English game, although at least clubs in England could hide behind government legislation in this instance. But for the clubs it is a fine balance. With the great atmosphere comes the occasional nuisance. Without the terraces the income could increase but it seems natural to assume that a more affluent, middle-aged support would neither generate the same volume of passion nor would it be a means of nurturing the passion in future generations.

While the Ultras have their own guidelines and ideas, the very nature of their organisation allows the individual Ultra to make his or her own decisions. In this respect they do not police themselves as such although some like to give the impression that they do. A tale that I've heard related in Nuremberg on more than one occasion tells of how a large, leather clad biker standing with some younger Ultras was told by an eager youngster that he wanted to find some opposition fans and give them a good hiding. The biker took the would-be street fighter to one side and explained why it was not a good idea to go around fighting. When the boy agreed, thanked him for the advice and went back to his friends to tell them that it was best to just watch the football, the biker's eyes allegedly filled with tears at the small amount of good he had brought to the world. So maybe those with violent intentions can be talked out of their aggression by those who know better. It probably has a bit more impact if it's a large biker doing the talking though.

And while there is maybe only a token amount of self-policing, the Ultras do have a legal team to rely on when trouble occurs. The *Rot-Schwarze Hilfe* (Red Black Help) was their idea and includes representatives of different section of the 1.FCN support with a lawyer to represent fans if they feel (and the evidence backs their claims) that they have been wronged in any way. And sometimes the issues have a high level of social significance. One Ultra was arrested in Dortmund for allegedly calling the police Nazis although the UN94 account of things is clearly different. Apparently trying to diffuse a situation and trying to speak to the police in a peacekeeper role, the individual involved told the police that he should be able to do this and that things should not be like sixty years ago. He received a lengthy ban from matches. Many other members of the Ultras have at some point experienced stadium bans for a whole range of other alleged offences. Julius Neumann himself served a one year ban when arrested for 'pyrotechnics' in 2000.

The confrontational and sometimes, some would say, ill-judged actions of the Ultras leads the official relationship between the club and UN94 to be, in the words of Jürgen Bergmann, "like the relationship between parents and a growing child. There is much love and pride when they are doing the good things but sometimes you wish you could just give them away for a few hours." The majority of fans would probably agree with the words of the *Fanbeauftragte*. The Ultras can be good for *Der Club* and when they pass around their flags and display their banners they provide an awesome sight. Occasionally though, they can either go too far or are less controlled than maybe some people would like them to be. Sometimes the actions of just one or two of their members clearly bring the reputation of the whole group into question, probably a result of the fact that the Ultras are highly visible in the stadium and the majority of them dress in a similar style. However, the price to be paid is probably small if the atmosphere is good and the amount of violence is minimal. They refuse to be accepted solely as customers of their city's football club and want the fans to have a greater influence in the running of the modern game. It is unfortunate for them that many of the other fans have already accepted their fate and are slowly being won over by the corporate football machine.

For some the Ultras might be a nuisance but for others they provide the only real power base to hold onto the game for the people. And at least their power comes from actions which are based on a generally good-natured support for 1.FCN without the need to go to matches to have a few beers and a fight.

As 1FCNUK was developing at a steady rate we were beginning to feel quite powerful ourselves. Not because we were about to change the footballing world but because we reached something of a crossroads. There was the potential to have become more than just a fan club of 1.FCN but also a whole focus for the fan who wanted to seek new footballing experiences abroad. The whole concept of what we were doing was pure fun. The football had now made the continuation of this concept absolutely necessary for some of us but we were almost starting to believe that what we were witnessing at 1.FCN was an era that would last forever. We were lucky that we could not remember the bad old days of the '70s and '80s when the football had been bad, and in many respects elements of the supporters had been even worse. Maybe like the Ultras we could have rebelled against modern football and become a far larger organisation. Our alternative was to just keep moving along, feeling our way as we went, without really knowing where we were heading. Of course, the latter won. It was the easy option and entailed the least work. Any allusions towards world domination would have to simmer beneath the surface. Besides, we were too busy booking flights, collecting membership fees, and selling our T-shirts, polo shirts and ties to think about a new world order against the corporate football of the twenty-first century.

The magnificent support in the Frankenstadion

Chapter 8

Cowboys, golfers and media tarts

It was all quite beautifully arranged. Twenty-eight of us would spend a long Easter weekend in Hamburg and take the train down to Bremen to watch Nuremberg play the mighty Werder on the Sunday afternoon. With the two week school holidays falling either side of the Bremen game it was a pity I couldn't extend my stay but financially it was a non-starter, particularly as far as my good wife was concerned.

That I spent the full two weeks before the Easter weekend in Germany was therefore something of a bonus. When presented with the opportunity to visit a German school near Düsseldorf for the last week of term I naturally jumped at the chance, not least because flights, accommodation and subsistence were paid for. And of course, play my cards right and I could manage to get down to Nuremberg for the home game against Hertha Berlin and then travel north again to meet the others in Hamburg.

I certainly played my cards right, although admittedly I was dealt a very good hand to begin with. After spending a week with extremely hospitable German teachers my subsistence allowance was in fine shape. I'd decided to skip the final organised event of the trip, a night out in Cologne, to instead travel to Nuremberg. When I found a flight for a reasonable price (and managed to get this paid for as an expense) I was rather pleased with myself and by mid-evening on the Friday I was supping happily in the usual Nuremberg haunts. I'd even managed to book a good standard hotel and cover the cost with part of my subsistence from the previous week. The rest was left to eat and drink at my leisure.

When I awoke late on the morning of the game it seemed likely that the subsistence allowance had taken a rather large hit. I had been about to return to the hotel at 1a.m. when I received a call from Klaus who had introduced us to the delights of the Indonesian karaoke the previous summer. Klaus had heard I was in town and as he could hear music in the background suggested that he could be with me in just a few minutes. And he was – for a few hours.

I could have just rolled over and gone back to sleep when I awoke the next lunchtime. With forty minutes until I had to meet Armin before the game, I should have called him, had an extra hour in bed and then gone directly to the stadium. However, there seems to be something of an unwritten rule when 1FCNUK are in Germany: we must be punctual so as not to be outdone by the exceptional punctuality of our German friends. With hindsight I should have let this rule slip, something which I wish I had done after leaping from bed, quickly dressing, running to the tram stop and purchasing a slice of pizza from a street vendor. Pretending that a hangover did not exist suddenly seemed a rather foolish policy to have adopted when I had caught my breath halfway through the journey to the stadium. As I eventually stepped down from the tram, relieved not to have caused myself any further embarrassment than looking as if I was a hardened alcoholic, I vowed that the rest of the day would involve no further sickening situations.

It seemed a good suggestion when Armin declared that he wanted to go to the *Fansprechstunde* before the game, especially when quite apologetically he told me that it would today be held in a tournament hall beneath the stadium rather than in a bar. I was able to sit there and generally tune out of the question and answer session between fans and officials of the club and then between fans and the injured star striker Robert Vittek. I was quite relaxed and was glad of the few minutes' rest the cool hall was affording me. Then Armin tugged at my arm. 1.FC Nürnberg Vice-President Schneider was beckoning me to the front of the hall, to say a few words Armin assured me. Why the hell did they want the unshaven, and ashamedly unwashed, Englander to say anything. In fact, with my basic German what could I say? I turned to Armin and pleaded with him to join me as interpreter. He did a sterling job and helped me to answer a few questions about 1FCNUK and our support one year on from our official welcome by the club. The response from the audience was positive and they were fortunately far enough away to not be able to smell the fumes that seemed to be venting from my every pore. They probably put my bloodshot eyes and nasal voice down to a heavy cold or the effects of having journeyed for many hours over land and sea from England. I even understood the question about whether I would be attending any further games that season. My response of, "Hamburg, Leverkusen *und natürlich* (and of course) *das Pokal finale* (cup final) in Berlin," was greeted with cheers and loud applause, not least because 1.FCN still had to play Frankfurt in the cup semi-final. They were certainly not applauding my German. Robert Vittek also seemed to approve and had his photograph taken with the flag. It was a shame that when we did make it to Berlin, Vittek was still injured and played no part in the final.

The Hertha Berlin game was not a particularly attractive affair. Nuremberg won 2-1 thanks to goals from Galasek and Engelhardt but it was now clear that every result between today and the end of the season would need grinding out if a league position sufficient to clinch a UEFA Cup place was to be attained. What less than eighteen months previously had seemed a distant dream for *Der Club* was within touching distance, although it would not only be a close run thing but on the evidence of today's game it might also prove to be somewhat nerve-wracking.

Several weeks had passed since Armin had emailed me inviting me along to see a live band on the Saturday evening following the game. Now, in some respects quite pleased to be avoiding the beer for a short time, we were driving out of the city and into the country. The drive allowed Armin time to try and 'sell' the planned evening to me. We were apparently going to see a kind of 'country folk rock music group' which seemed to me to mean either that Armin was not sure of exactly what they played or that they were a country and western band. As he explained more my second hunch seemed to be the most accurate and it was clear that no matter how far we drove now, it would not be far enough to make me believe that this band would be to my taste. My fears were all but confirmed as we pulled up outside a village hall, not because I have any problems with village halls but because there were lots of other people pulling up and getting out of their cars wearing Stetsons and cowboy boots. I left the 1FCNUK flag in the car and was glad I had as it would have looked somewhat out of place among all of the American Confederate flags on display in the hall. Although Armin had no cowboy regalia he did strip off his 1.FCN replica shirt and from the boot of his car pulled a Shania Twain T-shirt. After spraying himself with some 1970s looking after-shave from his glove compartment (this was obviously going to be a classy night) we made our way into the hall where long rows of tables led to the small stage. We were allegedly fortunate enough to have seats close to the band which to me translated in any language as unfortunate enough to have seats a long way from the bar.

As more cowboys arrived and the beer started to flow it was clear that these people were complete enthusiasts for the country music scene (I had already been corrected after calling it country and western). A woman well into middle age sat opposite me and I managed to gather that she was writing a report for a popular German country music magazine. Everywhere there were flyers for other events and even pilgrimages to the grand old U S of A to see country music played in its natural habitat. Surrounded by all of the denim, hats and boots, a small island of the American mid-west dubbed in German, it all felt rather surreal. I stood out somewhat wearing a 1FCNUK polo shirt. Armin explained to some of his acquaintances who I was and what I was doing in Germany. They were most polite but clearly thought I was some kind of freak, smiling graciously but then avoiding all further eye contact. I was over it as soon as I realised, so it left no scars but these people obviously thought I was a bit of a sad case. How ironic I thought to myself.

How ironic I thought to myself again thirty minutes later when, accompanied by the band, many of the audience were moving in formation on a dance floor to the side of the stage as they showed off their line-dancing skills.

The band, although not playing my preferred style of music, were certainly good musicians. I tried to focus on this fact for a while but kept wondering if they would be kind enough to change to a set of rock covers in the second half of their performance. They didn't but they clearly knew their audience. I recognised not one of the songs but most were greeted by varying degrees of excitement as the line-dancing continued. Only one song failed to be a floor filler. It might have had some deeper meaning and I'm sorry if I missed the point but what appeared to be the least popular song saw the dance floor empty apart from one would-be cowboy who line-danced alone. I know little of line-dancing and feel a little guilty for mocking it; live and let live I should say but there is something about it that I just don't get. To do it alone, well it's almost perverse. I was embarrassed for the guy because he was apparently a normal bloke. I hoped for his sake that he was completely inebriated and would not remember a thing the next day. I hoped his mates were not filming it on their mobile phones ready to publish on the internet. But he wasn't drunk and he wasn't being filmed. So then I started to hope that his mates would embarrass him more and start shouting abuse at him as he danced. But they didn't. This was strange. People sat and watched him perform a series of not very complicated steps with his thumbs hooked into two belt loops of his jeans. They were clearly full of admiration for these steps and applauded accordingly. Now I am admittedly not a dancer and all the rhythm had long since been handed out when I was in the queue for cool personal attributes but I know that I could have quite easily done what this guy was doing. I mused over the fact briefly and decided to make my current beer my last to avoid any potential personal embarrassment.

For the next song the shortest line-dancing line ever was joined by a couple of booted guys who clearly spent their lives lugging around huge and heavy pieces of farm equipment. You would certainly not want to mess with either one of them and I know I am wrong but liked to think that their size was why nobody was laughing at them as they added some twirls and kicks into a routine of fancy footwork. This was no longer just surreal. If they thought I was a freak they were now certainly out-freaking me. I was definitely not the saddest case in the building. In fact, I was now sitting in a sea of strangers listening to what was fast becoming rather monotonous music and witnessing some very strange goings on. Yet they thought it was me who was the oddball.

Things seemed to be improving when some younger couples entered the hall. They'd clearly had a drink and were wearing 1.FCN shirts, a sure sign that they had been to the game and were just stopping off for another beer. As they approached the dance floor I was intrigued and slightly worried. Was all hell about to break loose as football fan and line-dancer clashed? Briefly I almost wished for it to do so, just for the entertainment value but I was left more shocked than disappointed. These fans who just a few hours before were probably shouting themselves hoarse in support of their team were now all hooked thumbs, fancy twirls and flicking kicks with the best of them. Whereas when they had walked in I had hoped they might have spotted me as a fellow fan and come over for a conversation about football I was now trying to angle my body to conceal the badge on my chest.

To his credit, Armin decided it was crap before I had the heart to tell him so. But he thought it was crap because the music was not the hardcore country music he was hoping for. I just thought it was crap. And I thought it was just ridiculous. These grown men and women listening to their preferred genre of music was something that I had no problem with. Each to their own and all that. But why, oh why, did they have to dance around making fools of themselves and why, oh why, did they have to dress up to do so? Weirdoes.

I was still puzzled by it all when I awoke the next morning. Over breakfast I ruminated over what made people think that such behaviour was acceptable in the modern world. *Sad, sad, sad* I said to myself as I filled up on bread rolls to avoid the need to eat again until my evening kebab. *Sad, sad, sad* I thought as my phone buzzed to indicate an incoming text message.

We're all travelling to Hamburg in club ties, it read.

Sad, sad, sad. The irony was lost on me for a few minutes.

People who don't like football are sad, people who don't like sport are sad, people who line-dance are sad. In fact to take it to the extreme people who are different are sad. I sometimes wish I actually believed all this. It would mean I would not have to analyse what 1FCNUK was actually doing and could just accept it as normal behaviour. Maybe people who self-analyse so much are sad too.

It is easy to laugh at line-dancers or those with different tastes and different hobbies but one does not need to analyse too deeply to realise that travelling to Germany and obsessing about 1.FC Nürnberg, or even obsessing about Port Vale or any other team, is a close cousin of the line-dancing fraternity. Even the rituals of the average football fan – buying a football shirt, wearing it for the game each week, buying a pie at the match, listening to other results on the radio on the way home, tuning in for the TV highlights later that evening – are in some respects not particularly rational pursuits. Playing in a game of football is somewhat more purposeful because it enables one to, at the very least, get some exercise but then again how surreal is it to see twenty-two men, women or children chasing around a leather, air-filled sphere and giving it a kick each time they get to it. For the masses who pay huge amounts of money on season long rituals with the voyeuristic intent of watching such events then too much analysis would surely lead to us being classed as mentally unstable. Surely it is only the fact that so many do it that allows it to be accepted as normal on a weekly basis across the UK and the rest of the world. And maybe that is why line-dancing and country music are, in some places, confined to village halls thus preventing a no less strange but certainly less popular activity not to draw too much attention to itself.

When one takes football support to the extreme (and one has to admit that forming a fan club of a foreign team and travelling to matches several times a season is relatively extreme) then it is difficult to see any rationality in such a pursuit. Even of the insider, who has intentionally or inadvertently become completely engrossed with the obsessive support elements of it all, questions can still be asked. To those looking in, it must seem at best intriguing but more likely on a par with the purveyors of strange pursuits the world over. I've often wondered if this is at least partially the reason that we tie in our visits to Germany with so much socialising. If you tell somebody that you are going to watch a football match in Germany they will probably be quite puzzled but if you tell them that you are going to Germany to drink German beer and eat German sausages then they will be far more understanding, and I am sure this is because drinking lots and eating unhealthy food is far more normal and socially acceptable. The football, drinking and eating therefore complement each other with the latter two pastimes deflecting some of the attention from the former.

So why then do 1FCNUK end up drawing so much attention? As football fans we are no different than millions of others who go and watch their team play, with the exception that most of us have two teams to support. To be flying to Germany to watch football clearly pushes the boundaries of normally acceptable behaviour a little and it is here that outside interest seems to lie.

We've all seen regional TV news programmes that often have little news worth showing and therefore screen short features about such irrelevant stories as a local Women's Institute group making the biggest trifle ever made in the county, or the enterprising pensioner who sells his home grown roses to a member of the royal family who turns out to be the second wife of the fifth cousin of the eighth in line to the throne. There was a time when they even featured a new craze which was apparently sweeping the nation, had come all the way from America and was called line-dancing.

In the summer of 2006 we were approached by BBC Midlands who wanted to run a story about "The UK's FC Nuremberg supporters," as the introduction to the short film said, immediately following these words with, "So where's Nuremberg? Well it's in Germany!" What a superbly stereotypical regional news item. The World Cup had finished, the football season was yet to start but here was a football story involving an eccentric idea and the opportunity to give parochial viewers a geography lesson. They even had a real German in Herbert to add authenticity and asked various members about the support for the club with our flag as a back-drop. Herbert led some rather dubious chants which made those present sound more like a picket line than football supporters and the clip finishes outside in the sunshine surrounding LD's car – no ordinary machine but a barely road-worthy eastern European 4x4 with the FCN logo emblazoned across the bonnet. With more chanting the clip ended with a highly predictable *Auf Wiedersehen* from the reporter and a very dubious demonstration of footballing 'skill'. Half in and half out of shot, the frenzied chanting of my father-in-law continues as he picks up a football, tosses it a short way into the air and meets it with an awfully mis-timed header. As for me, well my cynicism and mockery of my friends and family was made quite easy as I watched on the internet while on my summer holidays. How glad I was that I had not been there because surely I would have caused myself plenty of embarrassment with mumbled words or ridiculous actions. Unfortunately my time would come.

Local radio also featured 1FCNUK at a similar time: cue more chanting, a potted history of our club and the concerning question, "Is this not just about the beer though?" Had we been rumbled already? LD's reply of "yes" was laughed off and the interviewer not only provided plenty of opportunity for us to convince listeners of our support but also called us media tarts in reference to our TV and various newspaper appearances. We had increased our membership significantly over a few months and had, I suppose, tarted ourselves to the media as we had sought publicity for our cause at home. Of course, we had plenty of help in doing so having (quite self-importantly) appointed a friend as our media officer, largely because she happened to work as a reporter for BBC local radio!

After the first couple of media appearances it seemed we had become something of a quick and easy story. Nothing to write about? Then go and get a picture of those crazy people who fly off to Germany to watch football. Jason, still not having much luck in securing image rights, was photographed for a local newspaper with the flag draped around him, unfortunately looking more like Count Dracula than a patriotic hero. The 1.FCN match day programme reported on our attendance at matches and our website was receiving large numbers of hits.

It was thought that our website would be a good place to publish a few photographs of our trips and tell anybody who was interested (not that we anticipated much interest) about our fan club. However, as soon as it went live, emails started to trickle in and for a few months we were constantly adding information and content. The use of 'we' is a little too broad actually. To make sure we were remaining completely self-important we had provided ourselves with grand titles such as President, Chairman, Treasurer, Secretary and Vice-Presidents. However, the one who really mattered on all things technical was our webmaster Darren. Darren is a computer geek. He hates football and he doesn't like line-dancing but he doesn't need to. If my previous comments about sad people are to be believed (which they should not entirely be) Darren is right up there with the best through his love of technology. Solo line-dancers and travelling supporters of foreign teams watch out. Darren is as obsessed with computers as any of us are with football or any phoney cowboy is with dancing in lines. But Darren is a genius. Not only did he learn how to build a website but he did so with the ability to ignore the content and actually focus on the structure. With his constant support we went from a few pages of information to having menus, downloads, online membership, adverts and a forum – fairly standard stuff by website standards but mind-boggling to anyone who knows nothing about computers when it comes to creating the pages in the first place. His obsession with them might sometimes be seen as sad but at least he was developing skills that would enhance his ability to make a living from his obsession. All we were left with was a forum and email system that provided us with the perfect opportunity to sit at the computer and talk about our football obsession all day and night. In the sad case stakes we were becoming quite highly regarded as experts in our field.

A football forum used by just a few friends who see each other most weekends anyway is probably of little use other than as a means of communicating which pub you will all be meeting in and at what time come the end of the week. Even this sort of use would soon lose any novelty value as everyone realised that it was easier to send a text message or make a phone call. We did not really know how our forum would be used when it was launched but a few of us started to post comments about 1.FCN, performances and proposed trips. Despite having over 100 registered users there are only a dozen or so who make regular posts on the forum but many more who view the posts. Any snippets of information that can be found about 1.FCN are added to the various forum threads with a high level of content coming from English speakers living in Germany. Particularly prolific are Liam, an Irishman living in Nuremberg and supporting *Der Club*, and Joe, an American who not only supports 1.FCN but has a son who plays in the youth ranks at the club. It is the ability of these two fans to translate articles from the German press into English that has helped to fuel our obsession further. And of course, communicating with other fans through a forum has led to many great days and nights socialising with them when in Germany. Once Darren had found a means of preventing computer generated forum 'members' posting all manner of pornography, adverts for Viagra and even invites to have penis enlargements (someone was obviously misjudging our level of sadness), the forum as a means of information exchange really took off. When Everton travelled to Nuremberg for a UEFA Cup tie many of their fans sought advice about tickets and bars through the forum. When Ipswich Town fans believed they were about to sign Nuremberg forward Angelos Charisteas, they visited the forum to seek reassurance about the prospective purchase. It is all very friendly, maybe even too friendly, but like the rest of the website it is one of the few places to gain information and share opinions about 1.FCN in English.

A second TV performance followed in the October, this time the extremely hungover affair before Nuremberg's home game against Dortmund. Iain's kilt became, and not for the last time, a focus of media attention as others were able to skulk away to the edge of the picture more than happy to let our friend take the limelight and taking pleasure in the fact that we ourselves were not Scottish. As with any of our TV performances, after this one had been shown on a Bavarian TV channel, our website received a relative spike in hits and requests for our merchandise increased for a short period. However, what would follow in the next spring would not only provide huge amounts of publicity but also portrayed part of a weekend where our support really lifted us high in the sad stakes.

The message I'd received about fellow fan club members flying to Hamburg wearing their club ties was not one to take lightly. On previous occasions members either wore their polo shirts or shirts and ties, as would be expected from any travelling sports team. The fact that we were not a team *per se* but a group of spectators was of little concern. At least on arrival we always wanted to look our best, taking pride in our collective identity and using it to show that we were a more serious organisation than a standard group of drunken football fans ready to rampage around a host city. It is always a good idea to at least set out with the correct image and intentions.

Having arrived in Hamburg at 7a.m., courtesy of a 20 Euro flight from Nuremberg, I had a full day and a half before the others arrived. For one night only I'd booked myself into a nice hotel with a sauna and swimming pool in the suburbs of the city. Having walked around for five hours with a pack on my back (which was considerably more than I'd managed in a whole week of backpacking the previous summer) I left the sights of the historical Hanseatic city to check-in and have an afternoon of relaxation. The short train journey took me past some rather splendid properties, demonstrating the wealth of Hamburg. As my eyes grew heavy and my head nodded with the motion of the train, I congratulated myself on the marvellous decision to look after my health prior to what would be a four-day onslaught on my already sub-standard physique. I slipped into my swim shorts in the room of my hotel, grabbed a towel and a change of clothing and took the elevator to the basement fitness area. As the doors slid open, the first part of my plan disappeared just as the room had done before me – most was under protective sheets and the rest under lashings of freshly applied white emulsion. With the pool drained of all water, the sauna surrounded by the tools of the decorating trade, brushes I guess and other things I never really intend to grow familiar with, I pressed the button to return to my room as decorators looked on and laughed at my disappointment.

Part two of the plan disappeared just as quickly. In the few minutes that it had taken me to enter the hotel, change and miss out on a swim, workmen had somehow managed to set about digging up the road outside the hotel. Even television watching would be impossible and so I was 'forced' to begin my reconnaissance mission of Hamburg's bar culture several hours earlier than planned. That this mission also finished several hours later than planned is testament to my dedication to the cause of finding suitable watering holes for my fellow 1FCNUK members.

When I met them the next day at our budget hotel a short distance from the notorious *Reeperbahn*, they were all resplendent in their club ties and I too had put mine on – it is one thing being sad enough to dress in this way but another thing entirely to be the only member of the group not dressed like this.

Better to stand out as a sad group rather than stand out as a sad individual!

The rest of the evening and the next couple of days went much as one would expect, judging by our previous excursions. The beer flowed and a rich mixture of fast food and Germanic cuisine was enough to regularly punctuate any activity which threatened to become too cultured. The ladies who had joined us for the jaunt decided to take themselves off shopping on the Saturday, with perfect timing it has to be said, as the men headed to the golf course.

Oh yes, golf. It takes little imagination to be able to see that this is a sport which has all the requirements to make it an extremely sad pastime right up there with line-dancing and football tourism. Obsessive, voluntary or otherwise dress-codes, its own language and the ability to make a normal person something of a freak for at least the time they are participating or talking about it.

And so the sadness of 1FCNUK was compounded further. And then further still: it would be slightly inaccurate to say that some of us even had our own clubs with us but only because some of us had our own *club* with us. The fact that this club was a putter of a folding variety almost makes me cringe as I write, although the cringe-worthy thought was I'm afraid to say, followed by a shrug of the shoulders that our putters are certain to make further trips with us at home and abroad. You see, and this is confession time now, we've got something of a liking, in fact quite an unhealthy interest in mini golf. For those who are still puzzled, allow me to puzzle you further: mini golf is far more like the seaside games of crazy golf than anything one might come across at St Andrews, Royal Troon, The Belfry or indeed any famous or otherwise golf course. While mini golf aficionados would dish out a severe reprimand for tagging their sport 'crazy golf', the principles are almost identical vis-à-vis the use of a specially shaped stick called a putter to strike a small hard ball (in an action known as putting) into a hole, passing under, over or through a different obstacle on each of eighteen specially designed lanes (also called holes just to confuse the layman). The fact that mini golf has a standard set of holes, albeit set out in a different order on each course, and avoids obstacles such as windmills, space rockets and lighthouses, provides it with a little more legitimacy as a real sport. The fact that throughout Germany alone there are hundreds of mini golf societies with thousands more across mainland Europe gives an insight into the fact that 1FCNUK are not alone in the sad habit of taking this game so seriously. In our defence we at least don't purchase the proper mini golf balls of differing weights and elasticity to use on different holes. Some players even go as far as regulating the temperature of their balls to optimise performance.

Now I have clearly mentioned mini golf to demonstrate that although line-dancing can be considered sad by many, our trips to Germany don't really put us in a position to criticise the leisure pursuits of others. I would have of course mentioned mini golf even if I had not scored the lowest combined score over 36 holes thus winning our own little tournament, despite having flung my telescopic putter to the floor in dismay after a particularly poor score on one hole. Its telescopic capabilities have never been the same since.

It was only after our golfing excursion that we were joined in Hamburg by Laura, a lovely lady from the BBC who had flown over especially to film us on our weekend jolly to watch *Der Club*. (Complaints about wasting TV licence payers' money should not be forwarded to 1FCNUK.) That evening she joined us as we ate, drank and sung – sometimes with, but generally over – a band in a large beer hall. Nobody, probably including Laura, can remember whether she did any filming that night but nothing subsequently appeared which was suitable for the consumption of the general public.

The next day however was different. We set off by train to Bremen for the late afternoon kick-off and found a picturesque square in which to take refreshment. Other Nuremberg fans were gathering and Laura decided to film. Although the broadcast footage only amounted to a couple of minutes it seemed to take an endless amount of time to film a group shot of 1FCNUK singing as we stood behind the flag, with our resident reporter either forgetting her lines, forgetting to switch on the camera or forgetting to switch on the microphone. Some of us were growing impatient as the dehydration and lack of sleep from the previous evening's activities started to take their toll. Interviews and filming with other Nuremberg fans followed as we headed off to the game. As we passed a group carrying an inflatable DFB *Pokal* we exchanged greetings and I held aloft the mock trophy which we all hoped we would see for real if the semi-final could be overcome. One of our new acquaintances decided that it would be a good idea to raise me onto his shoulders waving the air-filled cup above my head. As he walked around carrying my substantial bulk my initial thoughts were for the safety of his back, myself when it gave way and the small crowd should I fall on anybody. When the BBC camera began rolling it more than crossed my mind that my teaching career could be threatened by anyone misinterpreting these innocuous actions on television as stereotypical football hooligans rampaging through the streets.

Spirits were still high in the *Wesserstadion* before the game and more of our cheering was caught on camera as 1.FCN battled it out with Werder Bremen. Or rather it wasn't. Yes there were shots of us cheering and yes they were filmed in the stadium but for some reason Laura could only film from pitchside during the game (and only in the direction of the crowd) with little hope of getting much decent footage of the obsessed Brits at the back of the terrace. One member took a video camera onto the terrace and got some footage but the proper camera only came to us after the game had finished and most fans had left. Had *Der Club* managed a better result than a 1-0 defeat we may have provided some more spirited footage. However, for several of us the pure fun, enjoyment and banter of going to these matches was no longer enough. It was more than just a laugh now and the football clearly mattered more than we had previously imagined it could. Our team had lost, were looking as if they would miss out on a qualifying position for European competition and we were disappointed. To then have to pretend to be happy for the sake of a bit of film was not at all easy. When Laura's film appeared on TV a few days later, her report contained the comment that, "They're actually taking it all very seriously." There was no doubt about it. She was right.

It was typical that when we were waiting for it to be shown it did not appear on the scheduled evening. Apparently a man had been chased by a cow (I am not joking) and so we were pushed aside to make way for this groundbreaking story. Beware of cows.

A few weeks later we were contacted by *Deutsche Welle TV* about the possibility of filming 1FCNUK in England and on a trip to Germany for their *Bundesliga Kick-off* programme, broadcast in both German and English. Not only did they want to film us at a match but also wanted to film us socialising as a fan club in a bar in England and film some footage around our local area. Flights had already been booked months previously for the final game of the season in Hanover and the two man DW-TV crew decided to fly over to England on the Thursday, film our members in the pub, do some more filming on the Friday and fly back to Germany with six of us on the Friday evening. They would then film us before, during and after the Hanover game for a special cup final edition of their show to be broadcast the following weekend when, by this time having reached the final, *Der Club* would play Stuttgart in Berlin. When I emailed them to state that this plan was fine with the exception that I would not be able to do anything during the Friday because I would be at work, they clearly saw this as no problem and decided it might be a good idea to film me there. Against my better judgment I reluctantly agreed to this.

The results of the finished film were seen by some as amusing although personally I found them rather embarrassing. Teaching four very unenthusiastic school children to say *Berlin Berlin wir fahren nach Berlin* (Berlin Berlin we're travelling to Berlin) for the camera could have been my personal low point in the film. So could trying to explain that 1.FCN would win the cup final after a few beers during the 3-0 victory over Hanover in the excellent AWD Arena. Unfortunately these were relatively normal moments when compared to my responses to questions about supporting 1.FC Nürnberg. The answers themselves were generally acceptable, at least by our own sad standards when interviewed in the pub on the Thursday evening. My delivery however, left an awful lot to be desired. Maybe it is my lack of linguistic ability that causes me to begin to adopt what I consider to be a German accent when talking to a German (though strangely enough I do not do so to my father-in-law or wife). It sounds like I'm taking the piss but I'm not and I am quite unaware that I'm doing it until somebody points its out. After a drink or two, and with friends who would love to see you make a complete fool of yourself on camera, what chance did I have of being saved on this occasion? It is made even worse by the fact that nobody else except Jason does this, whether talking to Germans in England or Germany. (Just to deflect from my own embarrassment for a moment, Jason once told the wife of a German friend that he could, "zing like ze Robbie Vill-yams". How I now wished I'd hung back with my howls of derision.) Having managed to generally avoid the cameras on previous occasions, particularly as far as speaking was concerned I was now the bloody main focus of the film without the ability to speak properly or keep my damned head still as I spoke. Any dreams I may have once harboured of hosting a television football show were shattered in an instant. The viewer would find it far too disturbing.

It is quite fortunate that further embarrassment appears to have been avoided following an interview before the cameras in Lisbon prior to Nuremberg's UEFA Cup tie against Benfica. I assume, and hope, that the footage of me singing the club hymn in German after a few drinks was deemed unsuitable for general release and has now been forever deleted from records or is doing the rounds on a health service video about the dangers of alcohol.

Although there will clearly be some who think that 1FCNUK does fall into the category of extremely sad, we live in hope that there are also some out there who can see that the passionate support is coupled with having a laugh. Whether our activities can be classed as sad or not is really a non-issue as far as we're concerned. Like millions of other sad cases, whatever their chosen sad pursuit, we all get an enormous amount of fun from it. Maybe in the future I should try to be a little more tolerant of line-dancers and their ilk. But I probably won't.

Angela is caught up in the media attention

Chapter 9

Impossible is nothing

When our flag had been paraded around the *Frankenstadion* pitch at the end of October 2006 the game with Dortmund was Nuremberg's seventh consecutive draw, a record breaking run which had started with the goalless affair in the Allianz Arena two months previously. What at first was a solid continuation of the season's unbeaten start soon became a significant period without a win. In three of those drawn games a lead had been surrendered. *Der Club* dropped to seventh in the *Bundesliga* although were only three points behind second placed Bayern Munich and six behind leaders Werder Bremen. With just a little luck and the confidence of a couple of victories, the fans had faith that Hans Meyer's team would soon be challenging at the top of the table. Unfortunately two straight defeats and another draw followed as the league position now slipped to twelfth although importantly for some, the gap to Munich, now in fourth place (and on its own reason enough for some *Clubberer* to be happy) was still only six points and new leaders Stuttgart were just ten points away.

The first win since the opening two games of the season came over Bayer Leverkusen in mid-November with a 3-2 victory. The hope that it would act as a springboard to push *Der Club* back up the table was short lived – three more drawn games followed. Eleven games in the first half of the season had finished level but with a victory over Hanover in the last game before the winter break, 1.FCN were in seventh spot at Christmas and just four points from a much coveted UEFA Cup qualifying position.

It's not the winning, it's the taking part that matters. How the old ideals of sport make us feel better when we lose. As long as you have given your best and all that then nobody can ask any more. You should be proud to have achieved as much as you have. There's always next year or next time. Really? Such phrases may appease the least competitive school child but it is surely only the most pragmatic sportsman or woman, or even player of a board game, who can think along such lines in the moments following defeat.

Did the faces of the Bayern Munich players show any pragmatism as victory had been snatched from their grasp in the dying moments of the 1999 Champion's League Final? For them there was no next year, although at least the manner of their defeat meant that they would be a well-remembered runner-up. There is no pragmatism in the tears of the eyes of England players and fans as they suffer and witness another penalty shoot-out defeat (even though in this case there is always next time and even the knowledge that next time will probably have a somewhat familiar feel to it).

I've seen school children for whom winning is everything and they will do so at all costs, never mind all the pep talks about how proud you are of them and that they should just go out and enjoy the game. For them it is far more important than the school curriculum, friendships and life itself. And this is when the game is a thirty-a-side misshapen mismatch on a crowded school yard at playtime.

It would be hard to imagine the top professionals in the game managing to simply shrug their shoulders after a defeat in a crucial match. Rationalisation can come after time but in the immediate aftermath of the final whistle dismay, hurt, sadness and anger exist in a variety of mixes. It is important that they do so too. If a paying crowd of supporters could not see the obvious disappointment of the players they would certainly question their commitment.

During that first half of the 2006-07 season, the commitment of the Nuremberg players could not really be questioned. They had generally played well and many considered it unlucky that *Der Club* were not several more points better off and higher in the table than they were when the winter pause came along. Hans Meyer had maintained the respect of the vast majority of the support, largely because of the huge turnaround in fortunes he had orchestrated the previous season and in many respects also a result of the satisfactory current league position.

Something else was beginning to stir too. Without destroying what had so far been at best mediocre opposition, 1.FCN had progressed as far as the quarter finals of the DFB *Pokal*, the German FA Cup. Despite little interest in this competition in its early stages where as far as many fans are concerned even the taking part is met with apathy, Nuremberg had managed to do the winning during the first three rounds, although only just. A 1-0 victory at amateur side BV Cloppenburg in September was to prove to be a rare win among so many draws in the *Bundesliga* although a Marek Mintal equaliser only just managed to force extra-time against second division Paderborn before Robert Vittek's winner in the second round.

Having never been to a cup game in Germany even these narrow victories were greeted with far more enthusiasm than was apparently normal as I sat at home trying to keep up with the scores via the internet. Little did I know that the majority of fans take little interest in the competition before it gets to its later stages, and then only if their team are still in it of course. Maybe I should have realised the lack of interest as I searched various websites to just get the final result with no hope of any live video, commentary or ticker as far as I could see. It seemed that even the football crazy world of the web was not too enthusiastic about the *Pokal*.

Still, it was my theory that every game is important and as a fan I wanted to keep abreast of the situation whether *Der Club* were playing in the World Club Championships or against lower league opposition. As the former was unlikely to be occurring any time soon, I wanted to be able to settle for the latter via the cup competition, even if all but the hardcore supporters were not bothered.

The third round, or the last sixteen of the tournament, was held mid-week in the middle of December. Remaining deluded about how much effort one should give to following a cup game I was excited at the prospect of a victory putting Nuremberg in the quarter finals and then just two wins from the final itself. I'd also got something of a feeling that this could be Nuremberg's season. There was no rational reasoning behind this. Fans of many clubs seem to get the idea that their team's name is 'on the cup' after just one victory in an early round. Tottenham fans for example seem to have a range of factors that ensure that if the year ends in a numeral from 0-9 then this will surely be their year. Fans of the big four clubs in England have similar ideas right from the beginning of the season, although these hold more weight because surely the best teams have, on paper at least, the best chance of making the most progress. As far as Nuremberg were concerned it simply struck me that where there may have been some misfortune in the *Bundesliga* with so many drawn games, there may have been an element of luck working the other way in the first two rounds of the *Pokal* and I therefore based my cup-run hopes on this. As I say, not particularly rational but it is surely the prerogative of the football fan to make irrational and illogical judgments to keep their hopes high in support of their team.

Unfortunately, as 1.FCN were taking to the field against second division SpVgg Unterhaching, I was unable to sit at my computer and attempt to keep track of events in Franconia. Instead my role as Acting Head Teacher of a small village church school had necessitated my attendance at a pre-Christmas soiree for the staff as guests in the vicarage. Clearly there are times when professionalism has to take precedence over football although I do keep such times to a minimum and grapple with my diary to avoid any clash of interests where possible. This one had somehow slipped through my net. As pleasantries were exchanged and mince pies devoured I felt helpless, unable to will *Der Club* to victory in the same way I could have done sitting in front of a slowly updating website some 800 miles from the action. I then had a thought. I knew these *Pokal* games were poorly attended (indeed there were just over sixteen and a half thousand in the *Frankenstadion* for this game) but maybe, just maybe, Armin was there. After all, when it came to that prerogative of making irrational and illogical judgments regarding football, Armin was certainly up there with the best. I tried to send a text message but had no signal on my phone, not surprising really when sitting in a beautiful, old stone-walled house in the middle of nowhere. I excused myself and stepped outside into the cold, foggy night air. By contorting my body in a strange position round the corner of the building I was able to get a minimum amount of reception and gave Armin a quick call. He was indeed in the stadium and yes I would have loved him to provide a full commentary throughout the game but at some ridiculous cost per minute, the expectation that I should be inside, the cold and my currently uncomfortable position I reluctantly declined this offer, instead insisting that he listened out for subsequent calls to enable me to be kept updated.

At half time it was goalless. I called again midway through the second half. Still goalless. At full time it was still the same. At what I calculated to be half time of extra time I called again and sure enough the deadlock had not yet been broken. This game would be settled on penalties thought Armin. Then bring them on. German teams are great at penalties I thought so we should go through. But then of course the ridiculousness of this thought hit me. The first time I ever desperately wanted a German team to win a penalty shoot-out and would you believe it, they were playing against another German team. For fifteen minutes or so I stayed in the warmth of the vicarage making polite conversation but my mind was in the stadium. I looked at my watch. It would be over now. Either someone had scored and taken victory or penalties would be about to begin. I slipped away from the gathering into the lonely night once more. To my dismay there was no reception showing on my phone. No matter how I angled it nothing would happen. Surely this meant we had lost (according to that strange illogic). I stepped inside again and just a few minutes later my phone started to ring. Reception had returned stronger than ever, even penetrating the stonework in a cruel twist of fate which would now bring me the bad news from Germany.

I celebrated the penalty win with another mince pie. By the next morning I was able to read of the fine saves of stand-in goalkeeper Daniel Klewer who had denied Unterhaching four of their penalties. The rest of the game did not matter. That 1.FCN had taken part was of secondary importance to the fact that they had won and could now consider themselves as having a decent chance of reaching the final, particularly as they were now drawn against Hanover rather than one of the more threatening teams that season. Things were looking up and 1FCNUK harboured dreams of witnessing a top five finish, a cup final and European competition the following season, so unaccustomed were we to 1.FCN's track record of providing so many false dawns for their supporters.

The second half of the season started as the first half with victory over Stuttgart. This did little to dampen expectations as

Stuttgart were strong, above Nuremberg and only two other teams had managed to beat them. Then on 2nd February Bayern Munich made the short journey north. Despite the strengths over recent years of the likes of Werder Bremen, Schalke 04, Borussia Dortmund and Leverkusen, Bayern are still the benchmark, especially for Nuremberg. The game was scheduled for the Friday evening and so it would be impossible to get to Germany in time for the game after work. However, Setanta Sports were in the habit of showing the Friday night *Bundesliga* game live in the UK. An annual subscription was paid and twenty *Clubberer* squeezed into my house to watch the event. *Bratwurst* were fried and German beers popped open as we witnessed 1.FCN outplay their guests and secure a much celebrated 3-0 victory. As we continued our celebrations in a couple of local pubs people were puzzled by how we could be so delighted over what to them was a meaningless match but nothing would dampen our spirits other than the inevitable nausea the next day. One game it might have been and the season was far from over. However, those who dared to dream a little suddenly started to dream much more.

By the time the cup quarterfinal came along in February, Nuremberg had added another draw to their pre-Christmas tally but had just ended a run in which they had not been defeated in eleven games and six of these had been won. The crowd of over 31,000 was testimony to the air of belief building around the team and showed that the people of Nuremberg were beginning to sense the possibility of a first cup final appearance since 1982 and just maybe the first win in the final since twenty years before that. In keeping with previous rounds in the *Pokal* the game ended goalless with the main talking point arriving in the last minute of extra-time when Hans Meyer took a chance on substituting goalkeeper and captain Raphael Schäfer and replacing him with the penalty saving hero from the previous round in the shape of Daniel Klewer. Schäfer was angered, at least showing the passion that fans expect from the players, but Meyer was vindicated as his goalkeeping number two was once again the hero, saving two penalties and sending *Der Club* through to the semi-final. Now this competition had to be taken seriously. Much was at stake and as 1.FCN hopped in and out of the top five the cup could also prove to be a door into the UEFA Cup should Stuttgart also get to the cup final and finish in a Champions League qualification spot in the *Bundesliga*. The permutations changed each week and nobody seemed to be sure about the exact criteria but when Stuttgart and Nuremberg were drawn apart in the semi-finals I became more sure than ever that there would be a cup final appearance in May. Those who shared this belief were no longer in the minority.

The DFB *Pokal*, unlike the English and many other footballing nation's top cup competition, did not occur from, or near to, the beginnings of association football in Germany. Indeed, the existence of many regional leagues and the fact that the awarding of the national championship required some form of knock-out competition prevented the development of a cup competition for the major teams in German football until the 1930s. It was introduced by *Reichsportkommissar* (the head of German sport), Hans von Tschammer in 1935. Open to all football clubs in the country, only the teams playing in the top two tiers in each region were obliged to enter the competition. Originally a tournament to help keep players fit between seasons, the first cup was won by 1.FC Nürnberg.

The importance of the DFB *Pokal*, which now takes place during the regular season, is generally low when compared to the English FA Cup's historical significance. The opportunities the *Pokal* can provide for teams such as 1.FCN as a pathway to European competition add something to its appeal but it is the *Bundesliga* that still captures the imagination of the nation rather than a good cup run by an un-fancied team. Attendances for the games which, with the exception of the final are often played midweek, are generally low and TV coverage is sparse with only a few live games covered and at that only the games featuring the 'big name' teams. Live ticker for games is available on some websites although the quality of service never appears to be as high as it does for league matches.

None of this should really be surprising, given the fact that the *Pokal* was a relative latecomer to the world of German football and the fact that the commercial world of football now demands teams make a push towards Champion's League qualification (for the best resourced) or top-flight survival as their main priorities. Maybe it is a shame that the *Pokal* seems to hold relatively little of the history and romance of the English FA Cup, but even that old competition is losing some of its appeal as teams field weakened sides or, even pull out of the competition as did Manchester United in 2000 to enable them to play in the FIFA World Club Championships instead. In January 2007, then Reading striker Dave Kitson, declared that he could not care less about it, stating, 'I care about staying in the Premier League, as does everybody at this club. Our league status is not protected by winning the FA Cup – simple as that.'

Clearly this is a sign of the times but the apparent apathy for the cup competitions in Germany and England neglect the fact that for the fans the excitement and glory of winning the cup is an aspiration that many hope will become at least a once in a lifetime experience.

As Nuremberg rolled over Frankfurt in the semi-final, several British followers gathered around Herbert's television in England, cheering the team on. There was certainly no *Pokal* apathy amongst these gathered fans or those in the *Frankenstadion* that night who witnessed a rather one-sided 4-0 drubbing. The celebrations continued for long after the final whistle. Nor was there any sign of apathy as fans attempted for weeks, and by any means, to procure tickets for the final against the victors from the other semi-final, VfB Stuttgart.

Two further draws, three defeats and victories against Hertha Berlin and Aachen prior to the semi-final maintained *Der Club's* position in the top six but now Leverkusen were breathing down their neck and threatening to leave a UEFA Cup place totally dependent on Stuttgart's final few league games. The importance of the game against Leverkusen just a few days after the defeat of Frankfurt was not lost on 1FCNUK. Four of us took the short flight to Cologne yet again and were happily drinking in the city just a few hours after finishing work. In one bar we confidently re-arranged a cardboard league table to show where each club would be after the next day's round of matches. Foolishly we had tempted fate by keeping 1.FCN above Leverkusen, despite the protests of the barman. It is strange how confidence can often be the worst enemy of a football fan. Go to a game as pessimistic as possible and even a draw can seem like a good outcome but walk around telling everyone how well your team will do and that the destruction of Frankfurt just three days before proves how good they are then you are leaving the door wide open for disappointment to sneak in and take everything you own.

As we arrived at the BayArena (by taxi having remembered the walk the previous season) we were not really giving the game much thought. It would be a foregone conclusion surely and we instead set about talking to fellow Nuremberg fans to see if anyone, anywhere was able to help us to get tickets for the Berlin final. Handshakes, smiles and shared beers came with promises to try and help us in our quest. We were desperate and six of us had booked flights to Berlin, rather dangerously optimistically several weeks before the semi-final. 1.FCN had their place in the Olympic Stadium but now would we get ours?

The game against Leverkusen was a dull affair in which Nuremberg barely looked interested as the hosts took the points and leapfrogged *Der Club* in the *Bundesliga* standings. It was disappointing but the general feeling amongst the travelling fans was that this performance could be forgiven after the exertions of the semi-final. Indeed, before, during and after the game the away support sung of nothing other than the forthcoming trip to Berlin and the potential appearance in next season's UEFA Cup. Mock UEFA Cups and DFB *Pokals* were carried into the stadium and waved around with excitement as it seemed like the greatest celebration of a defeat ever to take place.

Following the final whistle we shared a couple of beers with fans on the official *Fanverband* bus. This luxury double-decker coach was purchased by the *Fanverband* for travel to matches and it seemed to us that it also doubled as something of a travelling bar, such was the quantity of beer we observed, all neatly stacked in crates. By the time we waved off the coaches as they set-off to Nuremberg, the area around the stadium was quite deserted so we headed through a park in the general direction of Leverkusen's railway station. Our walk was interrupted by a small bar in which Leverkusen fans were singing away and obviously enjoying celebrating their victory. We feel safe in most places in Germany although I doubt we would have entertained the idea of popping into this bar for a drink had 1.FCN won. As it was though we walked in and despite several initial strange looks we ordered our drinks.

When we left slightly worse for wear a few hours later we did so promising to return next time we visited the town. I was wearing a Leverkusen jacket I'd been persuaded to swap for my 1FCNUK polo shirt. After walking a short distance in the warm evening air I knew that I'd made a bad mistake. And what the hell did I want with a Leverkusen top anyway? My mistake however has to be put into perspective. My new jacket, if a little too warm when zipped up as it had to be as someone else was now the proud owner of my shirt, did at least fit me. Jason on the other hand had not fared so well. The cropped short sleeved top he was wearing had a previous owner who was certainly not petite but her garment was never going to cover much of the torso of six feet tall Jason. It made me feel a whole lot better about my misguided swap. Jason was only too keen to avoid a train ride back towards our hotel in the centre of Cologne and so we all jumped into a taxi. Despite my rather hot predicament I was fully supportive of the idea that we should sample other bars rather than go anywhere near to our hotel to allow Jason to change.

The form of the team following the defeat in Leverkusen was not that of a team threatening to break into European competition and win the German cup. Fortunately, Stuttgart's league position eventually secured the UEFA Cup place for 1.FCN by virtue of just reaching the final. A victory in Berlin would not be necessary although was obviously the main desire of the team and fans alike. To even contemplate a cup victory before the last league game of the season away in Hanover now represented something of a rather forlorn hope. A fifteenth draw and two further defeats had left *Der Club* in sixth place but with the potential to fall to ninth on the final day if other results went against them.

The Cup Final was dominating the minds of the 1FCNUK members who had flown into Hanover the night before. We arrived at the wonderful AWD Arena three hours before kick-off full of anticipation, not so much for the game itself but because we had arranged a rendezvous to collect our tickets for the following week's historical game in Berlin. Only a few days before had we received an email promising us the tickets. Now we were about to lay our hands on these much sought pieces of paper. We were kept waiting in the hot sun for over two hours as heavy traffic had delayed the arrival of many fan coaches from Nuremberg. As soon as the tickets were handed to us they were secured in Iain's sporran to be returned to the hotel immediately after the game. Who cared what today's match would bring now? The winning maybe would not matter so much against Hanover because at least we were now going to be in the

Olympic Stadium the following Saturday. The next morning it was considered rather foolish of us to have let Iain wander home alone in the early hours of the morning, our tickets still on his person, when we had still not returned from what had become post-match celebrations and the start of the calming of pre-match nerves for the next game.

1.FCN had beaten Hanover 3-0 with a score line that probably flattered their performance but it was enough to completely reignite the hopes of all *Clubberer*. Their team had finished sixth, the highest league position for nineteen years. They had qualified for the UEFA Cup courtesy of their cup final opponents Stuttgart being crowned *Deutscher Meister*. Even the fact that the cup final was against the team who had finished top of the league over a thirty-four game season was not enough to dampen hope now. After all, 1.FCN were the only team to beat Stuttgart home and away, scoring seven and conceding just one in the process. Surely it could be done again.

To add to the optimism Marek Mintal had been included in the starting line-up for just the second time since November having made a substitute appearance two weeks previously. When he scored the opening goal in Hanover his name rang out as the fan's prayers were answered that their living legend would be back to fitness and back on the score sheet. With a fit and hungry Marek Mintal in the team it was widely accepted that 1.FCN would be a far more frightening prospect for Stuttgart than without him.

A frantic dash from work to the airport on the evening before the final was followed by a simple flight and rail transfer to the centre of Berlin where we checked into our hotel and headed for the bar. Earlier in the day I had received a telephone call from BBC Radio Stoke and on air told listeners of our trips to Germany and my prediction that *Der Club* would beat Stuttgart by a single goal, probably after extra-time. As we stood drinking a nervous beer or two that night, we shared our predictions without doing so with any real conviction for fear of tempting a negative fate.

The morning of the game arrived. We set off in blistering heat to meet Herbert who had made his own way to Berlin via a business meeting. In front of the Brandenburg Gate a stage and huge screens were in place ready to welcome thousands of ticketless fans later that day. The *Straße des 17.Juni*, the grand tree-lined boulevard heading west from the Brandenburg Gate, was now also lined with many temporary bars and food stalls as slowly but surely a carnival atmosphere was beginning to build for the game some ten hours later. For some in Germany the DFB *Pokal* may have held far less significance than the English FA Cup does for their counterparts across the North Sea but today there was no doubting that the majority of those in this historic area of Berlin were of the opinion that this was more than just a game of football. History and glory were there for the making and taking.

After a brief walk to while away the time and take in a few of Berlin's sights we were soon back at the Brandenburg Gate seeking refreshment as the day became increasingly hot and humid. Before we had arrived in Berlin the previous evening, the heat of the day had broken down into thunderstorms and torrential downpours of rain. Herbert predicted that the same would happen today but for now we enjoyed the sun and the banter as thousands of supporters started to gather.

Back in the previous October I'd had a strange conversation in Nuremberg:

"King Guinness. You meet him?"

I hadn't, no.

"He guy who likes drink Guinness."

Well that figured.

"You meet him here in Nürnberg."

Of course I would. It's always the best way, to a point, simply agreeing with the drunken bloke who is trying to explain something quite incoherently. When he's trying to do it in his best attempt at English, which even when drunk is far better than your best attempt at German, then agreeing is the only polite thing to do.

So apparently, at some point in the future, I would meet a guy, a friend of the guy who was talking to me, who likes Guinness to the extent that he is nicknamed (or at least I hope it's a nickname) King Guinness. As the drunken guy would probably not remember any of the conversation the next morning, and as I would probably not be back in Finnegan's Harp Irish Bar in Nuremberg for another four or five months, it would be unlikely that *Herr Guinness* would ever have the opportunity to demonstrate his love of the fine Irish stout or indeed why he deserved the forename, King.

On and on went the drunk guy. He was unable to elucidate any further and certainly no friend or acquaintance was in any fit state to further explain the situation. My attention wandered. The bar was noisy and I was trying to listen out for opinions about the drawn game we had just seen against Dortmund.

A few months later, an email arrived in my inbox. From the email, I learned that the drunken guy in the Irish bar that night was called Thomas. The email had been sent after a copy of our newsletter had been found hidden away in a drawer, lying unnoticed since it had been folded and put there by its owner on returning home from Finnegan's all that time ago.

Reading through the email, which was again the sort of example of English that makes one slightly embarrassed when thinking of your own lack of foreign language skills, it turned out the writer had not only found his copy of the newsletter but had even remembered that he had told us that he would send some of the photographs that were taken at that time. One shows Thomas drinking some sickly looking shots with my wife, another shows some of the travelling Brits looking remarkably happy considering we were disappointed that *Der Club* had not won. The other shows us standing around a guy with a pint of Guinness. "That's me," the email informed us and was signed 'Andi King Guinness'.

Language inadequacies and beer had clearly caused a misunderstanding and the King had been in the building all along that night. Why had we not figured this out? In our defence the pub was busy. There was still some novelty factor about 1FCNUK and so many people were talking to us it was hard to keep up with all the new names and offers of hospitality. Only those who shouted loudest (such as Thomas) seemed to be remembered. And of course, we were drunk. Even if Elvis had been sitting in the bar that night, we would probably have not remembered.

The pictures served as a small jolt to the memory and we remembered that HRH Guinness was a member of a fan club called Irish Boys, who's members apparently had just two things in common – their love of 1.FCN and their love of Guinness. In fact we had been told that they sometimes visited Ireland to sample the black stuff but when on home soil had to make do with the ubiquitous Irish bars in the German cities they visited watching their team. Mostly they apparently made do with Finnegan's. I assume that night we had been in there to catch a live English Premier League game. I don't have anything against Irish bars but when away I'd prefer to try the local pub culture rather than the imported and generally homogenous 'traditional' Celtic offerings. That said, they do provide excellent places for viewing British sport and in some countries can be a saviour the morning after the night before with a full Irish/English breakfast or cheeseburger and chips (with Heinz tomato ketchup and genuine English PG Tips tea of course).

On our next visit to Nuremberg we somehow missed the King again, this time I assume by spending far too long in another bar while he was living up to his name. It was in fact in May when we next saw him. As we stood waiting to collect our tickets outside the stadium in Hanover, King Guinness walked over to us. The guy was transformed. He'd clearly lost a lot of weight and his Guinness drinking days were obviously no longer as prolific as they had been. He'd also dyed a thick crimson line into his hair. Had he now found that the Caribbean Red Stripe beer was a miracle dieting aid and was thus advertising this fact with his hairstyle?

"Hi Andi," we said as we shook his hand. I'm not sure I would be able to seriously greet somebody by addressing them as either 'King Guinness', simply 'King' or just 'Guinness', and by the look of him now, reminding him of his larger stout drinking days could have potentially reduced him to tears.

After a few more pleasantries were exchanged, the reason behind his prolific weight loss became apparent. The following week he explained would be the Cup Final in Berlin. Yes, we told Andi, we were going and had tickets. Yes, we were flying back to Germany again next week especially for the match and yes we had got accommodation, a rather nice hotel for a not too expensive rate. He clearly thought we were mad but stated that he would be there himself. Before I could advise him of a little Irish bar I had visited in the city before, he was already explaining that on Monday, he would be back in Nuremberg and setting off on his bike all the way to the German capital to raise money for charity. Now anyone who has the nickname King Guinness has, somewhere along the line, earned respect from some quarters for his drinking prowess. Anyone who decides that they will cycle to Berlin from Nuremberg deserves even greater respect and as Andi's sleek new figure walked into the stadium we were left to reflect that maybe a bit of cycling would be a good thing for some of us before we quickly got back to reality.

Standing on the Berlin 'fan mile', in close proximity to the big screen and stage and in even closer proximity to one of the main bars, the temperature was ridiculously hot. The crowds were beginning to get to a serious size and the bar queues were lengthening. There were still several hours to kick-off and we would eventually be heading off to the stadium. As the Nuremberg fans struck up another song, through the crowds came a cyclist. His bike bedecked with Nuremberg flags and with the red stripe still in the hair, there was no mistaking Andi. He really had cycled this vast distance and once again hands were shaken and he was passed a very well-deserved drink before leaving once again for the final few miles to the suburbs. Soon we also decided that it was time to make our way and head to the stadium to soak up the atmosphere there. As it happened we ended up absolutely soaking in the atmosphere as a huge thunderstorm and torrential rain hit, mostly as we journeyed on the *U-Bahn* but with its remnants still falling on us as we made the final part of the journey on foot.

As we had entered a *U-Bahn* carriage at Potsdamer Platz we were very quickly aware that the other end held a group of drunk and loud Stuttgart supporters. As the train pulled away their singing was apparently directed at us. Not fearing any trouble in Germany I decided that we should treat it as banter and sing back which the Stuttgarters seemed to find a little irksome. Their faces contorted a little and their singing became more aggressive as we pulled into the next station. To our relief crowds of *Clubberer* piled in between ourselves and the opposition fans who were now all but silenced as the suffocating atmosphere of the underground carriage became one filled with the songs of 1.FC Nürnberg.

The *Olympiastadion* is impressive. The old building retains its former glory and with it a fascinating history despite extensive renovation and modernisation to make it a stadium fit to host not only the German FA Cup Final but indeed the 2006 World Cup Final. As it is approached from the city the Olympic rings are suspended between two large stone towers in front of the stadium. We met Armin and posed for photographs before making our way inside. Our seats were just three rows from the front, slightly to one side of the goal and so vertigo would be no issue. Such a low position is certainly not the best from which to view a game of football but with huge screens posted around the stadium it was easy to check on the exact position of the players when the naked eye sometimes found it difficult to judge distance.

The build-up to the game itself seemed to take forever although to be in that electric atmosphere was very special. It is hard to imagine exactly how Herbert and many of the other older *Clubberer* were feeling as the teams took to the pitch, the anthem sung and play started. So many years had passed since they had witnessed glory. For a few it was once the norm, for others a fading memory illuminated once more by what they saw before them. The next generation saw it as a moment to savour, maybe the start of something new and a hike in status for *Der Club*. We could certainly get accustomed to such events. For the youngest generation present they must have wondered if the atmosphere would always be like this from now on, wherever they watched their football. For them the future expectations they would have of their team would be greater than those of anyone else.

Books containing football statistics will now always record that 1.FC Nürnberg won the 2007 German Cup Final, beating Stuttgart 3-2 after extra-time. They will record the fact that Stuttgart opened the scoring through former Nuremberg forward Cacau after eighteen minutes and that Marek Mintal equalized in the twenty-seventh minute. Mintal had been in the starting line-up and despite Nuremberg falling behind, he was showing some good movement and touches. As the script would have it, he connected with a Dominik Reinhardt centre from the right to get 1.FCN back on level terms. The stage was set for this to be his day.

Of course, this helped revive *Der Club* who eventually went on to lift the cup for the fourth time in their history. However, there would be one further twist of fate for the Phantom. In the thirty-fifth minute he was viciously challenged from behind by Meira of Stuttgart. *"Das ist Rot, das ist Rot"*, (that is red) screamed the commentator on German television station ARD. The assault, however, was somehow only punished by a yellow card. Many saw this as the referee losing his nerve having only a few minutes previously sent Cacau from the field of play for punching Nuremberg's Wolf. The consequences for Mintal were far more serious. He was carried from the field of play on a stretcher, tears in his eyes, and taken to hospital. Although the injury would only keep him out of action for a few weeks, Nuremberg had to play the remainder of the game without their hero. Marek Mintal had once again had a comeback curtailed by injury. However, as the match finished and the players received their deserved accolades from the thousands of *Clubberer*, a special cheer was reserved for the committed Slovakian as he limped around the track of the Olympic Stadium with his team mates, having returned from hospital.

Throughout the first half of the game I had yelled and sung and continued to do so until Marco Englehardt gave the Franconians a 2-1 lead in the forty-seventh minute. Now nerves took over. There was still almost one half of a football match to go and the question for me was whether *Der Club* could hold on. I stood mostly in a self-imposed nauseating silence until Pardo slotted home an eightieth minute penalty for the Schwabians after a foul by Raphael Schäfer. Now I felt I had to sing. A massive effort would be needed as Stuttgart were lifted by their equalizer. Another goal at this point would have been the end for 1.FCN. Heroically they managed to hang on for extra-time and as this ticked by, penalty saving hero Daniel Klewer was ordered to warm-up but to the relief of all fans, and without disrespect for Klewer, he would not be needed. In the 109th minute, Danish midfielder Jan Kristiansen collected the ball wide on the left. I looked up at the big screen to check his exact position as he cut inside and unleashed a wonderful shot in our direction that dipped over the head of the Stuttgart goalkeeper Hildebrand, clipping the bar as it sailed into the net.

When Kristiansen's *Traumtor* (dream goal) was scored the confidence of the *Clubberer* became high. With just a few minutes remaining both teams were exhausted and surely nobody had any more to give. What is more, the 74,000 people in the stadium had just witnessed a goal worthy of winning any match.

The jubilation and tears of joy that followed the final whistle were something to behold. The cup was raised into the air and paraded around the track, and it was a long time before the *Clubberer* made their way from the stadium, dispersing in all directions in a state of ecstasy and disbelief at having witnessed not only a famous victory for 1.FC Nürnberg but also a highly memorable game of football.

Arriving back at the fan mile in the city centre it was surprisingly quiet. A few fans milled around but the hour was now late and we were all emotionally drained. The majority of *Clubberer* would of course be on their way back south, ready for the huge street party that would follow in Nuremberg the next day. We sipped our celebratory beer congratulating ourselves on a successful season of watching *Der Club* perform and already looked forward to the next.

Our smiles remained for the next couple of days in Berlin although I was rather disappointed to see that the twice weekly *Kicker* football magazine focused their front page on their player of the season (Werder Bremen's Diego for the record) rather than on the famous victory for *Der Club*. What is even more surprising is that the offices of *Kicker* are actually in Nuremberg so the importance of the victory there can surely not have gone unnoticed. There were of course reports and reactions from the game on the inside pages but it was clear that as far as the world of football was concerned, the DFB *Pokal* was just a small blip on the radar. Fortunately BBC Radio Stoke did not see it this way. Receiving a call from them on the Monday morning I was able to tell the local radio audience of the drama in Berlin. As the presenter had the final word he introduced the next song, *We are the Champions*. Rather fitting I thought looking back to our drunken karaoke version in Nuremberg at the beginning of the season and the fourth Cup Final victory for *Der Club*.

It was a couple of days later back in England, that the immensity of that fourth *Pokal* really hit home. Here was a club who 18 months previously had been on the brink of another disastrous season and relegation. A club who had known little in the way of good times for the best part of four decades. Every brief glimpse of silver lining in those forty years would quickly turn into yet another cloud and there was rarely anything to suggest that things were changing for the better. Had somebody said to 1FCNUK, or any other *Clubberer* for that matter, as we watched Arminia Bielefeld score their last minute winner back in October 2005, that we would soon be witnessing *Der Club* win the cup and look like a team ready to take on the *Bundesliga* big boys on a more equal footing, such a suggestion would have been dismissed as ridiculous or even almost impossible.

The Adidas advertising campaign which states 'impossible is nothing' is supposed to be motivational. Wear Adidas and any hurdle can be overcome. Through footage of sports stars drawing cartoons depicting their own barriers and how they overcame them, it was a slick attempt to inspire the public to buy Adidas sportswear. Posters similarly depicted drawings or photographs of sports events when someone or something had flown in the face of adversity to claim glory. In the days following the cup final, the multinational company added another poster to its collection. A child-like drawing of a bus with an oversized DFB *Pokal* strapped to the roof and smiling figures inside has the title *Berlin, Berlin wir kommen aus Berlin* (Berlin, Berlin, we're coming from Berlin) in deference to the traditional *Berlin, Berlin wir fahren nach Berlin* sung by German fans if their team looks to be in with a shout of making the cup final. The signatures of the players surround the bus and the quite simple phrase of the advertising campaign finishes off the poster. It was not only a good gesture from Adidas but a very poignant comment on the past couple of seasons for 1.FC Nürnberg.

Another advertising campaign provided one *Clubberer* with the chance to highlight the victory further still. When a local radio station held a competition in which the winner had the opportunity to have a poster displayed in a prominent position in his local railway station, it just happened that the winner was a devoted fan of *Der Club*. Of course, he decided that his poster should carry a subtle message regarding the fantastic victory in Berlin. And it did. *München gratuliert dem DFB Pokalsieger 2007* (Munich congratulates the DFB Cup Winners 2007) it read and the radio station, Munich based Charivari, were good to their word. Much to the annoyance of some Bayern fans and the pleasure of the Nuremberg faithful it was displayed in Munich's main railway station. *Der Club* had haunted Bayern Munich throughout the season and now, even after its end the haunting would continue. The *Clubberer* delighted in this but took the greatest of pleasure in having overcome the odds and, despite the longevity of the journey back to glory, they had witnessed a season in which the improbable had been treated with respect and hard work but had been made to seem like nothing by this team of heroes.

Historic stadium, historic day in Berlin for 1.FCN

Chapter 10

Summertime blues
(and how to beat them)

The summer is a strange time for a football fan. Each year, the season finishes at the end of May and then a gap of anything from six to ten weeks follows in which the ubiquitous football of the rest of the year seems to fade into the background of life. Of course, there are the international competitions of the World Cup and the European Championships to fill the gaps every other year but they never quite replace the familiarity and banter of watching your team play. Yes, there can be excitement, lots of games to watch each week for the duration of the tournament, and many of the highs and lows of football all condensed into the space of a few short weeks. That many of the top 'stars' in world football fail to produce what we are told is their best at such tournaments is probably symptomatic of the fact that for the committed club player and the committed club fan too, the commitment is really more to their club team rather than the brief international sideshow. The definition of 'committed club player' is now more often a reference to the fact that the club pays his wages and his wages rule his commitment.

When the season ends and the height of summer attempts to pause the ongoing parade of football, the average fan has to find something else to occupy the mind.

In England, cricket is a pleasant sport to watch in the summer but it's rarely enough to produce the adrenalin rush of watching a glorious goal sail into the net or, as is more likely, screaming at your team's full back to get stuck in or sod off to somewhere else, or telling the ref that not only is he unacquainted with his father but he's also worthy of labelling with any number of vulgar terms for parts of the male or female anatomy. There is also another problem with cricket when discussing it in terms of 'a filler' in the pause between two football seasons. It is certainly a majestic game and, in its many forms, appeals to a widening audience, appreciative of the skill, complex tactics and varying disciplines it requires, but it is not a global game in the same sense as football. Yes, hundreds of millions of Indians love the game giving it a huge audience in the sub-continent, the Australians are the best in the world at it, it is played in the ghettos of Karachi, the beaches of Jamaica and the village greens of England, and that latterly mentioned location is the problem. It is a very English game and, generally only appeals where the English once ruled. (I know that these places were part of the *British* Empire but, with apologies to some excellent Scottish cricketers, it is hard to think of let's say Glaswegian shipbuilders playing the same game as a bunch of former Oxbridge university toffs and setting off to distant parts of the Empire to have a 'jolly good' game against the locals before making them servants.) The Englishness of the game of cricket and the fact that it is a game of the 'old Empire' has meant that it has largely been overlooked by the rest of the world.

 Of course, the English also lay claim to football, but this has travelled much better. Talk to your average German sports fan about football and it won't be long before he 'apologises' in a mocking tone (if you are English) for the better performances of the German national team when compared to that of the English, and then just maybe changes his tone into one which almost demands an apology in return for the 'luck' (as he sees it) of the 1966 World Cup Final. (Interestingly most of the references I've heard about 1966 and all that, have been through the playing of *Three Lions* in German pre-match entertainment. I assume that the German nation got over 1966 – helped by two victories and three further runners-up places – some time ago whereas the English still hark back to it as the most glorious moment in footballing history.)

If you are English, a generally good way to end a discussion about German footballing superiority is to start talking about cricket instead. In keeping with the majority of the rest of the European population (and in that one can also include the majority of the British population) the Germans *et al* find cricket very bemusing. Once, while entertaining a couple of Germans at home, both of whom knew about sport in general and football in particular, I happened to flick the TV channel to a cricket match. The guests looked puzzled but after receiving a short explanation they could understand the very basics of the game. Fortunately, just in case they had any plans to make Germany a superior cricketing nation to England (which would not be hard), I mentioned that what we were witnessing on the TV was the second day of play in a Test Match. They were astounded to learn that a game could go on for this long, and they then seemed to bear a huge anxiety for the sanity of cricket playing nations when I explained that the game could actually last for up to five full days. And still end in a draw.

Rarely do football fans take a break to the sun at a time when their team may, just possibly, perform some miraculous feat such as winning two in a row or, more likely, require their enthusiastic support (and as the game goes on, moans and groans) as another unsuccessful attempt is made to end that record-breaking unbeaten run. So, unless cricket (or anything else for that matter) is the sport you apparently live for, it is highly improbable that it can really replace football when the football season is over. Therefore, the close season is always a good time to go on holiday. For those without commitment, it can be a time for adventure away from the narrow existence of watching and reading about football for ten months of the year. For those with commitments it is a chance to impress, to show that you really are a caring individual who puts relationships and family before your favourite team and your favourite television sports channels. You can take your wife and kids away on holiday and maybe even go abroad to find the sun. And you can at least be safe in the knowledge that there is nothing that they can do to stop you thinking about the game during the summer pause (or winter pause which also exists for a month in Germany).

But when abroad the English football fan then finds him or herself drawn to English or Irish bars to catch the live game in the pre-season meaningless tournament from outer Mongolia in which top teams are playing as missionaries to convert the local population into shirt buying believers before anyone comes along with religion or anything else which could deflect the attentions and money away from the coffers of the English Premier League several thousand miles away. But we still go and watch the games and then sit on beaches longing for the season proper to be with us again.

In July 2007, having taken a few minutes refuge from the Tenerife sun in an Internet Café, I came across some cheap flights to Nuremberg scheduled for December. A couple of quick phone calls to the UK and a few clicks on the computer and several of us were booked for the weekend of the home fixture against Hertha Berlin. The added bonus would be that the wife would be only too happy to visit her home town when the *Christkindlesmarkt* (the famous Christmas market) would be in full flow. Another piece of ingenious planning. Almost. We were now at the mercy of the *Bundesliga* who do not confirm the exact date of fixtures until a few weeks before because of their kind-heartedness to the media who clearly pay them lots of money for television rights.

The phone call to the UK then turned quickly to the previous night's match which, as the conversation agreed, was a poor performance. My wife and I had taken a taxi from the holiday apartment to a German bar to watch the *Liga Pokal* semi-final between 1.FC Nürnberg and Schalke 04. The *Liga Pokal*, fortunately enough following a relatively inept defensive performance, is not part of the regular season.

A pre-season German football tournament of varying formats and popularity, the *Liga Pokal* this particular year comprised of six teams: the promoted champions from *2.Bundesliga* (Karlsruhe), the second, third and fourth placed teams, Schalke, Werder Bremen and Bayern Munich, the reigning champions, Stuttgart, and the cup winners, 1.FCN. The champions and the cup-winners were seeded and automatically gained a semi-final berth.

A pre-season tournament should not really set the pulse racing too much, but for the football junkie, it is the pre-season tournament that provides the methadone until the real thing comes along. For *Clubberer* in the summer of 2007, it provided a first look at the team we had last seen a few weeks ago, victoriously parading the DFB *Pokal* around the Olympic Stadium in Berlin, and a chance to see the new signings who would surely take *Der Club* to even greater glory in the next campaign. Maybe it would even provide the opportunity to continue the excitement and revelry of last season, the most successful for Nuremberg for thirty-nine years.

With rather Teutonic planning I'd taken my wife to the beach in Playa de las Americas the day before the game. We'd had a wander along the promenade past several bars until one gave a glimpse of the holy grail, written in chalk on a small blackboard, in German: *Morgen 19:30 Nürnberg – Schalke.* Now the sunbathing could begin in earnest. I lay on the beach reminiscing about the previous couple of seasons, playing over and over in my mind the *Traumtor* (dream goal) from Jan

Kristiansen that clinched the *Pokal*. Did I imagine hearing the 'dink' from my position three rows from the perimeter track in Berlin as that shot clipped the underside of the crossbar before hitting the back of the net? Remembering the brief moment of silence as the fact that the ball had crossed the line registered in the mind of the fans, then the roar and the jubilation as it suddenly dawned on me, and several thousand others, that we were on the verge of winning the game. Great memories which diverted my attention almost completely from the bikini-clad sunbathers on the beach. Memories of a game that would last forever but memories that would soon have to become a very important part of the past. For tomorrow the ten-month long roller coaster ride of life as a football fan would once again begin its exhilarating and often downright sickening journey.

Those first ninety minutes of the ten months were generally sickening. Wearing a Nuremberg shirt, entering a bar called *Zum Stuttgarter*, apparently owned by a Stuttgart fan (defeated cup finalists remember) seemed a good idea at the time and surely there would be no hassle involved in this. There wasn't. The majority of football rivalry in Germany is confined to banter in and around the game and certainly does not stretch to the Canarian waters of the Atlantic Ocean. We were greeted with mild surprise and a greater degree of genuine interest than amusement in the fact that an English thirty-something (albeit with his semi-German wife) had bothered to turn out to a quiet bar to watch a low-key game of a team from southern Germany. The standard questioning about why I was not supporting Manchester United or Chelsea was brushed off with the usual muttered phrase about German football being more 'interesting'. As so often happens, the landlord and landlady stood shaking their heads with puzzled half-smiles on their lips. Did they disagree with my consideration that their *Bundesliga* was more interesting than the Premier League? Quite possibly. Even I am not entirely convinced, only using this as a stock answer. Maybe they were hardly able to believe that I was prepared to sit in their quiet, homely bar and watch the game when English compatriots would be running amok in some of the resort's other bars, chanting drunken renditions of their favourite football songs and no doubt some songs with anti-German sentiment too. Or more likely, the hosts for the evening were feeling deeply sorry for my wife, this kind woman of German origin who had clearly and so selflessly taken this troubled Englishman, obviously harbouring a myriad of learning difficulties, under her wing. They stopped short of asking if she was in receipt of a National Lottery grant for my care and switched on the television.

"Learning difficulties it is then," they were no doubt saying when Robert Vittek put *Der Club* in front after twenty minutes and I made the four other customers jump by shouting, "Get in," followed by, "*Tor,*" in due deference to the little oasis of Germany in which I had just leaped to my feet. At that point I'd not consumed enough alcohol to strike-up an attempt at a discussion in terribly broken German about the lovely passing move that led to the goal, the finish itself, or indeed the excellence of Robert Vittek. All that was needed was a knowing nod from the landlord and a slightly more exuberant nod back from me which replaced the need to say 'good goal' and in return, 'aye, that will do nicely'.

But of course, football fans need to discuss the game and all its intricacies and so, without further delay (and with no disrespect to the footballing knowledge of my wife) text messages started to fly between Tenerife, North Staffordshire and London. Jason sitting at home watching the game via a live stream on a website, Iain sitting in a London pub watching it via a German TV channel. The footy was back after its short absence and wasn't it great.

Or at least it would have been great if Schalke had not scored three in the space of seven minutes just before half-time. Even better if the normally solid Nuremberg defence (at least normal for the previous season) had not looked so out of sorts and the new players had made little or no impression on the game.

Avoiding all eye contact with the landlord I sat through the second half which saw another goal for each side and the realisation that far from being the start of a ten month journey of new highs, the coming season could revisit some of the many lows I'd experienced in my life following football. With a few glasses of fine German Pils inside me I mustered up the courage to shrug my shoulders as I walked passed the bar en route to the toilet. "*Schade*," (shame) I said, trying not to sound too disappointed. "Shit happens," the landlord shrugged back in English, with a knowing smile that this could just be the start of it.

I'd been on board that roller coaster each season for at least the last twenty. I'd been on it before then but had always found it easy in my youth to get off or at least close my eyes when it got to the scary bits. The Port Vale of John Rudge in the late '80s had got me properly into this whole thing in the first place. Previous forays to Vale Park in the '70s and '80s were far from memorable. My maternal grandfather was an avid fan but after his death it was left to my dad to occasionally make the sacrifice of his time to take me to watch the Vale. Having being been brought up on the great Blackpool side of the 1950s, it is not hard now to see why he was clearly unimpressed with what Vale had to offer. Out of loyalty to my grandfather's memory I was somewhat blind to the unfashionable image and the crap football of Port Vale, and when I started to earn enough money through a shelf-stacking job in the evenings after school I was able to go to watch 'the Vale' increasingly regularly and became a season ticket holder eventually travelling all over the country during the course of several seasons. That this diehard support occurred alongside the incredibly successful Rudge era is quite probably no coincidence. In just a few seasons Vale achieved some fine

FA cup giant-killings (Tottenham in 1987 still a personal favourite), had some of their best ever players, made their first appearance at Wembley Stadium and won promotion to the second division for the first time in over thirty years. To label me a glory hunter would be wrong and more than just a little ironic in terms of one of the least celebrated and least fashionable professional clubs in England. However, it is true that my attendance started to wane in the mid-'90s, as did the success of the club on the pitch.

But once a fan, always a fan is surely the case with football and you cannot change allegiance. That is the realm of the school playground where one day it's Chelsea the next Arsenal and then maybe Real Madrid, all dependent on who was on television last night. True fans don't change though, do they? A friend who was a fully-fledged supporter of Port Vale's local rivals Stoke City, changed her allegiance to Manchester United, largely due to a relationship at the time. She's now a season ticket holder and has travelled all over England and Europe supporting United. I've never asked if she still has any feelings for Stoke, and perhaps it is best to let it be. From a purely footballing perspective I hope she does, from a football rivalry perspective I would be very pleased if she does not!

So why then, following my waning attendance at Vale Park, did I start to attend games of 1.FCN? And can you really support two teams at once? The first question is hopefully being answered in the pages of this book – if nothing else, at least see it as a self-indulgent confession. As for the second question, I've got to say that the answer is yes. But I've had to recall a rule which is really a refined version of something I did as a child. In those days I would have a favourite team from each division. The fourth division, and occasionally the third, belonged to Port Vale but then any season could see me following the fortunes, via the vidiprinter and the pages of Shoot and Match magazines, of teams as diverse as Leyton Orient (I liked the name) and St

Mirren (I liked the kit). Glory hunting was confined to a picture of Trevor Francis or Terry McDermott on the bedroom wall and the closest a Port Vale fan ever got to a decent trophy was the foil version for the Panini sticker album, although even that required the swapping of two Phil Neals, one Ray Clemence, a Southampton team picture and a Coventry club badge.

Now I've redefined that rule. One country – one team. This not only allows me to support Nuremberg and Vale but in future opens up a whole range of opportunities as the global village becomes ever more accessible and currently unfashionable leagues appear with more regularity on prime sports networks. Let's say I'm sitting pretty awaiting a football revolution that may never happen. Not that I intend to pick a team from every league in Europe and beyond, although the thought of becoming a multi-national football tourist is somewhat appealing. And of course, teams as diverse as Port Vale and Nuremberg are hardly ever likely to clash in serious competition, are they? If they did, who would I support? Port Vale. No doubt about it. They have been in my blood for longer. It's as simple as that. That my presence at the games has significantly reduced does not mean the love for the club has died. It's just that it is now shared with a younger mistress. And as for my fellow British Nuremberg supporters, they too have their favourite British teams who they have followed through thick and thin and I believe that they too would always put their British team first in the event of a competitive match against *Der Club* but it would always be a close call, and as I've already said, statistically it's very unlikely to happen.

When I learned that 1.FC Nürnberg *Fanbeauftragte* Jürgen also had another team I posed the conundrum to him. Having followed Würzburger FV in his youth he turned to *Der Club* at the end of the '70s as his home-town team fell into financial disarray before eventually folding in 1981. Even though the club reformed in the tenth tier of German football, Jürgen kept his support for 1.FCN but now makes sure he looks for the scores and information about his old favourites. Who would he support if the two ever met? "It will not happen," he informed me, "because they are too far apart. Würzburg are so far down the ladder now." I suggested that it could happen one day. Jürgen looked just slightly pained. I pushed him for an answer. Who would he support? A little more pain. He was clearly now thinking more seriously. What if they did meet one day? I thought for a moment he might crack but ever the diplomat Jürgen decided that a draw would be nice. I believed him too. I also felt a little guilty – it's not right to question diehard fans about their loyalties.

My attendance at Vale games from the late '90s onwards had become somewhat sporadic. A move of house eventually meant that even radio coverage became an almost impossible exercise in trying to get the best possible reception in the attic room. Having resisted the blatant commercialism of the Sky stranglehold on the Premiership for so long I gave in and was able to sit comfortably in my armchair watching all the action and results I wanted. A cold Vale Park was sadly losing its appeal yet I would still run laps of honour of the living room each time a Vale score flashed up, or kick an imaginary dog or cat each time a goal was conceded.

The trips to Germany started to reignite the old pleasures of being a football supporter and spending most of one's waking hours thinking about football and little else. The fact that I now had two teams to think about obviously came with double the pleasure and double the pain. Furthermore, the level of brain time devoted to football throughout the season results in a huge void when the season is over, at first bordering on depression and then turning into excitement as fixtures are released and trips are planned. The withdrawal symptoms when the obsession revolves around two teams is pretty miserable. During the summer months, if one did not think about football then surely insanity would set in.

When the German fixtures are announced the planning takes on a whole new approach as trips have to be matched to holidays and long weekends (not easy for those of us in the teaching profession) as well as paying careful attention to the cost and availability of flights, and departure and destination airports.

Of course, one advantage the teaching profession has is that August is when the 'big' holidays occur and the football season starts. Football matches clearly fit with cultural visits and the only debilitating factor is financial. The other great advantage, of course, is that I can satisfy my wife's desire for a couple of weeks in the sun, by beach and pool, and there is still time left for me to catch an early season game in Germany.

Nuremberg is, as you may probably now have gathered, a wonderful city to visit for a weekend break and to witness a game of football. If the city's premier football team has a rich history then this is certainly outdone by the city itself. The war saw vast destruction from allied bombers but slowly the city was re-built, much of it to its former glory. The city today is a vibrant place with a cosmopolitan population and a tourist industry of which that population is rightly very proud.

To go to Nuremberg for a week allows one to absorb even more of the atmosphere and culture of the city than is possible in a weekend and, therefore, it was decided that three of us, starved of football throughout the summer, would take an extended weekend break to do just that. We booked our flights and managed to fly out a few days in advance of the second home game of the season against Werder Bremen. A couple of days later we would be joined by further members of 1FCNUK.

We were collected from the airport by Armin who, in the excitement of welcoming the first wave of the British contingent first of all forgot where his car was parked, then drove around the airport complex several times before heading for the city centre and nearly crashing twice. To put this into perspective, Nuremberg airport is a small complex with well sign-posted exits and is just a few kilometres from the old town. Probably fearing that an accident was imminent Armin dropped us at our hotel before heading home to compose himself.

So what do you do in Nuremberg for a week? The football would take up the weekend when as well as the match we had also arranged to meet other fan clubs but until Friday we were left to our own devices. Surely all the sights had been seen on previous visits so what else could one possibly do except drink and eat?

The socialising is, as you will have now read on umpteen pages, a big aspect of the trips to Germany (and the meetings that we have in the UK). But there is a slight cultural shift in socialising in Germany. Yes, there is clearly a bar/pub culture very similar to that in England but, particularly in Nuremberg, there seems to be far less of the anti-social behaviour associated with groups of adolescents and twenty to thirty something's drinking to excess.

Maybe it's just because the whole German drinking culture is far more relaxed than in the UK. Far fewer places have a dress code for a start. When a German friend tried to enter a town centre bar in regional England, he was refused entry because he was wearing (smart) 'trainer type' footwear with a pair of slacks and a shirt. As he pointed out (and anyone who has ventured into an English town centre on a Saturday night will confirm this) most of the people in the trendy bar looked like they had just 'slept under a tree' but were allowed entry because they wore shoes.

Maybe the fact that everyone has to dress in pseudo-smart clothing and all look much the same in the UK to enter many bars is part of the cause of the late night problems in our town centres. People are trying to break free from the homogeneity of looking the same and being told what they can and can't do by doormen. Another friend was once asked to leave an English city centre bar (and not a particularly nice one either) by a bouncer, having already purchased drinks and found a table for himself and his partner on a Saturday lunchtime. His crime? Wearing a T-shirt!

It is certainly more relaxing drinking in (most) German city centre bars. Aside from a worrying few moments in Cologne, even when football is involved fans drink and laugh (yes, the laughing might be something we're a bit short of on a UK night out too) together until the small hours.

Of course, knowing the dress code (or at least that there really isn't one) helps with the packing – 1FCNUK members, after a few days away certainly look like they have been sleeping under a tree (which is rarely the case I will add). I've only once really felt stared-at in a German bar and that was on an early trip to Nuremberg when the league season had finished. It was also my first taste of the city's nightlife so I was unsure what to expect. Having, along with Angela, dressed for a night out, me in a nice shirt and trousers, my wife in a summer dress reflecting the hot temperatures of a late May evening, we were directed to a rock bar by the hotel receptionist who I had asked where we might be able to catch the German Cup Final live on TV. Entering the dark bar brought looks through the smoke from tattooed long-haired rockers. My wife wanted to make a sharp exit but I saw the small portable TV in the corner and braved it, telling her that we would have a drink and then find somewhere more suitable. The stares ultimately stopped, we never did find another bar that night and in fact, we generally frequent the rock bar in question on each visit, having made several friends that evening.

So of course, with a few days to kill before the Werder Bremen fixture, we visited Brown Sugar and several other bars we have come to know and love. We also had an important cultural visit to make. It just so happened that in the town hall that very week, the *Pokal* was on display with an exhibition dedicated to the victory only three months previously.

I'm not sure what it says about the importance of the German cup, the lack of English style hype surrounding the competition and the trophy, and indeed German society as a whole, but I could not envisage the English FA Cup being put on display in a large room with entrance (free of charge) directly from the street, with nobody telling you to queue here, don't stand there, no photographs (except official ones for £5 per person). Of course the great history of the English Cup gives it a special place in the hearts of the nation and demands that the trophy is afforded security and respect, while also lending itself to becoming a money making commodity, but the German cup also has its history and a celebration of the most recent chapter was now situated in a moderately sized hall in the city centre. Fine displays of images from the Olympic Stadium and the ensuing celebrations in the city adorned the walls, while the golden chalice itself stood in a glass case on a pedestal in the centre of the room.

In various sized groups, I visited that room on three occasions over the next few days, reliving the glory of Berlin and psyching myself up for the impending home game. Surely further glories would be on the way this season. Despite a 2-0 home defeat at the hands of newly promoted Karlsruhe, victories away at Victoria Hamburg (in the first round of the cup) and Hansa Rostock provided good reason to be confident about what the season would hold. There was an excited air of anticipation around the city as Saturday approached.

Amongst our travelling group and our friends in Franconia, anticipation was also high for the midweek game between England and Germany at the new Wembley Stadium. We took the short train journey to the university town of Erlangen to meet with Northern Irish exile Liam and Erlangen citizens Moritz,

Christoph and Frank. Moritz had had the pleasure of joining us in England to watch Nuremberg matches on the television when on a work placement. Frank was to soon follow in his footsteps. We then bumped into royalty in the form of Andi 'King Guinness' and with this final addition to our group we visited a beer garden before watching the international fixture in an Irish bar where the King could fuel his passion.

I'd heard of Erlangen before. I'd seen the phrase 'Twinned with Erlangen' on sign posts welcoming people to Stoke-on-Trent. Naively not understanding the urban twinning process, I'd expected Erlangen to be a rather dreary, uninspiring area of struggling industry and gritty inhabitants. It was therefore something of a pleasant surprise to witness the delightful buildings, and the upmarket and relaxed café culture. This surprise was about all that Jason and I could take away from Erlangen apart from all of the friendly but heartfelt stick we had been given as the Germans managed to once again make their mark at Wembley. (Iain clearly delighted in the *Auld enemy* being defeated.) To rub further salt in the wounds, Herbert had attended the game at Wembley before flying out to Nuremberg. He also took delight in the victory, calling from London to laugh at the English. Despite being on the wrong end of it, football banter was back and to socialise and share drinks and laughter with the beautiful game as a common denominator was the reason we were in Germany in the first place.

This common denominator became more intense a couple of days later. On the Friday, the evening before the Bremen game, we were invited to join a fan club in their 'fan pub' in the St Leonhard district of Nuremberg. The *Grüner Baum* fan club was founded around the same time as our own. Having seen our website and our plans to be in the city they suggested we join them for a drink. We left the *U-Bahn* at the correct stop and found the *Grüner Baum* bar, identifying it from the Union Jack which hung outside to welcome us as guests.

A somewhat heavy previous night (celebrating the fact that several more of our own fan club had flown in from the UK) and a long day of walking around in the blistering sun had dampened the mood and the last thing we intended doing was drinking copious amounts of alcohol with our hosts. Unfortunately they had other ideas. After a slow, almost painful start as we tried to force ourselves to drink beer and then a hastily provided gift of a bottle of whisky, the mood slowly changed. The fact that few of our hosts had no more than a couple of words of English and that our German was considerably less advanced did not matter. Here we all understood the language of football and with the names of players, references to teams and memories of matches came the inevitable facial expressions, gestures and glass-clinking enabling language barriers to be overcome and friendships to be formed. As the beer (at the insistence and expense of our new friends) continued to flow we somehow managed to be revived and as the *Grüner Baum* President, Kurt, produced a guitar and led a boisterous sing-along, the hours passed by and the evening eventually drew to a close.

As has so often been the case on our visits to Nuremberg, the morning before the match was non-existent. My parting words to Herbert the previous night, as he left our company at a more sensible hour than some of us quite mistakenly thought acceptable, were to arrange to meet him for a walk around the city, sharing a father-in-law to son-in-law bonding session and chat in his hometown. I assume he walked around on his own that morning as the rest of us managed to leave the hotel just in time to take the tram to the game.

On this particular occasion our self-inflicted suffering wasn't just limited to the fifteen minute tram journey. Unfortunately we'd been unable to get tickets for the standing terrace, some of which benefits from the shade of the stand above. For this game we had pitch-side seats and sat for two hours in the direct sun, slowly burning away and furthering our dehydration to new levels.

Prior to entering the cauldron of the stadium, we had attended the *Fansprechstunde* (or at least the last few minutes of it as we were running rather late). As we entered we were again recognised by some of the officials (not surprising really as we carried our flag with us) standing with injured left-back Javier Pinola, who was taking questions from the seated audience. Immediately, we were beckoned over and asked to share the stage with the highly-rated Argentine defender, all of us posing for photographs with our flag. Pinola then signed autographs from the audience, even adding his name to the 1FCNUK flag which was then draped around the player's shoulders. One hopes that the photos of this do not adversely affect his chances of selection for the Argentina national team.

Once in the stadium we were only kept sane by large cardboard signs provided to each fan. These signs were meant to be folded, fan-like, and then used to make as much noise as possible by striking them against whatever one could reach. Due to our location under the searing sun they became nothing more than sun shades as we witnessed a mediocre game which was won by Bremen by a single goal to nil. 1.FCN did not play well, though they did not deserve to lose the game, but the atmosphere created by the fans and the glorious summer weather was not sufficient alone to convince anyone that this would be another historical season for *Der Club*. Maybe the heat had something to do with the lacklustre performance on the pitch and maybe our general mood was not conducive to believing that the glories of last season could so easily be repeated. We left the stadium disappointed with the result from a team that our previous high-spirits had caused us to believe could always bring the elusive success that football fans crave.

Leaving the stadium, it was hard to say which was making us feel more sick. Was it the fact that 1.FCN had lost or was it the fact that some of us were by now suffering from sunstroke? No matter, we now had another appointment, an hour or so coach journey to a fan club *Stammtisch* (essentially a drinking session) with our friends from *Grüner Baum* and others. This journey was to be aboard the *Fanverband* coach that some of us had boarded very briefly in Leverkusen towards the end of the previous season.

Outside the stadium we met our friends and were told that we would be walking to the coach, parked several hundred metres away. As we set off it was apparent that the sun (and no doubt the previous evening) had inflicted too much damage on some of our group and regrettably (although probably somewhat sensibly) we slipped off into the shade provided by the large trees of a beer garden and never made the coach. That we felt some guilt about this was down to the fact that the hospitality we had received the previous evening was heartfelt and now we seemed to be letting down those very hosts who had provided so much already. However, it was clear that some of us would not have relished the journey to and from the drinking session, let alone the heavy consumption of beer that would inevitably be the order of the evening, and so comradeship kept us all together as we decided to head back towards our city centre hotel.

The German *Volksfests* are huge fun fairs that come to town periodically, stay for a few weeks and then move on. They are much the same as travelling fairs in the UK with the exception that the rides are bigger, brighter and look safer, although I personally would never class anything that spins you around, upside down high above the ground as particularly safe. The German fairground however has a big advantage over its British counterparts, namely a beer tent, or in the case of Nuremberg, beer tents. In fact, the Nuremberg *Volksfest* has two huge beer tents (and plenty of smaller ones) capable of sitting several hundred people at long tables and serving litre glasses of beer. Food is available and at the distant end of the tent is a large stage from which bands perform throughout the day. As the beer flows so the audiences become more lively and when we stopped off on our way back to the hotel after that game against Bremen it was only right to join in the dancing on the tables despite the sun stroke. Some members started to wave our flag around and someone invited them onto the stage as the band played, although the security team obviously disagreed that this was a good idea, eventually chasing them away. As the band finished their set and we had sampled the large beers we tried again to call it a night.

The following morning we awoke with a new mission. The previous evening, fearing going to bed too early, we had dropped into the excellent *Bierstüble* opposite our hotel. We had become well-acquainted with this extremely small bar on several previous visits and had the pleasure of sitting there speaking to the locals and the hospitable landlord, Ernesto. Not-surprisingly, when a large group of us enter the premises, Ernesto offers us a warm welcome, although does so with a somewhat perplexed look that suggests that he is unsure how more than a few people can physically fit into the bar. However, he must also like the fact that we generally stay in his bar far longer than would be medically recommended as healthy. This is largely due to the fact that, for some reason (I'm a customer not a publican), the excellent draught beer brewed in the nearby town of Leinburg, takes an inordinate amount of time to pour from the single tap. If you're desperately in need of a beer then you will be frustrated by this, as we were on our initial visits, but now wise to this problem we order a bottled drink while waiting. The fact that everybody, none more so than Ernesto himself, takes this for granted and is totally at ease about the time taken to pull a drink, is congruent with the relaxed nature of Nuremberg.

That particular night in the *Bierstüble*, we'd had a conversation with a regular who, impressed with our knowledge of 1.FCN and Herbert's Nuremberg heritage, told us that we should visit the grave of Max Morlock to pay our respects to the legendary player.

Maximilian Morlock was born in Nuremberg and played for 1.FCN from 1940 to 1964, accumulating approximately 900 games for *Der Club*. He was a member of the German championship winning teams of 1948 and 1961, finishing his career as a thirty-eight year old in 1964.

In 1954 Morlock sparked the revival of the German national team in what became known as 'the miracle of Bern'. Playing in the World Cup Final, the Germans were quickly 2-0 down against Hungary. However, after eleven minutes Morlock pulled a goal back and the Germans went on to win 3-2. In all he played twenty-six times for the national side, scoring twenty-one goals. In 1961 he was voted German footballer of the year. Max Morlock died in 1994 aged sixty-nine.

His fame in Nuremberg lives on through the memories of those who saw him play and who knew him as a true gentleman. Many *Clubberer* constantly campaign for the stadium to be renamed after their hero, even though the majority of them never saw him play. Such is the greatness that this man possessed and bestowed upon his team and city.

Having being guided to the small church and graveyard only a couple of stops from our hotel, we found the grave to be like the stories we had heard of the man himself – understated and straightforward. Without signs of his importance, and buried in the family grave of his wife, one gets the feeling that it is more fitting that the grave of someone who was so well-respected is no different than those around it. Max Morlock's legendary status lives on in the memories, stories and references to his greatness, not in a highly ornate tombstone.

Later that day we took the train out of town to eventually arrive at Buchschwabach, home village of Armin and his fan club *Clubfreunde* Buchschwabach. We were joined by a few members of this new fan club and also representatives of 1.FCN who thanked us for our continuing support. Among them was Jürgen. It is part of his role to give up vast amounts of his time to represent 1.FC Nürnberg at fan club events. As there are so many fan clubs, and as many of them have extremely active social calendars, Jürgen is kept busy, sometimes attending events each night. On any given weekend there are requests for 1.FCN representation at several meetings or drinking sessions. Jürgen does his best to please but some are inevitably left disappointed. On this day we had been lucky.

We returned home to the UK disappointed with the result of the game we had seen but delighted to have once again seen so much of the city and shared good times with so many people. At this stage we were largely oblivious to the signs that this season would be a real struggle for 1.FC Nürnberg, although subconsciously we knew that the *Bundesliga* and *Pokal* campaigns would not hold the excitement of the previous season. Our interest had, however, expanded and the UEFA Cup would hold our attention over the coming months. We'd sung about the European competition as the previous season ended in glory. We'd then kept the songs and the anticipation in our thoughts throughout the long summer. Somehow we had also managed to make the close season a more bearable experience.

Almost holding the DFB Pokal

Chapter 11

Europapokal

Erste Runde Bukarest, zweite Runde Rom,
in Kopenhagen schellt das Telefon,
vielleicht nach Rotterdam,
vielleicht nach Mailand,
vielleicht auch Teneriffa eine Woche Sandstrand!
Europapokal, Europapokal, Europapokal, Europapokal,
Europapokal, Europapokal, Europapokal, Europapokal.

Translation:

First round Bucharest, second round Rome,
In Copenhagen the telephone rings,
Maybe to Rotterdam,
Maybe to Milan
Maybe also a week in Tenerife on the beach.
European Cup, European Cup, European Cup… (etc)

The song is not quite up there with the lyrical genius of Lennon and McCartney and should certainly never be considered anything more than a ballad from the terrace but as football chants go, it is not a bad effort. Its origins are unknown although some say that it was originally sung by fans of Karslruhe when they appeared in the UEFA Cup in 1997. At least it made a pleasant change from hearing the English football chants of which so many seem to be about an opposition club. How must the Port Vale players feel if their fans are singing songs that are anti-Stoke City rather than pro-Vale? Are the fans so bored with what they are watching that they prefer to sing about the imaginary demise of their local rivals rather than concentrating on helping the players on the pitch to avoid their own demise? Or are they just so completely bereft of ideas?

Whoever penned the *Europapokal* chant, if indeed you do 'pen' a football chant rather than just make it up as you sing, can be credited with providing a hugely popular soundtrack to the end of the 2006-07 season and the first six months of the next in Nuremberg. As UEFA Cup qualification came and the fixtures were drawn and played, the *Clubberer* could be found singing this song until the *Europapokal* participation was over. Who cared if the places they were singing about would not be visited (with the exception of one)? What was important was the fact that *Der Club* were back in European competition.

We had quickly got the hang of the song and with a little help with the lyrics (found on the internet) we were able to join in with as much fervour and excitement as the rest of the fans at least for the first verse. We were now wondering if we would be able to get to any of the European games other than the final itself. Speaking to King Guinness before the season started I made a promise that should 1.FCN reach the UEFA Cup Final I would follow the example of his bicycle ride to Berlin and cycle all the way there. Was I serious? Could I really make such a journey, especially after the lame attempt at backpacking? Did I feel that I was safe in my promise because Nuremberg would not be good enough to reach the final? I was serious and I had a small amount of belief and a large slice of hope that *Der Club* would make it to the final in May 2008. After all, it would be held just sixteen miles from my home in The City of Manchester Stadium.

In the final weeks of the 2006-07 season the song would not go away. It kept coming into the heads of those who had heard it, such was its simplicity and the anticipation of events to come. Sometimes it became a little annoying when trying to concentrate on other tasks but as the summer came and went so the anticipation began to build and build.

In 1988 Nuremberg travelled to Rome and beat AS Roma 2-1. Qualification for the UEFA Cup had come via a fifth placed finish, the highest *Der Club* had managed since the glory of the 1968 championship. The victory in Rome, according to those who were there, was a deserved one for the fans who were packed into a small enclosure with a restricted view of the game. The home leg was lost 3-1 after extra-time but it is hardly conceivable that the *Clubberer* would have seriously thought that their place in Europe was anything other than the start of the return to former glories. But it was not. The mid-1990s would see to that.

When the draw was made for the first round of the 2007-08 competition I was sitting at my computer following the proceedings as near to live as the internet would allow me. Some *Clubberer* had gone to great lengths to find and share via various forums the possible teams Nuremberg could be drawn against. Apparently this was not as clear cut as putting the names of the eighty teams into a hat and pulling them out. Coefficients were given based on previous performances and the country from which each team came. Nuremberg's lengthy absence from European competition clearly gave them a low coefficient but I was still none the wiser and watched impatiently. It was all so new. When had a Port Vale fan ever had the opportunity to experience the excitement of a UEFA Cup draw? It can be considered at least a little strange that I found this such a momentous occasion but I paced up and down as I watched the screen, probably less nervous about the draw itself than I was about how one should react to it. There was, as far as I knew, no rule for what would be a good draw or a bad draw. In English cup competitions a good draw was either a very easy tie or a very difficult tie at a top club. But when you're looking at clubs from other countries how does one know who is good and who is not. Most of the teams will have finished high in their league but when you have never heard of the team, and in some cases only think you may have heard of the country from which they're from, it's easy to feel somewhat in the dark.

In some respects I was hoping for *Der Club* to be paired with a British team but also wanted a draw that would provide the best chance of making progress to the next round, the group phase of the tournament. Apart from wanting their team to win a cup competition outright, why should fans have an eye on the group phase? As a British contingent of *Clubberer* we should surely have been happy to settle for a game against Bolton or Everton, not too far from where most of us are based, or at a push Tottenham, a trip to London a far more realistic prospect than Germany for a midweek fixture. How fantastic it would be to travel to watch Nuremberg play in England, welcoming the team onto the pitch with a Union flag emblazoned with their logo. How puzzled the opposition fans would be. However, there was a nagging concern also. Some of us had spent plenty of time talking about the prospects of such games while downing beer after beer in Nuremberg. As the hospitality we were partaking of was so good it was only right to tell people they could stay with us if *Der Club* played in England. It is fair to say that there was the potential for a massive overcrowding problem if the draw was as many wished. The whole UEFA Cup affair could have required the hiring of army surplus tents and a local sports ground. It would be cheaper to take a couple of days off without pay and fly to somewhere else in Europe.

But the modern fan looks further forward than the next game and, in a similar vain to the chief executives and marketing gurus who now seem to run football clubs, the fans consider not just the next few weeks of the current season but also the next few seasons themselves. Of course, without any direct input to the club the average fan can formulate his own scenario of what could and should happen, safe in the knowledge that his expertise will never be put to the test. Football as big business and football as a game are now completely intertwined and both pull heavily on the fan whether it be on the strings of the hearts or those of the purse. In return fans feel they have the knowledge and the skills to take an 'informed' view on how their club should be progressing over the next six games, the next six months and even the next six seasons. They've done it on football management simulations on their computer so why should they not think they could do it for real?

I'm rubbish at computer simulations, probably because of lack of patience. Be it a case of car racing, alien invasion, flight simulation or football club management, boredom eventually sets in, risks are taken and a crash follows. However, I knew now that the best thing for 1.FCN would be to progress into the group phase of the UEFA Cup, getting through that and reaching at least the quarter finals. Coupled with a top five finish in the *Bundesliga* thus qualifying for Europe again the following season, a good UEFA Cup run would attract bigger sponsorship deals and the financial clout to entice a couple of big name players as well as very promising youngsters to the squad, building a team which would be consistently competing in the Champion's League in a few years time. In my mind I could also see how Port Vale could achieve the same outcome although I admit to my thinking being a little more creative and fanciful in this respect. Maybe a competition should be held for fans to enter their proposals for the development of their team, although I fear it would be won by the Abramovich's of this world whose policy would consist mainly of a blank cheque. But what a way to spend your time daydreaming. The glorification of the team you support takes just a few minutes of staring through the office window rather than getting on with your work. Who says football fans are increasingly difficult to please?

When Nuremberg were drawn against Rapid Bucharest the coincidence did not hit me straight away, busy as I was sending emails and text messages to those fellow fans who would not be in a position to be watching the draw being made. It was then a search on the internet to find out what I could about the opponents, somehow believing that any knowledge I could grasp would be useful to the progress of *Der Club*. It obviously would not be. Coincidence did not desert me for long as I started to whistle and then sing the *Europapokal* song. How prophetic the previous six months of singing had been. *Erste Runde Bukarest*.

There was never any chance of going to either Nuremberg for the first leg or Bucharest for the second leg. In fact, now armed with all of the dates for the UEFA Cup matches in the group phase, just in case 1.FCN got there, I would have to hope that Nuremberg would be coming to the UK in the next round as none of the midweek matches fell in line with my holidays. And without sounding too inhospitable I would have settled for an after work drive to London or Scotland rather than have to cater for too many *Clubberer* in our back garden. For now the television would have to do.

At the time of the first round draw, despite an inauspicious start to the *Bundesliga* season, there was still plenty of belief that *Der Club* would be going from strength-to-strength and making their mark in the league and on the European stage. Even after a 1:1 draw in the following day's *Bundesliga* game, away to Energie Cottbus, belief was still there. Watching live via the internet my joy at Andi Wolf's equalising goal five minutes from time was surely heard by the whole neighbourhood. Unfortunately so was my disgust at the disallowing of what appeared to me to be a perfectly legitimate Nicky Adler goal a few moments later. At least I had the decency to do most of my swearing in German, although the sentiment I am sure would have been clear to all who could not close their doors and windows quickly enough.

When the draw was made *Der Club* had won just one of the first five games. Performances had not been bad but confidence was beginning to falter. The defence which the previous season had been the joint meanest in the league was looking shaky with many blaming second choice Czech international goalkeeper Jaromir Blazek who had been brought in to replace the now departed Raphael Schäfer. Goals were also proving hard to come by and there looked to be a distinct lack of a cutting edge, even with the signing of Greek international Angelos Charisteas. Three weeks later when the first round, first leg tie was played in the *Frankenstadion*, Nuremberg were sitting in fifteenth place with just five points.

The atmosphere in the stadium as the Nuremberg and Bucharest players took to the pitch was something to behold. A huge banner covered much of the *Nordkurve*, flags were waving and *Europapokal* was coming across loud and clear. 1FCNUK were pumped up by it all – and this was just sitting watching it in Herbert's living room. Contrary to what many people seem to think, watching the game with a commentary that you don't understand is actually quite refreshing. For all you know the commentators and pundits could be reeling off bland and irrelevant facts, supported by inane comments and views of the game but at least when in German it is easier to be more or less oblivious to it although Herbert's tutting and shaking of his head does sometimes give the game away. I often wonder whether German commentators are as predicable as their English counterparts. If there is an English team or English player on the pitch do they make stupid stereotypical comments or make reference to the war as would certainly happen if an Englishman was remarking on German participation? Maybe the equivalent of an English comment about German efficiency would become a metaphorical sneer at English work habits – "The winger is not involved enough. He spends too much time away from his desk getting cups of tea. He needs to sharpen up his act." Alternatively, footballing stereotypes may come into play – "The English certainly won't look forward to scoring an equaliser and taking the game to a penalty shoot-out." Or what about reference to the war as so often seems to creep into British media coverage of the Germans – "They are under heavy fire at the moment but typically they're bringing on the American centre forward to try and help them out of the crisis."

As it was we watched the game without being bored by the usual diet of lowest common denominator satire, only listening out for the few words we recognised and providing our own expert views of course as both sides created chances in a lively game. There were plenty of opportunities to swear and shout at the television. There was also ample opportunity to throw our arms in the air only to bring them down to bury our heads within as another chance was not taken. So despite the 0-0 final score, there was at least some excitement as for the first time 1FCNUK and many other *Clubberer* witnessed *Der Club* in Europe. A win would have been nice but to at least not have conceded a goal was encouraging. Now a goal away from home in the second leg, maybe even two, would surely be enough to put Nuremberg into the group phase and more firmly back on the European football map.

By the time the second leg of the tie arrived two weeks later, any positives that had come out of the first leg were fading, or at least as far as the *Bundesliga* was concerned. Now in sixteenth position, third from bottom, already occupying a relegation spot and three points behind the team above, those who doubted the strength of 1.FCN were being joined by many, many others. There were of course a majority who still believed that they could explain away the poor start to the season in terms of changes in personnel, a new goalkeeper getting to know his defence and key injuries but their arguments were beginning to wear a little thin.

The game kicked-off at 3p.m. British time, which meant that under normal circumstances, I would not have been able to make it to the in-laws to catch the live coverage. As it happened however, by glorious accident rather than careful planning on my part, I was on a course that day. As with so many courses it failed to ignite any passions in the afternoon session with all delegates having being provided with a rather excellent and filling lunch. As the pace slowed, interest waned and the course faded. It was almost perfect as I set off with just forty-five minutes to make the thirty mile journey. Unfortunately less than half would be on motorway, the remainder along country roads with the inevitable obstacles of tractors, cyclists, horses and road works. But much to my shame and good fortune I made it in time for kick-off and what better way to forget a hair-raising journey than to hear the *Clubberer* in the stadium singing that familiar song. This pleasure turned to dismay after just fifteen minutes as the Romanians took the lead but the equaliser, and precious away goal, soon came from Peer Kluge. Shortly after half time another midfielder Zvjezdan Misimovic sent the Nuremberg faithful crazy (several laps of Herbert's living room for the TV viewers) as *Der Club* took the lead. These two goals helped to further diminish the argument about the new players at the club taking time to settle in; they had been two of the better performers so far this season and Misimovic would go on to be the leading scorer. As the game entered its final moments it became clear that 1.FCN would go through, even after Bucharest scored in the dying seconds. The away goals rule was enough.

I have met people who think the film version of Nick Hornby's *Fever Pitch* is funny. It is not, particularly if you just focus on the football side of the story. It's basically a documentary about proper football support as far as I'm concerned. People have been known to laugh at the part towards the end of the film when the main character launches himself through the air as his team, Arsenal, score the decisive goal to win the 1989 Championship. He embraces his friend and their celebrations are wild. This is not humour. This is what it's like to witness key victorious moments for your team. For each fan celebrating in that manner there is someone on the other side in complete and utter despair. I do believe that when Nuremberg scored their second goal in Bucharest I managed my first forward role since I was about eight.

For some reason, I was one of the many *Clubberer* who now thought that 1.FCN could go on to far better things this season, not just in the UEFA Cup but also in the *Bundesliga* and DFB *Pokal* too. The poor league form would be halted and a top five finish was still within reach and surely we would be capable of retaining that *Pokal* that we'd taken so long to get our hands back on. And European competition would take care of itself now as we'd done the hard part and made it through to the group phase. Maybe Premier League opposition would be handed to us with thousands of *Clubberer* flocking to England to see *Der Club* win on English soil. The draw could not come quick enough.

Sadly, all of this confidence and optimism represents the fairytale world into which football fans can sometimes be lured. Most of the time one can guard against it, trying to remain balanced and subjective but often needing some pessimism adding in to keep a check on things. However, a few simple emotions during and after a decisive game can cause all sorts of misguided aspirations. The evidence, of course, was against such dreams materialising. Two draws against the Romanians and in the last game two conceded goals, a lead thrown away and then, of course, the terrible league position. But it's the small things that the football fan holds onto. Hope springs eternal when your team is struggling.

Three days later and reality took its hold once again. 1FCNUK gathered in a local pub where we were able to watch Nuremberg's game against Bayern Munich. In fact what they were actually showing was Bayern Munich's 3-0 defeat of Nuremberg as the twenty British *Clubberer* present could do little more than look on in dismay, shaking our heads as the hosts had an easy ride. Other pub customers shook their heads at us wondering why we were so bothered.

Still, there was always the draw for the next phase of the UEFA Cup to look forward to. Even if the reality on the pitch was far less attractive than the scenarios conjured up in our minds, at least when the draw was made there would be the opportunity to dream and hope a little more. When drawn in the same group as Everton, albeit with the game to be played in Nuremberg, speculation immediately started about how the game would provide a benchmark for comparing the team we were following with the English Premier League. With both teams underperforming it would be an interesting encounter. The game would also surely be shown on English TV, especially important as none of our British-based members would be flying over for the match, having already paid for flights and accommodation for a few nights in Nuremberg for the next league game against Frankfurt.

Still without a home win, we held little hope of witnessing much of interest as we travelled over to Germany yet again. The usual socialising until the early hours did nothing to convince us the next morning that the *Bundesliga* form would return. As the teams were announced the lack of accomplished left back Pinola and solid centre half Wolf were of concern as was the form of lone striker Charisteas.

It seems unlikely that Angelos Charisteas will be remembered in football for anything other than his Euro 2004 exploits. Not that this is a bad thing. His quarter final winner against France and his winning goal in the final against Portugal provided Greece with an unexpected first major championship and turned Charisteas into a star almost overnight. However, as the next few seasons passed by it became increasingly clear that his goal against Portugal was the highlight of his career as far as his scoring feats would be concerned. Sure he would score other goals after 2004 for both club and country as he had before but that would have to be the one he was most remembered for on a wider scale. In some respects one also gets the feeling that he is something of a victim of his own success. *Clubberer* of course hoped that he would score goals to make him into something of a local hero in *Franconia* although by October 2007 it now seemed that this was something of a pipe dream. What people did not understand though is that while goals are part of his game, as they should be for a striker, Charisteas had other facets he could rely on too. Harry, as he is known, has strength, skill and a good work rate which should have endeared him to more fans and surely would have done if the team itself was achieving better results. But his reputation, that of the provider of Greek glory in 2004, had gone before him. Unfortunately, when the chips are down anyone who has been labelled a goalscorer previously is going to receive plenty of stick when goals are not going in, especially if he has got a lot of money and is rumoured to be on a rather large salary. The truth was however that Harry was never what could be termed a prolific scorer but has still managed a career average of a goal approximately every four games. With 1.FCN struggling for goals even a respectable return such as this would not be enough to impress some fans. As it was, Harry had scored just two goals so far, both against amateur side Victoria Hamburg in the first round of the cup and although many fans were beginning to question the acquisition of the Greek hero the fact remained that in the league, no centre forward at the club had yet found the net.

When the 45,000 plus crowd witnessed Nuremberg fall behind after just twelve minutes it was reasonable to fear the worst. Things were looking desperate but just eight minutes later Charisteas came good and stabbed home the equaliser. For the remainder of the first half *Der Club* rode their luck and managed to go in level despite a rather lacklustre display.

Any fears of a dire second half were quickly dispelled as further goals from Mintal and Misimovic within 10 minutes of the restart gave 1.FCN the cushion they needed to express themselves. Even substitute and Australian international Joshua Kennedy, or Jesus as the Australian media had labelled him due to his long hair and beard, got on the score sheet, although 'Jesus' was probably better suited as a remark of frustration when Kennedy missed a couple of great chances. Despite his height and experience in German football, the Australian never really got his Nuremberg career going, not least because an Achilles injury suffered in training immediately after signing in the summer of 2006 kept him out of action for a full year. However, when he did become available and was selected to play it was perhaps to his fortune that he did not get too many chances as he would have surely caused the fans of a poorly performing side even more frustration than Charisteas was doing.

In the bars of Nuremberg that night however there was much talk about how Harry's goal had allowed *Der Club* back into the game and how he had enabled 1.FCN to go onto a 5-1 victory, the first win since the second game of the season, and surely finally find the form that would now move them up the *Bundesliga* and back into a position which many assumed, and some even 'knew' they were more than capable of.

As for 1FCNUK, we could enjoy the rest of the weekend safe in the knowledge that the turning point had been reached. We walked through the streets sampling the delights of the Fish Festival and *Glühwein*. It is not clear how somewhere so far from the sea and with restaurants so clearly orientated to sell huge portions of meat to their customers can have a festival celebrating fish, with stall after stall selling all manner of fish dishes. However, in fine but cool autumn weather we naturally felt obliged to partake and were of course kept warm by the mugs of *Glühwein* on sale as the traditional winter drink was making its return as the days grew shorter.

Unfortunately the good feeling about *Der Club* lasted little longer than one of the small cups of spicy warm wine. Over the coming weeks three consecutive league defeats and a 2-0 victory for Everton in the *Frankenstadion* seemed to have sounded the death knell for the season. Gathering in our local pub in England several 1FCNUK members looked on as a reasonable performance against the Premier League side, in what looked to be a fantastic atmosphere in the stadium, ultimately ended with nothing. Something of an anti-climax as good-natured banter, advice about Nuremberg and well-wishing between *Clubberer* and Evertonians on our forum had provided us with a keen build-up to the game.

The death knell was silenced with a timely home defeat of Borussia Dortmund quickly followed by the first point of the UEFA Cup group phase away to Zenith St. Petersburg, another match necessitating a ridiculous break-neck drive to the in-laws after work. Once again the cruelness of hope had been sprung on the fans and now there was renewed talk about turning the season around.

Despite a league defeat at fellow strugglers MSV Duisburg, European glory dreams were firmly back just three days later when two Marek Mintal goals in the last ten minutes provided a 2-1 victory over Dutch side AZ Alkmaar. It was all starting to look just a little better as the home game against Hertha Berlin approached.

With our flights booked back in August we would have the chance not only to see the match but also to visit Nuremberg's renowned Christmas market – a brilliant piece of advance planning and a visit which we eagerly awaited. Unfortunately the *Bundesliga* officials responsible for deciding which games will be played on which day of any weekend do not recognise 1FCNUK plans as one of the factors they take into consideration. They provided Nuremberg with their fourth consecutive 5p.m. Sunday kick-off, exactly the same time we would have to be arriving at the airport to fly back to England.

This presented something of a test. While the social aspects of visiting Germany had been more than just enjoyable and had formed huge parts of our visits, I questioned whether I would really want to fly to the wonderful city if I was not going to see 1.FCN play. Of course, the Christmas market would surely be a wonderful thing and there were plenty of people to catch up with but it would surely be painful to be heading to the airport when everyone else was heading in the opposite direction. Some of us who were booked therefore dropped out, vowing to spend the money we saved on the hotel to travel to another game after Christmas. Those who did make the trip had a great time but not only had to miss the game but also sit in the airport just a few miles away awaiting their delayed flight. Frustrating but at least *Der Club* won with Charisteas still plugging away and starting the scoring after just five minutes.

Defeat the following week at the hands of Schalke saw 1.FCN finish the first half of the season in sixteenth place and in the relegation zone. With just four league wins to their name, how the draws of the previous season would have provided a welcome addition to the points total. However, 1.FCN still had the chance to remain in the UEFA Cup, a feat they achieved with a 3-1 away victory at Greek side Larissa five days before Christmas. This sparked something of a flight-booking frenzy the next day. The draw for the next round of the UEFA Cup was held at lunchtime with the matches scheduled for midweek in mid-February, a week in which I would be off work. With the *Bundesliga* having already announced the dates for the first few games after the Christmas break, a trip to Karlsruhe had been booked for the first weekend in February. Now I was hoping for a Nuremberg home fixture in European competition to enable me to watch a night of UEFA Cup glory ten days later. When drawn against the famous Benfica I was delighted but then frustrated that the first leg, the one I could get to, would be away from home. There was only one thing for it and that was to get a flight to Lisbon for the match. Within a couple of hours the plan was in place and flights were booked, all for a very reasonable price and not only would I be flying to Lisbon, I would be doing so via Nuremberg having watched the *Bundesliga* game against Hansa Rostock on the Saturday. Of course, it was not all plain sailing. When I informed Angela that I'd booked myself on a flight to Stuttgart, a train from Stuttgart to Nuremberg, a flight from Nuremberg to Majorca and then from Majorca to Lisbon before returning home a week later with a flight from Lisbon to Liverpool she was only mildly impressed. This did not last long when she realised that I would be in Lisbon on Valentine's Day while she would be stuck at home alone.

Before Nuremberg and Lisbon though there was the small matter of attempting to pick-up *Bundesliga* points at Karlsruhe. On a flight to Stuttgart the evening before the game, Iain and I ordered wine – they'd run out of beer – asking for two each expecting the miniature airline sized bottles. The flight was only just long enough to finish the larger bottles we'd been given but the wine was certainly enough to think that a midnight arrival at our hotel was no excuse for heading straight to bed and instead we hit the town. When we boarded a train to Karlsuhe the next morning three hours later than planned we found ourselves sitting in a carriage with several other *Clubberer* who had been aboard since Nuremberg. They had been well-stocked for the journey judging from the empty bottles surrounding them and the carrier bags full of additional bottles and sausages they still had remaining. It would have probably been better had they not recognised us as members of the British fan club but they did and we fought down the beer and sausages forced upon us. The *Clubberer* then lugged their provisions from the train and when we returned to the station in Karlsuhe after checking into our hotel they were now sharing their supplies with Karlsruhe fans and laughing and joking with a few police gathered to welcome any trains from Nuremberg. What a contrast this was to the scenes one would have witnessed outside railway stations when visiting fans arrived in the 1970s and '80s.

We eventually made our way to the stadium ahead of the drinkers as they seemed happy enough to leave their departure until the very last minute, probably to give them time to finish their supplies. Jürgen provided us with the match tickets and also those for the following week's game against Hansa Rostock and for the UEFA Cup tie in Lisbon. Today's game though, was of great importance. Desperate for points, *Der Club* had signed the giant Czech forward Jan Koller during the winter pause and despite his age it was hoped that his height and goal-scoring prowess would achieve that which the centre forwards already at the club had largely failed to do before Christmas. He would certainly have to take the place of Joshua Kennedy as the tallest outfield player at the club as the Australian, unimpressive in the few chances provided by Hans Meyer, had now been snapped up by Karlsruhe.

I'd always liked Koller. When I'd seen him playing against Nuremberg for Dortmund a few seasons before he'd not only scored two goals but was also a constant threat. For the Czech Republic he seemed to score goals for fun and with over fifty goals in less than ninety performances for his country and a similar goals to games ratio in club football he would hopefully add an Indian summer to his career at 1.FCN.

Naturally things did not work out like this. Koller caused problems in the air against Karlsruhe and most other teams he played against up until the end of the season but the ball seemed to have a habit of leaving his head and landing anywhere but at the feet of a Nuremberg player. As an imposing figure on the pitch there was no doubting Koller's presence but as an effective force in helping *Der Club* out of the doldrums – well he probably wished he was a little smaller to enable him to hide better.

Not that it was only Koller who could not find the net against Karlsruhe and other teams. That day the loyal travelling fans were rightly frustrated at having spent several hours on coaches and trains to stand in freezing conditions watching a team who were seriously underperforming even by the low standards they had set themselves so far that season. Patience was running out and just to test it a little further, Kennedy looked lively for the hosts. Not long after the biggest cheer of the day came from the *Clubberer* for a Kennedy miss, he scored his new team's second and left *Der Club* two points from safety behind the opponents for the following week, Hansa Rostock.

Yet there was still hope for some. Largely it came from the fact that there were still games to play against all relegation challengers. That night in Karlsruhe, for Iain and I, hope came in the form of the local beers but even these were not able to fully convince us. At least the social aspects of our support remained strong as we were provided with a tour of some excellent bars by a Preston and Karlsruhe fan and his German wife. Kirk had made contact through our forum and shared humorous tales about his experience of moving from north-west England to Germany, with plenty of advice in case we ever wanted to follow in his footsteps.

I was a little more optimistic the following week after flying into Stuttgart again and then taking a train to Nuremberg on a beautiful morning. Maybe the sun and blue sky would convince the players, too, that today's game was yet another opportunity to turn the season around. Their minds however seemed to be on the game against Benfica the following Thursday and, despite a Jan Koller opener, the lead lasted just nine minutes. Things were beginning to look rather desperate but still hope lingered. If only we could get a result in Lisbon then who knows where the season could go.

Now with time to spare in Nuremberg I could explore and Armin gave me a room for a night in the hamlet of Buchschwabach. The next day he inadvertently provided me with what is surely part of the answer to why the German national team has greater success than the English. On a crisp Sunday morning, perhaps trying to excuse his performance in goals after several 1FCNUK members had appeared in a second game for the Rot-Schwarz Franken Oldstars back in October, Armin showed me some of his personal footballing heritage. In that last game we had played, the kits had been new – black and white in honour of Port Vale Armin had told us after announcing he would today be player coach and put himself in goals. An early acrobatic save gave us hope that if the rest of us could chip in with a few goals then the match could this time be won. However, the course of the game and the final outcome were pretty much the same as on our first outing and as the opponents started to shoot for fun, Armin both lost interest and avoided getting in the way of some of the more powerful shots.

Now, with the intention of showing me some of the beautiful countryside to the south of Nuremberg, Armin also showed me several frost covered village football pitches of a variety of teams for which he had played or coached in his younger days. Each of them had the main pitch and at least one training pitch. The striking thing about it all was that the training pitches, without exception, not only appeared to be better quality than those pitches reserved for Saturday afternoon local league games but were also floodlit whereas the match pitches were not. In England it often seems to be the case that the best floodlit pitch cannot be touched until the day of the game and the training pitches are often little more than mowed fields. That or the training and matches take place on the same pitch rendering any semblance of anything other than a muddy slog all but impossible. The Germans clearly took training very seriously even at the grass roots of the game, something which Armin could clearly see that we did not by half time of each match we had played for his team of footballing hopefuls and hopeless cases.

Two days before my flight to Lisbon I sat in a favoured Nuremberg bar listening to the radio with the landlord and the only other customer. When the music broke for the news I understood little of it but then came an announcement from *Der Club*. I understood enough German, tone of football reports and looks upon faces to realise that the Hans Meyer era was over. Just two games after the winter break had finished and Meyer had been allowed to add players to his squad he was now deemed unsuitable to keep the club in the *Bundesliga*.

It is true some fans were beginning to lose patience with Meyer though the majority were supportive of the coach but less so of some of the players. After all, Hans Meyer had gained *Der Club* their first silverware for thirty-nine years and had taken them into European competition. Now on the eve of the biggest European game since the 1960s he was out of a job. If not surprised, many were devastated. The man had given hope to 1.FCN and sustained it for longer than many of his predecessors. He was charismatic, loved by the fans and the media and was undoubtedly the force behind the uplift in fortunes. However, having taken the team from relegation contenders, to cup winners and UEFA Cup qualifiers, then back to relegation contenders in two years the senior management of 1.FC Nürnberg had lost patience, clearly wanting to keep top flight football in the city at all costs. Whether Hans Meyer could do this would now never be known but the fans knew he had done it before and he was one of the main reasons for keeping alive hopes that relegation could be avoided again. Unfortunately for Meyer his managerial style seems to have not helped his cause.

Quite authoritarian in his ways it appears that while there were the good times, the good results and enthusiastic crowds, those among the management and players who disliked his style could barely be heard. When the results started to falter these same people started to be heard much more clearly and any amount of unrest, coupled with the desperate league position, saw Hans Meyer's reign come to a rather abrupt and sad end. As more people entered the bar that night there were mixed feelings.

There was one man who could not see what all the fuss was about. I don't remember his name but I think he was from Essex (highly probable as he was certainly a Manchester United fan) and he was something to do with the toy industry, visiting the Nuremberg Toy Fair. He found it difficult to accept that I could travel to Germany to support a football team and asked me why I did not follow my local team. When I explained that I did he seemed perplexed that this was not Manchester United and the irony seemed completely lost on him that his allegiance was to a team two hundred miles from his home. However, he was a pleasant guy and took no offence when I informed him that I thought he was a complete and utter bastard staying in the hotel I usually stayed in but had been priced out by businessmen such as himself. We managed to drink long enough for his wife who was travelling with him to get to her third call to his mobile phone telling him that he should be in bed as he was working the next morning. I felt quite proud that I'd managed to lead him astray and considerably reduce the amount of time he would spend in his already extortionately priced bed!

Hans Meyer's replacement, Thomas von Heesen, could not have had a more difficult start to his role as coach. The game in Lisbon would be followed just forty hours later with the thankless task of an away game in Bremen and the necessary flight between the two cities. But at least the players would have their flights paid for and would be flying at reasonable hours of the day on direct flights. My passage to Lisbon involved a

4.30am start to get to Nuremberg airport in time for an early flight to Majorca where rather than finding a beach I'd be boarding another flight an hour or so later to Lisbon, such is the lot of the football fan trying to keep the costs down while seeing as many games as possible.

The warmth and brightness of midday Lisbon contrasted sharply with the icy and dark Nuremberg streets just a few hours before. As I awaited other 1FCNUK members at the airport, a few *Clubberer* were gathered to see the 1.FCN team arrive. A few club songs started and fizzled out as the players made their way to their waiting coach. So this was what European away days were like then. Little to get excited about so far.

However, later on as the warm day became dusk more and more *Clubberer* were gathering in the city centre drinking outside bars and the banter was beginning. An atmosphere was coming together and it would surely have been even greater if several hundred Nuremberg fans had not decided to go to watch Sporting Lisbon play Swiss side Basel, frustrating the Swiss fans by singing Nuremberg songs louder than the outnumbered Basel fans could sing for their own team.

As we stood in a side street drinking bottles of beer bought from a small snack bar owner who must have thought he'd won the lottery, Bavarian TV filmed the *Clubberer* singing, drinking and enjoying their evening. Talking to several fans they were amazed that there were Brits who'd made the effort to travel to Portugal to support their team. Several members of the Red Devils fan club wanted to relate stories about their experiences of English football in bygone days when occasionally they'd travel over to England to marvel at the hooligan firms of West Ham and Millwall. Of course they were now well-behaved individuals who were only interested in the football, so they said as yet another crate of beer was dragged onto the street. Sure enough, though, they replaced their empty bottles in the crates and returned them to where they had come from. I mused over how many members of the London firms they talked of would be able to converse as well with a foreigner in that person's language. Would they have respect for European hooligan firms and talk about them with such excitement as tales of street fights and run-ins with the police were retold as if they were yesterday? And would they then put their empty beer bottles neatly away ready for recycling?

That night I also spoke to Heino Hassler. I'd met him on a few occasions in Germany and he was always happy to offer advice and talk about *Der Club*. He had been a member of the *Seerose* fan club in its more notorious times but was now extremely affable with the interests of 1.FCN at heart. This was not his first trip to Lisbon to watch *Der Club*. In 1962 Heino had flown over for the European Cup quarter final second leg tie, a rather unusual trip for anyone to be making in those days, never mind a six year old child. However, Heino's mother was an air hostess for Lufthansa and had secured his passage to allow him to see maybe for the first of many occasions in his life time, 1.FCN turn great hope into despair. Having a 3-1 lead from the first leg it would be fair to say that there was a good chance of *Der Club* making it through to the semi-finals but the class of Eusebio's Benfica turned the tie around that night as the hosts controlled the game and finished the proceedings as 6-0 victors in front of 70,000 fans. Heino and everybody else was certain that such a fate would not await Nuremberg the following evening.

The next day provided an opportunity to take in some culture. A walk through winding, narrow streets and passages climbing up one of the cities seven hills into the Alfama district was rewarded with magnificent views over the city from the imposing Castelo de Sao Jorge. Tourists photographed each other at this high vantage point and even I, with my fear of heights, was enjoying the sunshine and vistas. It all felt rather strange, too. Here we were in the middle of February, in beautiful warm sunshine gazing upon this historical Portuguese city, passing other visitors every few metres with the Franconian greeting of *Servus*. There were few people we passed who were not wearing an item of clothing identifying them as *Clubberer* and as we made our descent towards the streets below, the distant songs of the 1.FCN faithful could be heard rising above the rooftops. Restless fans now ended their sightseeing and headed toward the sounds emanating from the Praca Dom Pardo IV. They were ready for the game and ready to join the singing.

Arriving in the large square with its central column and ornate fountain, it was clear that many had commandeered positions at bars around the perimeter though most had purchased crates, bottles and cans from various other outlets. And they certainly needed the liquid as the heat was beating down. The singing continued and the crowd grew in size as the whole square became a sea of red and black. This then was what the European away day was all about.

The authorities had placed huge bins around the square as receptacles for beer bottles and the *Clubberer* dutifully filled them with their empties. A few police arrived, largely to prevent the crowd spilling onto the road and stopping the traffic flowing. Somebody had a football and to great cheers it was being kicked high into the air time and time again by whoever it happened to land nearest as it fell back to earth. Unfortunately, after a couple of bounces too close to the passing traffic it soon landed close to a police officer who failed to see the funny side and stopped the game before it ended in tears.

Amidst all of the fun I had almost forgotten the fear I held inside ahead of this game. Not the fear of defeat of course but the fear of the hell that would torment me inside the stadium – the hell that was the steep high stand for which I had mentally prepared but now I feared, not nearly enough.

It was time to head to the game and rendezvous en route at our hotel with the others. Earlier, a time had been set to leave the hotel. Somehow I arrived twenty-five minutes before that time giving myself the perfect opportunity for last minute mental preparation for the huge psychological task ahead of me. I opened the hotel room door, and was about to lie on the bed, close my eyes and have one final visualisation of my triumphant entry into the stand. Then I realised that a day in the sun, mostly walking and standing, coupled with a few shots of local Ginga and a couple of pints had made me somewhat sleepy. Lying down and visualising would surely lead to me falling asleep and missing the game. I panicked. The hotel room was warm. I was tired. In less than one hour I would be entering the stadium.

Visualising was now out the question. A little way down the street from the hotel was a small bar. A large brandy to settle my nervous stomach and then probably too much rather excellent port recommended by the English speaking, Sporting Lisbon supporting, barman were now becoming my main weapon against my fear. When a glance through the doorway along the street revealed that my friends were not yet waiting for me, I indulged further and then a little further still when they joined me for a 'quick one'.

The metro ride to the *Estadio de Luz* and the walk through the turnstiles was easy and something of a blur. Climbing the internal staircases, it was clear that we were gaining plenty of height but I was feeling immune to it all. Even walking into the stand itself was, although not quite as easy as I had wished it to be, relatively easy compared to that day in Munich's Allianz Arena. It seemed that few people were bothering finding their allocated seats and so I quickly sat myself down on the nearest one I could find and told the others I'd see them later. After a few minutes of acclimatisation I even had the bottle to stand up. I like to think that the mental preparation had worked but I'm not convinced it did so alone. But here I was, feeling safe, relaxed and happy in the *Estadio da Luz*. So I wasn't quite as far back as my allocated ticket and maybe I did have to ask a group of young fans behind me if they wouldn't mind waving the 1FCNUK flag around a bit for me but I was ready to witness the game. If I could raise myself to a new level, quite literally, then surely 1.FCN could do the same and win the match.

The 1-0 defeat was only slightly more disappointing than the manner in which it happened and the fact that the home fans had not really bothered to turn up. In the early stages of the game the *Clubberer* had done all they could to lift the team but when police entered the stand with batons after arguments between fans and officials, the fans were almost silenced. Only 25,000 witnessed Benfica score with their first shot on goal just before half time, a harmless effort that somehow trickled through goalkeeper Blazek and into the Nuremberg net. *Der Club* had looked the brightest in the first half but as the match went on it was clearly not going to be their night. And even Angelos Charisteas, kept out by injury, would not be able to repeat his heroics of the Euro 2004 Final in this stadium. What was an anti-climax following the afternoon of revelry in the city centre was now only buoyed by that familiar feeling of hope – the hope that the 1-0 scoreline could be overturned the following week in the *Frankenstadion*.

As 1FCNUK made their way home so, too, did many *Clubberer* although there were of course those who made their way to Bremen with the team. Watching once again on the internet, a 2-0 defeat against the second placed team ended a thoroughly miserable week for *Der Club*. Points were hard to come by, the strike force still looked weak, the trap door was open in the UEFA Cup and the position in the *Bundesliga* was even more precarious. And now there was no Hans Meyer to save the day.

The home leg against Benfica clearly had so much resting on it. As 1FCNUK watched once again from Herbert's living room Nuremberg looked capable of turning the tie around. The performance was far more like everyone knew they were capable of and as the game went on *Der Club* came into the ascendancy. It was Charisteas who broke the deadlock in the fifty-eighth minute and when Saenko made it 2-0 in the sixty-fifth the *Frankenstadion* and a living room in central England went wild. Finally, as the end of February approached, the season had really got going. The way the team were playing oozed confidence and even a little class. 1.FCN were back and going through to the quarter finals.

In just a few minutes we went through many of the emotions of a football fan. The relief at making the tie level, the joy of taking the lead, the anxiety of holding onto that lead as the final whistle approached. But because it was *Der Club* and because *Der Club* are notorious for the ability to flatter to deceive we were not to feel the emotion of ecstasy of victory at the final whistle. The final moments of the game made sure of that. Like the whole season in microcosm, those last couple of minutes saw 1.FCN so close to turning their fortunes around but then in the eighty-ninth minute an attempted clearance in the penalty area by defender Glauber somehow hit Koller and rebounded to Benifca player Cardozo who scored the vital away goal for the Portuguese. With hope now wafer thin Nuremberg pushed forward deep into added time but were caught out as Benfica broke forward and made it 2-2.

A silent disbelief filled the room. We stared at the screen unable to speak of or even quite believe what we had seen. Now would have been a good time to not be bothered. We could then have simply sighed and walked away having seen a good cup tie with a twist of fate at the end. But we were far too involved to do this and all we could do was feel devastated that our team had not won, just as those 40,000 or so fans in the stadium would do. It was one of those moments when you just hate being a football fan. The *Europapokal* dream was over.

European away day - sun, beer and a big square in Lisbon

Chapter 12

The long road home

When your team are fighting relegation every defeat, or even draw as the hunt for points becomes more desperate, can make the journey home feel like a long one. All you want to do is get back so you can do something other than travelling and get the dire situation faced by your team out of your mind. You know deep down that this will be almost impossible as everything you try to do is punctuated by a feeling of nausea that the season is practically over already. After a few hours, if you're lucky, or sometimes days if you really want to beat yourself up about something completely out of your control, you start to come round and hope takes over again. In your mind you run through the remaining fixtures and calculate the points your team will gain and the points their opponents will gain and start to believe that everything will work out well in the end. The following week you go through the same procedure after your first prediction turned out wrong but again hope prevails.

Flying back from Germany it never seemed to matter whether Nuremberg had won drawn or lost. We'd still got great memories of the weekend away and at least the flight provided time to catch up with some sleep. However, as the support became more serious the journey home started to feel longer when the results had not materialised as we'd hoped.

It was quite strange really because I'd more or less become accustomed to the feeling with Port Vale. In successful times a defeat had been something of a devastating blow and as the 'glory days' started to slip away, each defeat hurt and piled on more misery. But then it became almost accepted. Maybe it was because for Port Vale it often felt like the results on the pitch were only of secondary importance. Of course, positive results would help the situation but it was the club's very survival as Port Vale FC that became more crucial. As money poured into the English Premier League the ability of lower league teams to compete and hold on to any talent that came into their ranks diminished. So did their ability to remain financially viable as sky-high wage demands filtered down to even the most mediocre of players. The fans are now often left satisfied if their club is still in business from one season to the next.

Yet sometimes we forget this very basic necessity as the season goes on and from game-to-game still get the sick feeling following defeat. With Port Vale struggling even more than Nuremberg, 2007-08 was turning into the worst season in memory. Even had I (and some other 1FCNUK members) only being following the fortunes of one of the teams it would have been depressing but as fans of two teams who were both spending most of the season in a relegation position the only way we could suffer more would be if the two teams had not moved up the table by the end of the season.

For Port Vale many of the players had worked hard and there were a few encouraging glimpses that, just like Nuremberg, the second half of the season might see a change of fortune in the league. As with Nuremberg, Port Vale had already by this stage of the season been knocked out of the Cup, Vale doing so against non-league opposition and thus playing a major role in keeping the 'romance' of the English FA Cup well and truly alive. Unfortunately they had also maintained their tradition of never qualifying for the UEFA Cup and so unlike Nuremberg did not have the pleasant distraction of that competition to at least provide a couple of decent results. Vale first hit the relegation positions after just three games and then only briefly flirted with the idea of building a successful escape plan before finally succumbing to the bottom two. This did not mean however that everyone gave up hope. Even entering the final weeks of the season, three consecutive wins saw them move off the final place that they had occupied for fourteen games. While there is still a mathematical chance of surviving there is still some hope. I was left to contemplate the figures of two clubs and create ambitious scenarios which would see both avoid the drop at the end of the season. It was not only the fans who would have a long road home. End of season survival for the clubs seemed a dream far beyond the horizon as Easter and the final reckoning approached. Everyone could only hope that it was not too far.

Now with the UEFA dream over 1.FCN could concentrate fully on the *Bundesliga*. How hard would it be for the players to pick themselves up after the disastrous ending to the Benfica tie? Surely they could take so much from their good performance that in the remaining fourteen *Bundesliga* matches enough points could be amassed to reel in some of the teams above and make a miraculous escape even without Hans Meyer at the helm. A good way to have started would have been to beat Energie Cottbus, the team sitting two places below *Der Club* at the foot of the league. Even by simply beating other relegation-threatened teams Nuremberg would surely stay up. Wouldn't they?

It seems stupid to have expected a win now. When only four league games had been won from the previous twenty the position was far from enviable although admittedly it was just a little better than that of Cottbus. Unfortunately, though, the game ended in a draw and watching live coverage via the internet made it even more frustrating. At least in a crowd it was easier to let out your frustrations with those around you, especially as Nuremberg's lead lasted for just a minute. The following week however a group of us would again be flying out to Germany for another match in Hanover.

The previous season we had witnessed a victory in the AWD Arena on a day which allowed us to test our vocal chords to the limit the week before the Cup Final appearance. The weather was hot and the spirits were high. This time, flying in late on a Friday night in fierce winds and driving rain we only just made it to a bar a few yards from the hotel hoping that by the next morning the meteorological conditions would have improved. They had not, and a couple of hours avoiding them was followed by a tricky walk to the stadium as the wind and rain stung our faces. Naturally we took shelter in a couple of watering holes along the way but even a few pre-match drinks could not relax our nerves and lift the mood.

As the wind tore at our backs in the stadium we had with us a couple of newcomers. Despite the conditions they were excited but hadn't really got the hang of things as they yelled at the Hanover centre half to get stuck into the forward (Koller I think) because he looked like a useless carthorse. When I pointed out their error (the one which involved the team they were shouting for, not their judgment of Koller) they settled down and were almost as gutted as the rest of us when the final whistle signalled a 2-1 defeat. The wind and rain seemed less important now as we headed back to the city centre. They were there alright, threatening to soak us and lift us from our feet but nothing was soaking in more than the reality of the situation facing *Der Club*. I was finally realising that escape from the relegation zone was looking more and more improbable. For the first time I was becoming resigned to the fact and recognised that in the grand scheme of things it wasn't all that important. Disappointing yes but there would still be 1.FCN next season and whether they were in the *Bundesliga* or *2.Bundesliga,* I and other members of 1FCNUK would be giving our support. As once again we took refuge from the weather in the bars of Hanover I naturally started to calculate that of course *Der Club* could make their escape. Thankfully I had had enough to drink to not be able to remember if I thought they could even just about qualify for Europe again. But I probably did.

A hangover is always a good way to bring one back to reality. For me that reality was the worrying gaps beginning to appear between the bottom few places and safety as I glanced at a newspaper while walking to a bakery for a cheap breakfast. And all around me there was litter, branches and small pieces of rubble. What had become of our German dream? The high performing football team, the bright mornings, the clean streets? Little did we know that the storm of the day and night before was the tail end of Hurricane Emma which wreaked havoc across central Europe even causing deaths. Suddenly defeat in a game of football did not seem so bad. I guess it was just one of the miracles of alcohol that we'd managed to not notice the worst of the weather as we returned to our hotel in the early hours of the morning.

The next two games would have to be watched via the internet as a goalless draw against Hamburg and a 4-1 whitewash at the hands of Leverkusen in the BayArena, which was thankfully on Sunday afternoon and thus made it all but impossible to attend, added to the 1FCNUK woes. Not that I would have preferred to watch the Leverkusen game on a screen rather than in the stadium had there been any choice about it. It's just that with the increasing regularity of our visits to Germany it almost naturally followed that the number of nights spent drinking until the early hours of the morning were also increasing, with each trip treated like a mini-holiday. If you party the nights away in a holiday resort for a week or so each year in the summer that is one thing but we were getting to the stage where we were doing it every few weeks on a Friday and Saturday night with precious little time to recover before the working week. I for one was certainly starting to wish I was at least ten years younger. If only there was some way of getting a flight the morning of the game and one straight back afterwards then some of the liver pounding nights out could be avoided. Obviously we were under no obligation to go out and drink to excess each time we visited Germany but on the other hand visiting bars was the best way to meet people, discuss football and maybe even pick up a little German, too. The beer fits in quite naturally. It was also a means (in a purely sociable rather than problem drinking sort of way) of easing the pain after a glance at the league table. The defeat in Leverkusen left *Der Club* one place above bottom club Duisburg, courtesy of having scored one more goal than them. It was looking as bad as ever, particularly with the next two games being against Bochum, some thirteen points above Nuremberg, followed by table topping Bayern Munich. Although both games were at home, few expected much from them.

The Bochum game over Easter weekend saw a large group fly from the UK. For several it was their first time and some were not even bothered about the game itself. They had flown over for the pre-nuptial celebrations of two members, Steve and Gail, who thought it would be a good idea to party the weekend away in Nuremberg. Some of us just hoped that the football would not spoil the fun. On arrival we hit the town, this time with a real excuse. Steve, a former holiday rep from Derry, Northern Ireland has a habit of singing and break dancing when under the influence. He had memorably had something of a singing competition in a Nuremberg beer cellar on a previous visit when a glamorous older lady from a family group decided to sing something quite operatic probably as a gift for one of her party. Steve immediately saw this as his cue to wow everyone with a drunken rendition of Danny Boy. I think most of the packed bar applauded out of politeness to enable them to then get on with their drinking and eating. Steve though saw it as evidence that they clearly wanted more and dazzled his captive audience with a just about comprehensible version of the The Fields of Athenry. Fortunately, on that night there was no room for break dancing. However, in the early hours before the Bochum game a handful of us found ourselves in an almost deserted Karoake bar. It smacks of desperation when you enter such a premises for another drink, particularly as the very fact that you are in there at all suggests that you've had far too many already. Of course, when Steve realised it was a Karaoke bar his glazed eyes lit up a little and he immediately tried to grab a microphone. After he realised that the microphone was going to be hogged by a couple who clearly spent their whole lives practising to try to entertain drunken football fans at 3a.m., our own singing star gave up and lay down on what was supposed to be a dance floor. We were about to be treated to a display of his finest moves when another member of our group decided to help him to spin round, grabbing his legs and inadvertently slamming our street dancing hero's head straight into the stage. The only thing more miraculous than the fact that he was not knocked unconscious was the fact that he seemed not to notice. I mention these shenanigans not because they are macho manifestations of nights out on the town but because there was not much fun to be had in the stadium itself on the Saturday afternoon.

There was still clearly belief amongst the *Clubberer* as over 43,000 packed out the stadium but what we witnessed on the field of play was not encouraging. A goal down after five minutes and an equalizer a few minutes later then that was it. *Der Club* managed to keep things tight in defence and at last showed considerable improvement in this department but too many errors when going forward saw the game end level.

Before the game we had been approached to see if any of our members would like to appear in a large rubber coke bottle on the pitch trying to compete against another coke bottle as part of the half-time entertainment. The performance of Jason and Steve with two other fans hidden in one of the Coke bottles in a race towards the goal with a large ball was as good as it got for 1FCNUK, although I'm sure that the majority of the attendance in the *Frankenstadion* don't recall that our boys led their bottle to victory or even that Jason raised his arms as he emerged from it before falling to his knees and kissing the pitch.

Unfortunately what many fans will remember are the strange scenes on the *Nordkurve* as the Ultras decided to stage a silence for the opening period of the match. Today there was no choreography, no flag waving and for much of the first half they had also decided that there would be no singing or getting behind the team. It was their way of showing how important they were to 1.FC Nürnberg and of showing their dismay at the current state of affairs at the club. Via the internet and word of mouth the Ultras had requested that others join in with their action but not everyone agreed with it and probably more importantly not everyone knew about it. What occurred was to be one of two moments in little over two weeks when 1.FC Nürnberg could have no pride in their Ultra fan movement.

As the fans who wanted to sing and cheer did so, there was clearly some anger from the terracing of Block 7 and the seating of Block 8 where the majority of the Ultras were gathered. Pockets of fans then started singing songs clearly directed at the Ultras and fingers were raised on both sides. Even when the Ultras broke their silence there was still an atmosphere and in Block 8 trouble occurred as maybe not before time the sides in what was essentially a battle to be the controlling voice in this block became clearly defined. It did however at least bring the situation to a head. It also showed that while the importance of the Ultras in creating an atmosphere was undeniable, there were many, many fans who wanted to make up their own mind about when and what to sing.

Members of 1FCNUK had not travelled to Germany to be silent in our support and I for one have a clear belief that when the team is struggling it needs support more than ever. As a Port

Vale fan it was not an entirely alien situation to me. How many times had I seen the loyal fans booing the team or individual players as results and performances reflected a low confidence which would subsequently become lower still? That evening I was talking to a *Clubberer* in a bar and he told me that he was one of the silent Ultras in the stadium. When I asked him why and what he thought the action would achieve he seemed to have little idea other than saying that it was important. His excellent English meant that he most certainly understood my gripe about people not getting behind the team and he was almost apologetic as the conversation ended. Now he was probably not representative of the hardcore Ultras but he was young and impressionable and clearly fitted with what had been described as those fans who go along with the current 'fashion' just to belong. For me football is deadly serious, not just something to use for a statement that you belong to a group or a movement. It's about people and bringing people together and it's about getting the ball into the net and beating the opposition. Why had Jason kissed the pitch after the Coke bottle victory? Because he had been victorious of course. And that mattered. If there is a stone or a can in the street it has to be kicked into the grid or underneath a parked car as a commentary is instantly triggered in one's head. "And that should seal it. Goulding slides the ball [tin can] past the 'keeper [a dog turd] and into the net [a hole in a fence]. Port Vale will surely now clinch Champion's League glory." And so on. Whether you're walking down the street or are part of an eight-legged caterpillar advertising the world's most famous soft drink, if there is something to use as a ball and something to use as a goal it is the natural instinct of most football fans to make sure the ball hits the back of that net. With the 1FCNUK self-proclaimed *Fussballgott* and our all action former holiday rep inside, there was only ever going to be one winner. It's just a shame that issues off the pitch were being taken too seriously by some in the stadium that day. But having said that there would always be something to argue about even if the rubber bottle game ever became mainstream. At least 1FCNUK had one thing to cheer.

The pre-nuptial celebrations of the weekend were in sharp contrast to the match and result. Plenty of fun was had and despite a trip to Nuremberg zoo to keep some of the female members of the party happy, as snow lay on the ground (and most animals were therefore well out of sight indoors) the tradition of keeping the cultural aspects of a group trip to a minimum were upheld. It was simply too cold to do much else anyway.

The result against Bochum did not bode well for the visit of Bayern Munich the following Saturday. As it was the Easter holidays I would also be attending the game but returned to England for forty-eight hours in the interim to attend to a few things at home. Now of course it would normally be the obvious thing to actually stay in Germany for an extra couple of nights and not have the hassle or expense of flying back and forth but this was all part of a grand scheme hatched much earlier in the season to ensure that I had plenty of options for this final week in March. Some members were travelling by train to Vienna before flying home (obviously to make up for the cultural void created by a weekend of partying). In case I made this trip I had booked a flight from Vienna to Nuremberg in time for the Munich game at a cost of £12. I'd also booked flights from Germany to England and back again as Angela was not sure if she would be able to make the Vienna trip and I was therefore in two minds whether to make it myself. Maybe this was the last great opportunity to take advantage of low-cost airline tickets as even in the months since they were booked, the price of oil and taxes made such cheap flights almost non-existent. However, I managed to cover my options for around £100, no more than I would have spent on accommodation and refreshment had I stayed in Nuremberg for a couple of extra days.

It was still cold in Nuremberg as we landed on the Thursday, although the snow of Tuesday morning had now cleared. While my travelling companions decided on staying in Erlangen for a couple of nights for a change, I opted to stay in Nuremberg alone and have some quiet time before the match. I explored the city by tram and the forest to the north on foot, seeking out places I had not yet visited over the previous few years. I bought a map showing forest walks and then decided not to use it leaving my exploration to instinct. The area is beautiful with so much space and cleanliness. If your task was to design a city and surroundings from nothing, you would be pretty damn pleased if you could come up with something like Nuremberg. After four and half hours of meandering I was somewhat tired, thirsty and lost. I consulted the map which was little help in the forest and walked until I eventually came to a road. Not only was I several miles outside Nuremberg but also had only a few cents remaining having purchased the map which I'd neglected to use until too late. It was dusk by the time I reached the hotel and with a nasty blister I wished to simply climb into bed.

The following day as we made our way to the stadium there was that air of anticipation that can only precede a derby game. In the *Nordkurve* it felt like everyone was united again even if this was not entirely the case, and the atmosphere generated was surely a big factor in the players raising their game and putting in one of the best performances of the season.

Despite coming close to conceding to Luca Toni after just thirteen seconds, Der Club more than matched their opponents and deservedly took the lead with a fantastic strike from Misimovic just before half time. In the second half Koller fluffed a glorious opportunity to seal the points and it was a shame that Nuremberg could not hold on. There would be no fairytale today however as substitute Podolski levelled the game and broke many hearts in the *Frankenstadion*. The previous season a goalless draw in Munich had been celebrated with some fervour as it put 1.FCN at the top of the league. This time, other results conspired to mean that even this good performance and deserved draw saw *Der Club* hit bottom spot. And it would have to be Podolski who scored the Munich goal. How many times does it happen? Having maligned an opposition player at some point during the game or at some point in the past, your words suddenly come back to haunt you. I'd never criticised his talent but I certainly took an element of dislike to the player two years before during that superb game in Cologne as he whinged at the referee and appeared to go down far too easily when challenged. When Bayern brought him on as substitute I feared the worst, even though he had struggled with injuries and form all season. With nine minutes remaining he compounded those fears and made me wish I'd never spoken a word about the man.

The feeling that this was just not going to be Nuremberg's season was really beginning to take over now. What else can one do after witnessing a good performance, matching the league leaders and falling to the bottom of the league? Even as the Franconian spring arrived and people sunbathed by the River Pegnitz just a week after it had been too cold to be outdoors, hope for *Der Club* was becoming a fading shadow of its former self. Any permutations I could work out were almost instantly dismissed as a rather forlorn case of clutching at straws. The sun may have brought a change in the seasons but as far as the footballing one was going the winter of discontent would now surely be followed by a spring of sorrow.

Little was expected from the game in Frankfurt the following week. I was sitting in front of my computer once again. Looking at a full stadium and seeing the thousands of *Clubberer* made me wish I was there but that soon changed. Not because Frankfurt took the lead in just the third minute. This strangely gave some hope as I remembered their early goal in the *Frankenstadion* in October. All that was needed now was a Charsiteas equalizer as we'd witnessed on that day when he brought Nuremberg back into the game and 1.FCN went on to record their most decisive victory of the season.

In the eighteenth minute the Greek forward obliged and *Der Club* were back in the game and looking like a team who were determined to continue their good form from the previous week. It looked like a victory, the first since December, could be on the cards. Then all of a sudden I was glad I was at home. With no commentary on the live stream I was watching it was hard to be exactly sure of what was going on but it was more than clear that a firework had landed on the pitch and that the referee was taking the players off the field.

The pictures coming from the Commerzbank-Arena were not conclusive but it appeared that a group of Nuremberg fans, probably the Ultras or at least some fans dressed mainly in black as the Ultras have a tendency to do, were the focus of police in riot gear who were now standing in a line in among the Nuremberg supporters.

Goalkeeper Blazek, who had not had the best relationship with the fans, kicked the firework from the pitch before looking at the block of *Clubberer* and pointing a finger at his head. He may not have had much German but it was not hard to agree with the sentiment he was portraying that the perpetrator clearly had a screw loose. The *Clubberer* continued to sing even with the players back in the changing rooms and it certainly appeared that for a time the continuation of the game was in doubt.

It was easy watching to criticise the foolish behaviour of those who had thrown the offending firework onto the pitch but then again surely it was not the first football match in recent times where such an incident had occurred and surely other matches continued. However, there had been other bangs in the stand and now was not a time to consider why the game had been suspended but how it could be recommenced as quickly as possible. With Nuremberg starting to get on top it was surely to the advantage of the home side to have a break and regroup. As far as the home fans would be concerned, the events would almost certainly provide them with further motivation to get behind their team.

1.FCN president Michael Roth appeared on the pitch and stood in front of the *Clubberer* with a microphone. His address (as I found out later) asked them to not repeat the incidents and to calm down otherwise the game would be abandoned. The *Clubberer* continued to sing, something they did very well and which they could be admired for at most games. They even hastily arranged games in which some of them ran at each other wrestling on the terrace – something probably not so wise in the present climate in the stadium.

Watching from home I was wishing they would just shut up, calm down and let the teams get back on the pitch, particularly as I was now beginning to fear that *Clubberer* initiated 'crowd trouble' could lead to a disastrous points deduction. As it was, the referee eventually returned the teams to the pitch some twenty minutes after suspending play. The scores remained level at half time but Nuremberg went on to win the game 3-1. The points were much needed of course but the shine had been taken off the occasion by the disturbance from the terraces.

Recriminations went on for a long time. Certainly without firm evidence it would be wrong to say that this was the fault of the Nuremberg Ultras but everybody seemed to think that they were to blame in some way. Even if, as was extremely unlikely, they had 'officially' planned to set off fireworks in the stadium there was obviously the possibility that some of them had been involved. Although libellous to categorically state that the UN94 were to blame for the unsavoury events it seemed that the message board's general talk among fans was that the Ultras were the culprits. As for the club, had they not been proud of their Ultras movement after the Bochum game, now there was widespread despair. Even the *Fanbeauftragte,* months after the event was happy to go on record as saying that although one has to be careful of making accusations without evidence, this was a moment when there was a wish that the Ultras could be given away for a while. The majority of the vast community of 1.FC Nürnberg, official and otherwise, clearly felt, rightly or wrongly, that UN94 had disgraced the club.

Maybe, just maybe, the incident showed how well-controlled German crowd behaviour had become. If for one moment you forget that somehow fans managed to get fireworks through the turnstiles, the swift action in suspending play and sending police into the stand could have prevented an escalation of events. Of course indignation followed as the *Clubberer* (with only a few guilty members among them) were made to stand in the rain for a long, long time after the final whistle and were then escorted to the railway station, man, woman and child without opportunity to purchase provisions for the journey home. However, the police felt they had good reason to do this – the avoidance of any incidents with Frankfurt fans who might have come looking for trouble with smaller groups of *Clubberer* (some of whom would surely have obliged) without a police escort. Reading about such scenes in the aftermath made it seem like a throwback to English (and probably German) football in the '80s and early '90s. Had we been there that day it seems that the treat would have been nostalgic rather than refreshing.

1.FC Nürnberg were handed a hefty fine for the events in Frankfurt. With hindsight a points deduction could have been deemed as harsh. The actions were not violent but just plain stupid. As a letter from fan representatives *Rot-Schwarze Hilfe* to the DFB pointed out, if points were deducted a dangerous precedent would be set. It would only take fans from another club to set off a few fireworks amongst the fans of a relegation or title contender and their club could gain an advantage. It goes without saying that there are plenty of fans or idiots around who would be more than willing to try such an action, if only to amuse themselves. It may have been extremely fortunate though that President Roth addressed the fans and helped to avoid an abandonment of the game – an outcome that would surely have had more serious consequences for *Der Club*.

An abandonment of the game was the furthest thing from anybody's mind the following Friday as Jason led a party of 1FCNUK members around Nuremberg in hot sunshine prior to that night's match against Wolfsburg. Back in England I was purchasing *Nürnberger* sausages and German beer after work when he sent me a text message saying how hot it was and that they would soon be on their way to the stadium. There were pangs of jealousy that I was not there but at least the game would be shown live on Setanta and therefore a large party of *Clubberer* would be gathering at our house for the evening, hence the Germanic theme to the food and beverages.

As the sausages fried away gently (courtesy of the women who were generally not as interested in the game as the men) I passed comment that Jason must have been joking when he said how hot and sunny it was; the pictures on TV showed some rather heavy rain. As it happened he had not been joking but the rain had started as they arrived at the *Frankenstadion*. As the game commenced the rain continued to fall and by the time Saenko made it 1-0 after thirty-five minutes the ball would not roll on certain parts of the pitch. However, as long as the rain eased over the remaining ten minutes of the first half and ceased at half time then Nuremberg seemed set to continue their good form of late and seal a second successive victory. The scenes at half time showed various methods being used to remove water from the pitch, including large tables dragged across the surface on their side. It may even have worked but when the game did not restart after the break it looked unlikely that it ever would as the rain had continued as heavily as ever and was still doing so. We were quite warm and dry as we ate our *Bratwurst-Brötchen* and supped our beer waiting for the decision to abandon to be made. In sharp contrast, our members in Nuremberg stood soaking in the only open part of the stadium.

Eventually, for the first time in the *Bundesliga* since 1976, the game was washed away and with it not only the three points that were so vital for *Der Club* but also the new-found confidence that would surely have helped the team to gain something from the midweek fixture that followed in Stuttgart. As it was, the *Englische Woche* (English week) as the Germans call any week where there are midweek league fixtures, was something of a disaster with Stuttgart easily winning 3-0 and *Der Club* left two points adrift at the foot of the table and five points from safety.

The rearranged game against Wolfsburg happily ended with a 1-0 victory, lifting Nuremberg off the bottom and then all eyes turned to the *Kellerduell,* the relegation battle against Arminia Bielefeld, now just two points away. A win was the only result that could be contemplated and the 2-0 half time lead courtesy of goals from Mintal and Saenko were not only going to take *Der Club* above Bielefeld but would now surely keep them in the *Bundesliga*, particularly if that first half performance could be repeated a couple more times in the remaining matches. But the old cliché about football being a game of two halves was probably coined with Nuremberg's second half performance in mind. Quite simply they came out for the second half without the fire that they needed to ensure the three points. Bielefeld scored twice and the one point from the game would surely not be good enough. Once again, a false dawn in terms of the halftime lead had been smothered in the darkness of another game thrown away. Although a mathematician would say otherwise, the *Bundesliga* was slipping from the grasp of *Der Club.*

Even now, though, the situation improved with a no score draw at Dortmund and a 2-0 home victory over Duisburg who 1.FCN now leapfrogged. With two games remaining Nuremberg were just one point behind Bielefeld and two behind Cottbus. It was quite feasible that a couple of draws could be enough to stay up and even more feasible that *Der Club* could achieve them. Going into those last two games I, and many more *Clubberer*, had Hope back with us. Our long-term travelling companion had returned and, as the end of the road approached, she was riding up front and giving directions. There was just the nagging doubt at the back of the mind that Hope might just be holding the map upside down.

1FCNUK try to smile despite a drawn home game

Chapter 13

Full circle

Back in the previous summer when the fixtures had been released, it was clearly some sort of prophetic coincidence that the last away game of the new season would be away to Hertha Berlin at their home in the Olympic Stadium. We had just played our last game there and lifted the cup and would surely return almost twelve months later challenging for the title or at least a qualifying place for the Champions League. The flights were booked as soon as they became available and we paid very little for them. All that we had to do in the interim was watch Nuremberg get themselves into a position where the Olympic Stadium could witness another great performance as three points propelled us into another new chapter of the club's history.

After the first few weeks of the season, I started to have some concerns about the game in Berlin. The far from perfect results soon put paid to any hopes of a Champions League spot and even re-entry to the UEFA Cup looked beyond the team as the thought started to cross my mind (and that of all but the most desperately disillusioned fan) that a mid-table finish was on the cards. Hertha Berlin would probably be in a similar position and Saturday 10th May would provide an end of season mid-table affair in which the teams were simply going through the motions and looking forward to their summer holidays.

I started to get further concerns at the beginning of October, at the same time that, to great joy, my wife announced that she was pregnant. The feeling for both of us was nothing short of euphoric. In less than nine months' time we would welcome a child into the world. It was a feeling to savour and one which started to sink in slowly as the day went by. I remember the day well. Thursday 4th October, 2007. It was the day I had to make that crazy and almost certainly unlawful dash down the motorway to get from a course I was attending to the in-law's house to watch the away leg of the tie with Rapid Bucharest.

It was only after *Der Club* had got past the Romanians that I was finally hit by the significance of the other big story of the day. In the last week of May another fan of 1.FCN and Port Vale FC would be born. The footballing allegiance of my first offspring would not be in doubt as far as I was concerned. However, what was in doubt was the exact date of arrival. Apparently a due date for a baby meant any time in a five or six week period depending on whether it was an early or late arrival, and that would clearly put the end of the football season into serious doubt for me. Would I get a pass for Berlin? It was unlikely.

The final nail in Port Vale's coffin was hammered home with a goalless draw at home to Huddersfield in April. Having witnessed the abandoned Wolfsburg fixture in the *Frankenstadion* on TV the night before, Vale Park was the only place to be on the Saturday. It was pointless going with any hope of a miracle turnaround to the season as for the past few weeks it had just been a matter of when, rather than if, they would go down. Hope now came in the form of what was considered a very generous season ticket offer for the following season and before the game several of us handed in our application forms. At £183 for a season we all agreed that it was an offer that could not be missed, though we had to put to the back of our minds the fact that this would be for the fourth tier of English football and avoid comparing the price with that of a season ticket in Nuremberg (approximately 100 Euros for the cheapest). This season was practically over for the Vale so now we had to start looking forward to the next.

It had been something of a tiring season as a supporter of Port Vale and Nuremberg, not to mention an expensive one largely due to the number of trips to Germany I had made. As the Berlin game approached and Angela grew ever larger I took the decision to do the honourable thing and stay at home. She said I could go, of course, and that she did not mind etc. etc., but when put in such a situation it is always the etc. etc. of which one must be wary. Not minding on a Friday morning is one thing but imagine receiving a desperate phone call in Berlin or simply arriving home and the mood not being quite right – it could put pay to future trips (of which I was sure there would be plenty despite the imminent new arrival). While friends flew off to Berlin I did the shopping and some housework to at least ensure that come Saturday afternoon there would be no demands on my time other than the pull of the internet and a live video stream.

In many ways I was pleased I was not there. What would there be to do in Berlin if results went against us and we were relegated that very afternoon. Certainly there would be nothing to celebrate. But when the live stream appeared on the screen in front of me I wanted to be there, singing away with the *Clubberer* in a penultimate desperate attempt to spur the team on to victory.

As it was, *Der Club* lost the game 1-0 but somehow managed to avoid relegation. For several minutes they were practically down with Bielefeld leading Dortmund 2-1. However, a freak goal in that game saw Dortmund pull level and save 1.FCN for another week. As Dortmund forward Frei curled a free kick over the wall and past Bielefeld goalkeeper Fernandez, the 'keeper turned his head to see the ball rebound from his right hand post straight into his face and into the net. Maybe this was the lucky break Nuremberg had sought all season.

It had gone right down to the wire and victory against Schalke in the *Frankenstadion* could still ensure *Bundesliga* football the following season. Nuremberg and Schalke have history. Both great teams in the pre-war era, more recently the two sets of fans were probably the most feared in Germany in the 1970s. Certainly as the '80s came around they were untouchable, largely because they had formed a unique and strong friendship – the *Fanfreundschaft*. There are several stories of how this famous friendship started, most involving some allegiance born out of a clash against a mutually despised group of fans from another team. It is likely that only those who were actually there at the conception know the true story, however one which I have heard several times from different sources suggests that a love (or lust) was involved too. A group of Nuremberg fans, so the story goes, were escorting their friend to meet her Schalke fan boyfriend. He was waiting with his posse who wanted to make sure that the Nuremberg supporters did not give him any trouble for seeing one of their girls. It seems that as the two groups were about to meet one group was set upon by a group of fans from a third club. Fortunately the others heard this and the *Clubberer* and Schalke fans were together strong enough to see off the attackers. Love was not only blossoming between the Nuremberg girl and the Gelsenkirchen boy – a friendship grew between the two groups and eventually extended to thousands of supporters of both teams. Surely it should be turned into a Broadway musical.

Whatever the exact origin of the *Fanfreundschaft* it is now a big thing. Jürgen Bergmann described it as a beautiful thing for both clubs and said that the only shirt other than a Nuremberg shirt one could wear on the *Nordkurve* and not expect at least some verbal abuse is a Schalke 04 shirt. When the two teams play each other, the sets of fans sit and stand together and sometimes create jointly choreographed displays of flags and banners. When they are both playing elsewhere the fans will stop off to support each other's teams when convenient. Many fan clubs are dedicated to the *Fanfreundschaft* and their membership is made up of fans of both teams. Merchandise is available in the Nuremberg shop celebrating the friendship and displaying the blue and white of Schalke alongside the red and black of Nuremberg.

There are, of course, those who are against it and their arguments focus on how it is possible to give support to two teams and that all energies should focus on 1.FCN. Some members of the Ultras do not really relate to the friendship although they do have a link to the Ultras Gelsenkirchen. UN94 President Julius Neumann once told me that he found the concept of friendships such as the *Fanfreundschaft* problematic because he felt that you have to live friendships and not just have them in name alone. The UN94 main friendship is with the Ultras of Rapid Vienna and members of both sets of Ultras do meet regularly. It was a good point that Julius made though. It seems that too many people want to say somebody is their friend but then never really have anything to do with them. Social network sites such as Facebook seem to encourage people to collect friends in the belief that he who has the longest list of them is the most popular. But does meeting someone on holiday for a couple of days and tagging them on a photograph really constitute friendship? Friendly maybe. But friendship? Probably not. The more I think about it the more Julius was right. 1FCNUK have met many people and other fan clubs but to have a *Fanfreundschaft* with them would be somewhat fraudulent unless the friendship could be lived with regular opportunities to meet and communicate.

But for some, the dominant friendship with Schalke is all they know. They have been brought up with the *Fanfreundschaft* and when Schalke come to town it is party time and when they are not in town the fans make excuses to party together anyway. They hold joint events and do lend support to each other's teams. In footballing terms this is something of an unusual phenomenon.

It was something of a long shot but we hoped that the final game of the season would be reason enough for us to party in England. Jason had his newly installed satellite system ready in time for the game and was able to receive live *Bundesliga* matches. As we sat in his living room we could do nothing more than simply watch and see if *Der Club* could win and Bielefeld would fail to do so in Stuttgart. This was the only permutation that would work. There was not much hope left. The season had seen too many moments of misfortune and even more of underperformance to suggest that there was a Nuremberg victory on the cards. And with Schalke chasing down second placed Werder Bremen and automatic qualification to the Champion's League, *Fanfreundschaft* or not, there was no way they would be taking it easy on *Der Club*. And why should they? The *Bundesliga* has to be seen as a fair and open competition and 1.FCN could not suddenly rely on help from a friendly club. Besides, Schalke operate at the 'money end' of football in Germany and the difference between second and third place for them could be worth millions.

We sat and sipped at bottles of dark German beer, nursing them in our hands as if they were some kind of lucky charm. They were not. Bielefeld only managed to draw but a Schalke goal in each half condemned *Der Club* to relegation. Herbert left to walk home alone, clearly distressed at what he had witnessed. In a way I was more relieved than anything. In the same way they say it's a relief when somebody who has been seriously ill for a long time finally passes away, the end of the season was something of a release for some of us. As football fans we expect to take the rough with the smooth but on two fronts that had been a season we'd love to not have to witness again.

I wanted to laugh when I thought back to the previous Monday's article by Raphael Honigstein on The Guardian website which suggested that defeat would provide Nuremberg with a record less enviable than anything ever produced by David Hasselhoff. After becoming the first team to be relegated the season after winning the German Championship, Nuremberg had now become the first team to be relegated the season after winning the German cup. And defeat against Schalke also confirmed *Der Club* as the team relegated more than any other from the *Bundesliga*. This was the seventh time they had gone down. Honigstein joked that this would be a record to put even Monica Lewinsky to shame. (I bet she wishes that the moment she would be remembered for was a Euro 2004 winning goal like 'Harry' Charisteas.)

And just to rub salt into the wounds, as a Port Vale fan, the big local rivals Stoke City had gained promotion to the English Premier League and in Germany Bayern Munich had already once again claimed the crown of Deutscher Meister. Still, there was always next season to look forward to and surely the fortunes of Nuremberg and Vale would be reversed. Hope would last at least throughout the summer.

So as far as football is concerned there is no fairytale ending to this book. The period chosen coincided with the start of the fantastic experience of supporting 1.FC Nürnberg through thick and thin, not to just celebrate a wonderful moment in their history. And as with Port Vale it seems that there could well be more thin than thick as the years go by but the enjoyment we have and the passionate support will last forever.

On Wednesday 11th June, Angela gave birth to Thomas Ben Goulding. Two weeks late and a full month after the game in Berlin, he had done well to avoid the end of the season. I just wish he could have somehow communicated his intentions to his mother a few weeks before. We avoided purposely choosing the names of Nuremberg or Port Vale players for the names of our son. Thomas was chosen as a name used in both English and German while his middle name came from my maternal